ALONE, ON STAGE

SOLO PLAYS FOR MEN

ALONE, ON STAGE

SOLO PLAYS FOR MEN

edited by
DD Kugler and Brian Quirt

Playwrights Canada Press
Toronto • Canada

PLAYWRIGHTS CANADA PRESS
The Canadian Drama Publisher
215 Spadina Avenue, Suite 230, Toronto, Ontario, CANADA M5T 2C7
phone 416.703.0013   fax 416.408.3402
orders@playwrightscanada.com • www.playwrightscanada.com

For professional or amateur production rights, please see opposite page.

The publisher acknowledges the support of the Canadian taxpayers through
the Government of Canada Book Publishing Industry Development Program,
the Canada Council for the Arts, the Ontario Arts Council,
and the Ontario Media Development Corporation.

Front cover painting "Krak Krek Krik" by Robert Dempster, 28.25 x 19.75 in.
Mixed Media. Courtesy of Rand and Cath Harker, and The Collector's
Gallery, Calgary. "Krak Krek Krik" from *Watt* by Samuel Beckett.
Copyright © 1953 by Samuel Beckett. Reprinted by permission of
Georges Borchardt Inc. on behalf of the Estate of Samuel Beckett.

Production editor/cover design: JLArt

LIBRARY AND ARCHIVES CANADA CATALOGUING IN PUBLICATION

Alone, on stage : solo plays for men / edited by DD Kugler and Brian Quirt.

ISBN 978-0-88754-878-9

1. Monologues. 2. Men--Drama. I. Kugler, DD II. Quirt, Brian

PN4305.M6A46 2008   812'.045089286   C2008-905773-2

This book
was printed
on 100%
recycled stock.

First edition: December 2008.
Printed and bound by AGMV Marquis at Quebec, Canada.

Table of Contents

INTRODUCTION

• • •

Shortly after being asked to edit an anthology of male solo Canadian work we had a series of discussions about the criteria we might use for determining selection. Our much-reduced final list—in descending order of importance—looked something like this:

1. range of solo performance strategies
2. scale of content
3. quality of line-by-line writing
4. geographical representation

We were initially tempted to discuss the six texts in terms of each of these four criteria. Upon further reflection, we decided to deal briefly with the final three criteria, and devote most of the introduction to our primary consideration: the range of solo performance strategies employed by these writers.

Our concerns about **geographical representation** were minimal. If we had inadvertently chosen six plays from any one locale, we might have felt obliged to re-think our selection. As it turned out, this volume features playwrights based in Prince Edward Island, Quebec, Ontario (2), Alberta, and British Columbia. We were pleased that, in spite of non-geographical criteria, so much of the country was represented.

We also wanted to include only plays that evidenced high **quality of line-by-line writing**—engagement at the level of the sentence, a delicious sense of language. This highly subjective value is perhaps best understood as a reverse criterion; work that didn't meet that standard, simply didn't make the shortlist from which these plays were ultimately chosen. It seems to us fruitless, however, to quote sentences removed from their immediate context in an effort to demonstrate their strengths. So we encourage you to read the plays aloud, to taste the words as you speak them.

In thinking about **scale of content**, we looked for scripts that, however auto-biographical—and three of the texts can be seen as autobiography—rise above per-ceived limits of the solo performance, to examine the surrounding human society. We had no predetermined appropriate content; we were interested in playwrights who demonstrated reach, who dealt intelligently and passionately with social and political issues. We are pleased that the six selected plays present not only dynamic examples of theatrical visions, but equally demonstrate how effectively the solo form can address large ideas: Burkett's revisiting of a singularly dangerous era for artists, indeed all individuals, in a time of collective consensus; Diamond's self-reflective rant on prop-erty—in the family, in art—within the murderous world of capitalism; Verdecchia's questioning of "home," and his attack—personal and historical—on all borders that accentuate and promote belittling stereotypes; MacIvor's investigation of the need for love, the big lie of hope, the fear of death, the knowledge that everything ends; Mouawad's depiction of an imagination encountering the terrifying world of the invisible; and Garnhum's complex weaving of personal and public loss, with the healing process of art-making. None of the content of these plays is easily summarized (a fact that attracted us), and they stray across topics and issues with great skill—that too is a part of their strategy.

Discussions during the selection process eventually revealed to us that our primary criterion had become the **range of solo performance strategies**—an umbrella heading that included such closely-related issues as structure, theatrical vocabulary, and audience relationship. The one-person show is a difficult theatrical form. While other theatrical forms rely primarily upon dialogue, the solo performer finds himself alone on stage—to whom does he speak? Of course the audience is every performer's implicit partner, and the solo performer, as in other theatrical forms, may choose to make that relationship explicit by breaking the fourth wall and speaking directly to the audience. The plays in this anthology exploit that strategy to varying degrees.

But we were interested in celebrating a wider range of theatrical strategies that solo performers employ to meet their unusual circumstances. None of the strategies listed below is the exclusive domain of the solo performer—they are strategies accessible to any theatrical production. But what follows, we hope, is a partial catalogue of the most significant strategies that the solo performers in this volume have employed specifically to help populate and complicate the difficult simplicity of one body alone on stage.

Central Character(s)

Neither *Beuys Buoys Boys* nor *Here Lies Henry* employ voices beyond those of their central characters—Ken Garnhum as himself, and Daniel MacIvor as the fictional (in more senses than one) Henry. You could argue that Garnhum's Barbie doll plays a puppet-like function—embodied, but unvoiced—in her progressive theatrical roles in "Barbie Does Beuys!" Still, both of the solo performances essentially feature a single central voice.

In addition to *Beuys Buoys Boys*, two scripts present an autobiographical central character. Guillermo Verdecchia appears as himself in *Fronteras Americanas*, but he also assumes the persona of Wideload McKennah with whom he shares alternating units of text. In *Property*, Marc Diamond creates a similar division of his central character: the Actor who is on stage recounting the story; and the thinly disguised M___ who always speaks from the past, in the moments immediately following the arrival of the letter.

In addition to *Here Lies Henry*, two scripts would not be considered autobiographical. Wajdi Mouawad provides a Narrator in *Alphonse*, but he appears infrequently, and only to reassure us by providing clues about the progression of the story ("Actually, Alphonse was walking along a country road but we're not supposed to know that just yet.") As the puppeteer in *Tinka's New Dress*, Ronnie Burkett has at once an odd aura of invisibility, despite his physically dominating presence; but he speaks in his own voice only twice ("Tinka" and "Fly").

Additional Characters

Inside his portion of the *Fronteras Americanas* narration, Verdecchia briefly assumes the additional roles and voices of Doctor, Jorge and Bruno, as well as the voice of Sharko in his video audition. The Actor, in *Property*, pursues a similar strategy, but takes on a much wider range of additional roles and voices: Robert Crow, while reading the letter; his family (Mom, Brilliant Cousin), partner (Ariadne), and friend (K); his mentors at the Collaborative Vision (Beaver Winslow, Tibor Lumax, Cleigh McNab, Franco Hermes, Maggie Klue, Ben Scham, Richie Orex, Conrad Shadow, Assistant); a couple minor characters (Nurse, Lawyer); and most significantly, the ominous voice of London Ontario. Although they are not "characters," Verdecchia and Wideload also give "voice" to points of view expressed in a variety of sources—Fuentes, *The Atlantic, Elle, Mirabella, Gentleman's Quarterly, The Economist*, the Kerry Sub-Committee Report—often accompanied by a slide (more on this later).

Given the limited role of the central fictional Narrator, the majority of *Alphonse* is told from the unmediated views and voices of the wide range of characters who populate the story: Alphonse's family and best friend, Walter; the police inspector Victor, and the many people he interviews, including Alphonse's schoolmates. Inside the Pierre-Paul-René story we have the additional characters of Sabayan, Flupan, the Old Man, and even the Cave. Although the play is about him, the title character Alphonse, and his alter ego Pierre-Paul-René, don't introduce themselves until the conclusion of the tale. This incarnation of the one-man show has become quite populous; the single performer plays a total of 22 characters.

Ronnie Burkett takes this strategy one step further in *Tinka's New Dress* by providing not only additional character voices, but eleven physical puppet bodies who also populate the stage. Although their voices remain the same, several of those puppet characters appear in successive physical forms—Tinka (7 times), Mrs. Van Craig (4), Stephan (3), Carl (3), Morag (3), and Isaël (2). There are also the puppet puppeteers (Franz, Schnitzel, and Madame Rodrigue), as well as another seven characters who form The Populace. Finally—much like Diamond's voice of London Ontario—Burkett includes an unembodied Voice that speaks for The Common Good.

The use by these playwrights of additional characters as a theatrical strategy can been seen—as can each of the following strategies in our introduction—as points along a continuum: from *Beuys Buoys Boys*, which includes no additional characters (if we exclude Beuys and Barbie) to *Tinka's New Dress*, the most populous of these "solo" scripts.

Fourth Wall

Garnhum is clearly on a stage and speaks directly to his audience. Diamond's Actor is also on stage recounting the story in present time to the audience; although for his alter ego, M____, the fourth wall remains securely intact. Most of the characters in *Alphonse* introduce themselves directly to the audience with their first appearance, but their implied circumstances are somewhere other than the stage. Burkett's puppets in the central story also remain behind the fourth wall, but for the puppet show of Franz & Schnitzel the fourth wall disappears (for example, they prime the audience for Madame Rodrigue's arrival). Both Verdecchia, and his alter ego Wideload, break the fourth wall, speak directly to the audience, and are acutely aware of their theatrical presentation ("Okay, [The lights come up] let's see who's here, what's everybody wearing, let's see who came to *El Teatro* dis evening.") MacIvor's Henry also speaks directly to the audience, and even repeatedly enters the audience: for his demonstration of "just kidding," his request for cigarette and light, and his retrieval of the reserved chair. In short, all six plays—using a variety of strategies—make the audience their explicit partner.

Sound

Most of these scripts make important use of recorded sound. Garnhum twice uses a German-accented English voiceover to provide text by Joseph Beuys. One imagines that Burkett's limited sounds—a police whistle, barking dogs, and shattered glass to create chaos, for example—would be incorporated into the larger musical score which accompanies the play. Verdecchia's script calls for his own voice in a voiceover ("This play is not a plea for tolerance. This is a citation, a manifesto."), as well as for gunshots and a loud buzzer (twice, to signal the beginning and end of the "break"); there is also one "silence" notated in the same style as other music cues. The recorded sound of a telephone (nine rings, seventeen rings, one ring, fifteen rings) is critical to Diamond's *Property*, as is the sound of a toilet flushing. However, the most significant use of sound occurs in *Here Lies Henry* in which MacIvor wears a microphone throughout; this allows the sound operator to modify his voice, often to startling effect. This use of sound helps create the unsettling impression of MacIvor responding to himself as is he were somehow alien—a theatrical strategy similar to splitting the central character's persona.

Music

Music plays no significant role in the texts of *Alphonse* or *Beuys Buoys Boys*. The only song in *Property* is "Baa Baa Black Sheep," although Diamond uses three separate occasions in the script to complete singing the song. Verdecchia, however, calls at least fifteen times for specific recorded music by title and performer—a wide range of Latin music—that is used primarily as a transitional device.

Here Lies Henry makes extensive use of music, often combined with sound and light, "as an indication of a level of reality outside Henry's control." MacIvor's "Note to future productions" continues: "These moments are not notated in this text. Use your imagination." Musical notation in the script includes: emotional qualities (ominous, deeply eerie), dance accompaniment ("Finally," nightclub), and gestural support (cuts in and out with stabbing motions), as well as the show's *coup de theatre*: "building rain and then a thunderstorm… should take at least thirty seconds."

The extensive use of music in *Tinka's New Dress* becomes underscoring. Burkett comments in his notes that "Cathy Nosaty's score and Brian Kerby's lighting are integral to the overall design and performance." The script's cornerstone musical moment is the second appearance of resident diva Madame Rodrigue—"the fat lady who sings"—during which Burkett improvises a song "written that day and commenting on topical news, to one of five standard bedtracks composed by Cathy Nosaty."

Slides

Of the six scripts, only *Beuys Buoys Boys* and *Fronteras Americanas* use slides as a theatrical strategy to populate the stage.

Garnhum calls for three slide sequences—of literal and figurative monuments, of Beuys's sculpture, of buoys and the sea—which serve as a shifting visual backdrop for his text. He also indicates several one-word slides that appear sporadically throughout the show—Fear, Guilt, Compassion, Complicity—to emphasize thematic elements. Verdecchia makes extensive use of more than sixty slides. There are ten titles, fifteen slides recounting the history of the world, nineteen Latin lovers, five quotes, six definitions (Chicano, Hispanic, cajones, cojones), as well as nine other images (map, passport photo, Morris dance, X-rays, brain scans, a ferret, a bee, shooting photos, therapist drawings). Both plays, clearly, employ slides as an on-stage partner.

Video

Of the six scripts, only *Fronteras Americanas* uses video as a theatrical strategy, and Verdecchia employs it on three occasions. The first occurs during the "break" seemingly required by the audience at the forty-five minute point in the show. Accompanied by "cheesy music," the video is comprised of "clips of cartoons and movies featuring, among other things: Latinos, Hispanics, dopey peasants, Anthony Quinn and a certain mouse." The second video, entitled "The War on Drugs," is "an edited drug-war movie" that plays without sound during Wideload's Drug War Deconstruction; he identifies the characters, fills in the narrative, speeds up and slows down the tape as he comments ironically on the film's implied themes. The final, and the most inventive, use of video is Verdecchia's audition for an "overweight Hispanic in a dirty suit"; he sits in front of a video camera, and a close-up of him appears on a large monitor.

Costumes

Costumes may well play a significant role in the theatricality of the solo performer, but surprisingly little information is included in the stage directions of these scripts. There are no explicit costume notes for *Alphonse*. In *Property*, M_____ discovers with delight that he is wearing the greenjeans that he had longed for as a child. Fecundo Morales Segundo first appears in *Fronteras Americanas* "wearing a bandito outfit" which he shortly removes ("Ees an old Hallowe'en costume. Scary huh?") and introduces himself as Wideload McKennah; Verdecchia slips on a red bandanna for his video audition. Although *Here Lies Henry* indicates only "Henry should be dressed up, looking his best," the costume becomes a physical element: he checks his fly several times, takes off both jacket and tie, exhales cigarette smoke into his shirt, and finally, throws his jacket aside. Garnhum dons the Beuysian grey felt hat and boots in *Beuys Buoys Boys*, wraps himself in felt, and even his Barbie gets costume changes; although the script doesn't indicate it, a production photo reveals Garnhum wearing a chef's hat during the Madame Benoit section.

Not surprisingly there is considerably more attention to costume in *Tinka's New Dress*. In his "Notes on Staging," Burkett includes a one-sentence paragraph: "The play progresses from light to dark emotionally, and each scene is assigned a palette dictating colours and tones for costumes to further enhance this": yellow (park), red and blue (cabaret), black and white with orange and pink (Franz & Schnitzel), rust and blue (cabaret backstage), green and mauve (camp), brown and gold (party), grey (camp), and black (camp). There are more than forty puppets in *Tinka's New Dress* and, as production photos attest, each is costumed in exquisite detail; for Burkett, every costume performs a critical role in the telling of this story. We draw your attention, however, to only one costume—a costume that becomes a set: in a highly theatrical moment, Fipsi's wide hoop skirt "a bizarre reminiscence of the Court of Versailles" separates like a theatrical curtain to reveal miniature Franz and Schnitzel puppets.

Set and Props

Four of the scripts rely minimally on what would be considered set and props. There is no mention of set or properties in the text of *Alphonse*; choices are left entirely to each new team of interpreters. Diamond's *Property* limits itself to a bare bones inventory: an envelope, a butcher knife to open it, the letter inside, a garbage can and toilet to dispose of it, a telephone to interrupt, and the refuge of his Adirondack chair. Burkett, on the other hand, provides a detailed description of the staging of *Tinka's New Dress*: the carousel containing twenty-one animals on which the puppets ride, an outside acting ring on which The Populace stand, the Franz & Schnitzel puppet show stage left. *Fronteras Americanas* mentions neither set nor props, but Verdecchia interacts dynamically throughout (as mentioned above) with slides, video, music, and sound. A front row chair clearly marked "reserved" is the only addition to *Here Lies Henry*'s simple set description ("a bare stage"); but MacIvor interacts throughout with the exceptionally detailed and complimentary score of the light, music and sound—including his miked and manipulated voice.

It is in *Beuys Buoys Boys*, however, that set and properties play the most significant role. None of Garnhum's prop elements remain static, but rather transform into stage-partners through his dynamic interaction with them. He first enters in darkness carrying the flashlight. When he visits the miniature stage-set at intervals we discover three distinct versions of "Barbie Does Beuys!" From the microwave he takes the lunch pail; inside the lunch pail are rice cakes, and a mug of coffee that he heats in the microwave; he drinks coffee and munches rice cakes while talking about Madam Benoît—correlating cooking and drawing. In two long sequences he draws on the chalkboard while reminding us that Beuys thought of drawing as "notation" or "gesture"; Garnhum's drawing enacts gesture. In conclusion, he removes the wheels from the red cart and mounts them on the tree-chair to create a unit for removing materials from the stage and, in a *coup de théâtre*, Garnhum slowly assembles the final monument/buoy topped by a light-emitting pyramid.

Lighting

There are no significant indications about the use of light in either *Property* or *Fronteras Americanas*. The first monologue in *Alphonse* is entitled "Voice In The Dark"; in a play without stage directions of any kind, this is perhaps a theatrical strategy to encourage the audience, from the outset, to use their imagination. Garnhum also first enters in the dark; he carries a flashlight, and shortly after, stars appear in that darkness. The few additional light-related stage directions in *Beuys Buoys Boys* suggest that light was used to create an emotional space: "During the next scene, the set and lights conspire to create an atmosphere of bleak confinement." Similarly, Burkett's "Notes on Staging" indicate that *Tinka's New Dress* "progresses from light to dark emotionally," and (as discussed earlier) he assigns a scene-by-scene costume colour palette "to further enhance" this progression of light. MacIvor first enters "through a dim tunnel of light" in *Here Lies Henry*. Light, almost always in concert with music/sound (as mentioned above), becomes his dynamic partner: "The Lighting in the original production consisted of a series of boxes that grew increasingly smaller until only Henry's face was lit." One early sequence demonstrates the partnering which occurs throughout: Henry says "I had a strange dream"; the "music and light shift: deeply eerie"; Henry says: "It wasn't that weird"; then "music out and light restore." MacIvor's final text describes in detail a lighting cue that will NOT happen, and then—clearly partnering with theatrical elements—the cue happens precisely as he has described.

Verbal and Physical Gesture

All plays employ repetition to some extent, but two of these plays elevate that impulse to a theatrical strategy in which the repeated units become building blocks to create connection.

Diamond's repetitions within *Property* are primarily, although not exclusively, verbal. Variations on the phrase "to tell you the truth" or "the truth is" occur thirty-nine times, and there are thirty additional references to "lies" or "liars"; "I don't blame" occurs twelve times; the Brilliant Cousin's "by the way" occurs seven times. Stage directions twice indicate that M____ "repeats final sentence until convinced": "But all in all things aren't too bad"; "I have escaped." The singing of "Baa Baa Black Sheep" is segmented so that it occurs three times. Some verbal repetitions, like "ching ching" (repeated four times), suggest an accompanying physical score; as well, both Actor and M___ share the "tap dance" which is repeated four times.

The physical impulses largely implicit in the text of *Property* become explicit in *Here Lies Henry*. There are verbal/physical gestures which immediately follow Henry's trigger words: the cough which follows "Father," the laugh which follows "Mother," and the sneeze which follows "Nietzsche." Even more distinctive are the physical gestural scores: the fly check (3), hands on genitals (8), arm check (3), mime birds (2), and the uncomfortable pause (7).

Given the detailed verbal and physical gesture that both scripts explicitly provide, it is not hard to imagine productions that would take enthusiastic advantage of this theatrical partnering strategy.

Conclusion

Each of these six scripts represents—uniquely—a pinnacle in meeting the distinct challenges of the solo performance form. We feel honoured to collect and offer them to you in this anthology. We hope, additionally, that our introduction usefully highlights the diverse strategies these six playwrights have employed so successfully in confronting that most exceptional circumstance—alone, on stage.

DD Kugler, Vancouver
Brian Quirt, Toronto
August 2008

Alphonse

or the adventures of Pierre-Paul-René,
a gentle boy with a one-note voice who was
never surprised by anything

Wajdi Mouawad

Translated by Shelley Tepperman

Wajdi Mouawad was born in Lebanon in 1968, and fled the war-torn country with his family; they lived in Paris for a few years, then settled in Montreal. In 1991, shortly after graduating from the National Theatre School, he embarked on a career as an actor, writer, director and producer. In all his work, from his own plays—a dozen so far, including *Journée de noces chez les Cromagnons* (*Wedding Day at the Cro-Magnons'*), *Littoral* (*Tideline*), *Incendies* (*Scorched*) and *Rêves* (*Dreams*), all published by Playwrights Canada Press—Wajdi Mouawad is guided by the central notion that "all art bears witness to human existence through the prism of beauty."

From 2000–2004 he was the Artistic Director of Montreal's Théâtre de Quat' Sous, in 2005 he founded two companies specializing in the development of new work: Abé carré cé carré in Canada (with Emmanuel Schwartz), and Au carré de l'hypoténuse in France.

He is the recipient of numerous awards and honours for his writing and directing, including the 2000 Governor General's Literary Award for Drama (*Littoral*), the 2002 Chevalier de l'Ordre National des Arts et des Lettres (France) and the 2004 Prix de la Francophonie. He is currently Artistic Director of the National Arts Centre French Theatre.

Shelley Tepperman is a Toronto-born, Montreal-based writer, dramaturg and translator. Working from French, Spanish and Italian, she has brought more than thirty plays into English, including three other plays by Mouawad: *Wedding Day at the Cro-Magnons*, *Tideline* and *Pacamambo*. Shelley's translations have been produced on CBC radio and on stages from coast to coast, and she was twice nominated for the Governor General's Literary Award in translation. Shelley also writes, story-edits and directs for documentary film and television.

This version of *Alphonse* was commissioned by Theatre Direct Canada in 2001, and premiered at DuMaurier Theatre, Harbourfront Centre, Toronto in November 2002 with the following company:

ALPHONSE   Alon Nashman

Artistic Director, Theatre Direct Canada: Lynda Hill
Directed by Lynda Hill and Alon Nashman
Set and Costumes designed by Vikki Anderson
Lighting designed by Michael Kruse
Original Music and Sound Design by Cathy Nosaty
Stage Managed by Tamerrah Chiyoko Volkovksis

Theatre Direct Canada would like to acknowledge Theaturtle and Artistic Director Alon Nashman who produced the Toronto premiere at the Toronto Fringe Festival in 2000.

• • •

The original French version of *Alphonse* was first produced in Beloeil, Quebec on December 12, 1993 by the Théâtre de l'Arrière-scène. It was directed by Serge Marois with a set by Paul Livernois assisted by Pierre Tremblay. Lighting was by Claude Cournoyer, costumes were by Georges Lévesque and music was by Pierre Labbé. *Alphonse* was performed by the author, Wajdi Mouawad, who is also an actor. The actor Emmanuel Bilodeau also performed the play occasionally.

A staged reading had previously taken place at the theatre La Licorne, directed by Alexis Martin, on Tuesday, April 6, 1993, as part of the seventh edition of the Semaine de la dramaturgie québécoise.

Since 1993 Wajdi Mouawad has performed *Alphonse* more than one hundred times, in Canada and in Europe.

Characters

ALPHONSE/NARRATOR

ALPHONSE
or the adventures of Pierre-Paul-René,
a gentle boy with a one-note voice who was
never surprised by anything

VOICE IN THE DARK

When we're little,
No one tells us very much.
So we imagine.
Later,
Imagining gets kind of complicated.
So we ask for information.
And so we become grownups and there's nothing wrong with that.
It's the natural order of things.
And things are well-designed
Because they prevent us from going backwards
Which is a very good thing.
And things are well-designed
Because they prevent us from going backwards
Which is a very good thing.
Because,
If by some impossible twist of fate,
A man crossed paths with the child he used to be, and they both recognized
each other, they would both crumple to the ground, the man in despair, the
child in terror.

ALPHONSE'S FAMILY

I have a little brother.
His name's Alphonse.
He's a brave kid, Alphonse: his green eyes look right at you. When he walks
down the street, people don't notice him. He doesn't want anyone to notice
him. Anyway, he's just not the kind of kid people notice.
Tonight Alphonse didn't come home from school. My mother's sitting in the
living room, her knitting beside her.
My father's smoking by the wide-open window staring into the night,
my sister's asleep (actually, she's just pretending)
and me, I'm sitting in the kitchen, worrying about Alphonse. Where the hell can
he be? The little weasel.

Something must have happened or he would have called! the mother exclaimed
from the living room. The father turned and spit in her face to shut her up.

The father had already thrown in the towel. It's understandable, he was too upset.

After working like a dog my whole life, sweating away my youth, sweating away my good looks, my elegance, all for my family.

And what a family!

An ugly wife who knits non-stop, a daughter who still isn't married and who nobody wants,

and an ungrateful son who just stands there in front of me smirking superciliously.

And the last one, the youngest,

Alphonse,

the one I'd put all my hopes in,

now he's gone: No one knows where.

What have I done with my life? Why didn't I listen to myself back then "You aren't made to have a family" and now look what's happened! Your youngest son's just disappeared! I don't blame him, I'd have done the same thing!

Actually, Alphonse was walking along a country road but we're not supposed to know that just yet.

I really love Alphonse. He listens to me when I speak, and when I need help he's always there. Where is he? Life has given me nothing: my daughter's crying into her pillow, my son, the eldest one, must be reading in the kitchen (that one doesn't give a damn about anything!) and my husband who used to be so handsome, a man now all alone in life, a man who used to be so strong, has to steady himself on the door frame so he doesn't fall. My goodness! They say it's going to be cold tomorrow. And Alphonse didn't take his sweater with him! I mustn't forget to buy cheese for tomorrow.

We mustn't scold Alphonse. We'll have to try and understand why he left. That's it.

In her bed, the sister started to cry. She had said one or two prayers but what good was that? Alphonse won't be coming back. She was used to looking after him. When he was little she took him for walks, she bathed him, she gave him little presents. He was her baby brother. At night, when Alphonse would awaken, she'd wake up right away too, stirred by a feeling of protectiveness.

Alphonse, where are you going? I'd ask him every time.

I'm going to get a glass of water.

Do you want me to get it for you?

No thanks, Sis, I need to stretch my legs.

He always said exactly the same thing: it was to stretch his legs!

But I know it was really to sneak into the pantry and stuff his face with marshmallow cookies.

Actually, the real reason Alphonse would get up was very very different…

THE REAL REASON ALPHONSE WOULD
GET UP IN THE MIDDLE OF THE NIGHT

Alphonse would get up each night to meet—in the hallway that led to the kitchen—Pierre-Paul-René, a gentle boy with a one-note voice who was never surprised by anything, and who only he, Alphonse, was acquainted with. In the time it took to go from the bedroom to the kitchen, Alphonse and Pierre-Paul-René could live out a thousand adventures in the dark.

Pierre-Paul-René always appeared to him at night since it was during a ferocious stormy night when Alphonse had gotten up to get a glass of water that they met for the first time.

On that unforgettable night Alphonse had found himself sitting up in his bed, his eyes wide open; the surrounding darkness stuck its tongue out at him. In the next bed his brother was fast asleep and seemed totally consumed by mysterious affairs no one else had access to.
The closed shutters painted the room a thick jelly-black. The storm was magnificent. Alphonse was very thirsty. The kitchen was far away. Very far away. Between the kitchen and Alphonse lay the hallway, and in the hallway anything could happen. Because first, Alphonse had to go all the way down the hallway to reach the switch that would fill it with light. The hallway. That cold hallway that led to a bottomless living room and a dining room that was loudly digesting creaky wood. Alphonse's pyjamas were too big, too long. Getting out of bed seemed unthinkable under such conditions. But he was so thirsty and the water would be so nice and cool in the earthenware jug.
His brother rolled over. Waking him up would unquestionably jeopardize his internal affairs.

The hallway furrowed its eyebrows at him. Alphonse was terrorized! And he knew very well that he couldn't even *consider* waking up his mother. Because she was certain to get angry and that would be awful. Really, Alphonse, you're not a little boy anymore was what she said to him the last time. But now the horrible thirst ravaging his throat was so unbearable it made him forget his fear for an instant and coaxed him out of bed. By the time he reached the edge of the hallway, it was too late to turn back! The storm kept on crashing louder and louder, and in a flash of lightning the hallway filled with sordid characters lurking at the foot of the wall... the floor was nonexistent, and falling into the void seemed inevitable. And then! Right then, in a flash of lightning, Alphonse saw, at the other end of the hallway—for just a brief moment—a boy looking right at him.
Alphonse! he thought he heard in the middle of the storm.
—Who are you?
—I'm Pierre-Paul-René! A gentle boy with a one-note voice and I'm never surprised by anything. I've come to live inside your head, Alphonse. From now on you won't be afraid when you get up in the middle of the night and unafraid you'll cross the hallway to get your glass of water because I will always be there.

And that was it!
That night, when he went back to bed, Alphonse dreamed about Pierre-Paul-René... strange dreams, very strange dreams...

Pierre-Paul-René was sitting at the foot of a building. Children played serenely in the shade of some brontosauri frolicking gaily in the grass. The wind gusted through the falling rain. Pierre-Paul-René was happy. Little by little, the rain died down and the wind took a bow, having chased away the clouds. The daylight dissolved into silence, the children had disappeared, and the brontosauri were levitating. Suddenly, sucked up by a giant vacuum cleaner that appeared out of a cottonosity of clouds, Pierre-Paul-René found himself inside a tube that smelled like seashells and sausages and which was pulling him along at an incredible speed. Pierre-Paul-René thought it was the end of the world and therefore decided it would be pointless to scream, since he was a gentle boy with a one-note voice and was never surprised by anything. He remained absolutely calm and let himself be dragged through the dark when he felt himself slow down and land on a wooden floor. There were five nightlights that lit up nothing but Darkness, that fallen Princess famous for frightening children. Pierre-Paul-René decided to play it safe. He called out: Yo, is anybody there?
—Yes there's somebody, came the reply. There's Sabayon the Fourth, your king, and I've chosen you for a mission!
—Why me?
—Because you're the only child left.
Sabayon the Fourth continued: Yes, this mission is crucial, Pierre-Paul-René, to bring back the children of our country, because there are no more cakes, the pastry chefs have all disappeared, some dead, others eaten by the enemy and the rest turned into popcorn!
Pierre-Paul-René, who's a gentle boy with a one-note voice who's never surprised by anything, was nonetheless a bit surprised.
No more cakes? he said.
—No!
—Drat!
—What is the world coming to? People don't believe in miracles anymore. The pastry chefs have disappeared! The situation is critical. Pierre-Paul-René, you must go to Pastryburg, that savage land teeming with legends and traps. There you must find the cake recipes the pastry chefs took with them and bring them back here. Go, Pierre-Paul-René, you must go to Pastryburg. Go. You must also beware of the infamous Flupan, the prince of excessively gluttonous gluttons. Go, Pierre-Paul-René, go, go, go, I tell you, you must go to Pastryburg, go—
—Okay, okay, I get the message.
—Go, run, fly, don't forget the children, and remember me!

Then Sabayon the Fourth opened the great vacuum cleaner that was his body and Pierre-Paul-René walked out. The landscape around him was extremely indecisive. The sky kept changing from white to blue and back again; the trees, not knowing what season it was, kept losing their leaves but new ones would sprout immediately; the sea turned to desert and the desert turned to wind which multiplied among the stalks of the flowers, which were frantically opening and closing. Faced with so much indecision, Pierre-Paul-René was overwhelmed. He didn't know which foot to put forward first to begin his journey, and he didn't know what direction to take either.

I have to make a decision, he thought.

ALPHONSE'S FAMILY NOTIFIES THE POLICE

The brother, still in the kitchen, kept silently repeating to himself that yes, something might have happened to Alphonse, and that would be awful. And if he'd been kidnapped, taken prisoner, yes, dragged off by sinister characters, raped even, yes, then tomorrow they'll find his body in the river! Call the police! We'll wait a bit longer, the father shot from his window. It's already after midnight, Dad!

So call then, go ahead, call.

Alphonse was still walking on a country road. It was night. The trees, on either side of the road, opened their arms to welcome him. Immersed in his story about Pierre-Paul-René, Alphonse was straining his imagination to extricate his hero from the most ludicrous of situations. It's quite a job to make up a story like this one! Alphonse said to himself.

Obviously, a child who doesn't come home one night, that's rather vague! What do you want us to do! We'll wait a bit, and tomorrow all the police stations in the capital will have all the particulars, and that's all we can do, and then we'll keep on waiting! People expect us to perform miracles! What's his name? Alphonse? Right, well… we'll see what we can do! My name is Victor, I'm the Police Inspector. Tomorrow I'll go do a little investigating to see what I can find out!

There was a picture of Alphonse on his desk and Victor looked at it distractedly. Victor is a really good policeman. Affable and understanding. Thank you. Alphonse. For once I'm not dealing with some hoodlum or scumbag…. Alphonse. Now all we have to do is find him.

Hello. I'm François, I live next door to Alphonse's family. I heard through the wall that Alphonse still hasn't come home! No, I don't sleep much at night. Alphonse, I know him a bit, we run into each other sometimes on the landing, in front of the elevator. We chat a bit. Hello, Alphonse. Hi, François! That sort of thing. Poor Alphonse! When they find him, they'll want to know why he left, they're going to ask for an explanation! Poor kid. As soon as you have to explain yourself things get complicated, because explaining yourself means justifying yourself, and justifying yourself is the end. Something's up, somewhere. The clues seem clear to me. Alphonse has disappeared. The whole world of the invisible is speaking to us through his disappearance. But no one teaches us to tell the difference between lies and fiction.

GATHERING INFORMATION AT ALPHONSE'S SCHOOL

Alphonse is quite a strange boy. A bit disturbed... yes, disturbed, in the clinical sense of the term of course! He's the kind of pathological case I see quite often in my work with young adolescents. Child psychology holds very few surprises for an experienced clinician like myself. A boy has disappeared. Well, we can understand his parents' anxiety, but the desire to run away is simply a stage of adolescence. Some kids do it, some don't, but all think about it at one point or another. Isn't that right, my dear colleague?

Yes, yes, if you say so. Well, then I'll introduce myself, since we have to introduce ourselves. I'm his French teacher, Monsieur Gayaud. They just called me because I'm his main teacher, that is, his homeroom teacher. Look, I have no idea where Alphonse could be... and I don't care all that much. You know, the teaching profession is very demanding, you have to answer the students' questions, know everything, and then there's the pressure from the parents, and then whoops, a child just disappeared and *I* get called! What do you want me to say? It all gets very tiring. Alphonse! He's probably just getting into some mischief with his friend, if you want my opinion.

The two men smoked their cigarettes in silence, then went into the classroom where all the students were at their desks. The principal was there, as well as the superintendent.

I'm Leon. I'm in Alphonse's class! Wait, I haven't finished—
—I'm Albert! I'm in Alphonse's class too (it's not just Leon)! So they told us Alphonse disappeared, and they like want to know what happened to him. Like, what we think and all that. Wait, no wait, I'm not fini—
—I'm Arnold! *I'm* in Alphonse's class too! I told the principal, and Monsieur Gayaud and the psychologist, I told them what I thought of Alphonse. That I hadn't talked to him that often, but that I didn't mind him as long as he didn't talk to me!
—Shut up Arnold! I'm Roger, the school jock. In sports everyone wants me on their team. Alphonse was kind of puny. But I like Alphonse. He was an ace at marbles, and I'm the same at sports so we had something in common! So my question is, Mr. Principal, is Alphonse dead?
We don't think so. Your schoolmate has probably gotten lost. Which one of you knows him the best, or spent the most time with him?
Jules turned around.
I think Alphonse talked to Walter the most.
And where is Walter? the principal asked.
Monsieur Gayaud leaned over and told him that Walter hadn't come to school

today because he was very sick.
Well then! All we have to do is call Walter and we'll know where Alphonse is!
concluded the old Principal as he left the room.

WALTER, ALPHONSE'S FRIEND

Walter and Alphonse met one day. Nobody knows where or how. They say it
happened very simply. Hi, I'm Walter. My name is Alphonse. And that was that.
Walter gave Alphonse his cookies, and Alphonse won at marbles and shared his
winnings with Walter.

Alphonse.... We didn't know where he came from. One day, just like that, I just
saw him coming around the corner. His eyes were very gentle. He wasn't very
good at grammar and when he didn't know how to answer, he would just look
up and stare into space. I'm Walter; Alphonse used to be my best friend. I don't
know what's happened since, but anyway… I still like Alphonse. Alphonse is
so fantastic! He plays marbles and, you gotta admit, Alphonse is awesome at
marbles! He could decimate *anyone* at marbles! But Alphonse doesn't like to
argue, so if the other kids got too upset, not only did he never hesitate to give
back all the marbles he'd won, he would smile and very discreetly slip in some
of his own as well. Then he would always raise his head and gaze for a long time
at the rooftops where every so often you could see people's laundry drying in
the sun.

Before, when we were still talking to each other, we would meet in the morning
to walk to school together. I would carry his bag and Alphonse, in a burst of
morning enthusiasm, would launch into stories of his nocturnal adventures.
His nocturnal adventures, give me a break…. He told me lies. He made me
believe incredible things!! And I have to admit, I did believe him! For a long
time I thought he was telling me the truth. Yeah, man, it was awesome! he
would always start off.
Oh yeah? Let's hear!
And then he'd be off. And now that I'm telling you, I suspect he even made it up
as he went along!
Guess what? he'd say. Last night, Walter, last night, an awesome thing happened.
Three shady-looking guys were after me, and I had to run all the way to the
outskirts of the city where they park the boats for the winter!
No way!
I swear to you, man! Yeah! I thought I was a goner. I swear, I'm not stupid, you
know, so I said to myself, Alphonse, you gotta ditch them. So I climbed into
a boat and there, in the boats, there were all these sailors lying down—they were
sleeping! Then one woke up, he had tattoos up to his eyeballs. The shady-
looking guys got there and a fight broke out. They were going at each other
like you wouldn't believe! I let them beat each other up and I took off and so
last night, I ended up sleeping in the subway!

No way! And he would have bags under his eyes, so I believed him and I would worry! He made me promise not to tell anyone! He swore me to secrecy! And I believed him! I know now that they were just stories he'd made up. But that's what he was like. He'd lie awake all night so he could think up incredible stories to tell me in the morning. I used to ask him: Alphonse, what the hell gets into you wandering around at night like that?

At night, Walter, there are lights that don't go out until the first sign of daylight. They're just standing there in the middle of the night. Windows of light. On the other side of the light are things. People too, I guess. But you know, Walter, people and things have never really interested me. There were those lights, that was enough. It'll always be enough. At night everything is so different: there isn't enough light to see where the trees end. Everything merges with the night: buildings, people, cranes and bulldozers you can make out by the smell of their metal, they all climb towards the night and embrace it, caress it. That's why love, Walter, is especially at night. Yes, because everything loses itself in us and we become bigger, more beautiful, more generous with our bodies. At night, Walter, there's only the orange moon that slips in slivers through the window grate and lingers softly over languorous bellies. The night sculpts you, Walter. It's true, you can't see for miles around the way you can in broad daylight, no, Walter—at night, out of fear, you can only hold onto the things that are right around you, and the darker the night, the more you see inside yourself, Walter, because you're really the only thing you can still see.

Walter, I love the night and the people who inhabit it. One day you'll come with me and you'll see.

VICTOR QUESTIONS ALPHONSE'S FAMILY

Alphonse, like I said at the beginning, is my little brother! Sometimes, when my parents were asleep, we would hang out in the kitchen talking in whispers, and even though I had exams in the morning he would keep me up till three a.m. "My brother, do we have to experience different cultures to truly grasp the fact that we all only seek to be loved?"

Did he have a girlfriend? Victor asked.

You know, Inspector, we're a respectable family! My husband earns an honest living, and my son to whom you're referring is a very intelligent boy! We're upstanding people, you know!

All right, all right Ma'am! We'll wait a while longer.

We've been waiting for three days! exclaimed the father who got up and left the room. The mother started crying again, moaning: What on earth could have gotten into Alphonse?! The brother remained standing, and the sister kept her head bowed, her hands in her lap. The sun, radiant and orange, gently lowered itself onto the smooth tiles of the kitchen floor. Victor got up and left the apartment.

They must be in an absolute panic at home, they must be worried half to death! That's what Alphonse was saying to himself as he walked along his country road when suddenly a phone started ringing. Pierre-Paul-René whirled around with a start and looked everywhere for some semblance of a telephone but there was nothing in sight. Not a leaf, not a stone, much less a telephone jack! Still, the ringing continued loud and clear. Confounded by the absurdity of the situation, he shouted just in case: Hello?
—Pierre-Paul-René?
—Speaking.
—Go north!
—Who is this?
—It's Flupan. Flupan-the-Evil-Flupan-the-glutton—Flupan!
—What do you want?
—Me? I don't want anything, my boy, I want the best for you, I'm telling you which way to go: Pastryburg is to the north.
—Why should I believe you? Huh?
—Because my goal is to lead you right into my clutches. I spend my time eating cookies and cakes, a little boy like you would make a succulent appetizer!
—Shut up!
—You see? You don't have a chance, you snotty-nosed brat, go back to your village, go away before I unleash my powers on you!!
—Go away!
—I can't go away because I'm not there!
—Hang up!
—I don't want to, I'm having too much fun!
—Then *I'm hanging* up. "Click."

Instant silence. Just the drone of the dial tone that soon gave way to a voice that insistently repeated: Please hang up and try your call again. Please hang up now.... Pierre-Paul-René continued on his way towards the north, towards the night. Soon, when darkness kneeled over the entire countryside, he could see a tiny glow, just above the horizon. It was the fortress of Pastryburg. The closer he got to his destination, the worse he slept at night because of horrible dreams in which a horrible Flupan used a cake recipe to turn him into popcorn. Not to mention the enticing smells of caramel custard, whipped cream and chocolate fudge that sometimes floated towards him from Pastryburg, teasing his nostrils.

THE PICTURE OF ALPHONSE IN THE
NEWSPAPER (JUST A SMALL ONE)

For several days now, Alphonse's picture had been in the papers. (Just a small one, since the situation wasn't serious enough yet.)

Hello, I'm Judith. I just saw the picture. I wanted to introduce myself right away because soon—not right away, but soon—my name is undoubtedly going to come up. See you later.

VICTOR DOESN'T UNCOVER ANY NEW
INFORMATION, BUT HE HEARS A STORY

Victor is a calm and thoughtful police inspector. On his way out of Alphonse's apartment he met François who was waiting for the elevator.

Inspector, you have to understand. You're dealing with a dreamer.
—Yes, he's a child!
—He probably doesn't even know himself why he didn't come home, and now he can't turn back, since he knows full well that everyone's going to want to know what made him leave!
—True, said the Inspector. A young romantic.
—Listen, Inspector, I can't help you.
—So help me out then… you knew him well.
—Since you're asking my advice, I'll simply say that to find Alphonse, you have to search within the invisible.
—And what is this "invisible" you're always talking about? How do I access it?
—There might be something in this story, Mr. Inspector, that Alphonse told me one night when we ran into each other on the street. We walked home together taking our time, and Alphonse told me a story that he was incredibly excited about.
—What was it about?
—It was a story of a journey, about a strange man who went off on foot in search of a wild child. There was a mountain and a storm, I think.
—Tell it to me.

François couldn't remember all the details perfectly, but as the narrator, I don't want to repeat his hesitations since that will only slow things down. Here then is that famous story as it was told to François by Alphonse.

A man set off one fine morning along a country road that led to the foot of the mountain where, they said, a wild child who was a gentle boy with a one-note voice who was never surprised by anything lived among wolves in a cave near stretches of ice which at that altitude formed a plateau where ancient trees grew.

The sun rose weeping, and swept the fog off the road; the fog stretched and curled up, trying to snuggle even closer to the earth; the purple dawn glided towards the distant plains, and the night disappeared on the other side of the horizon. The opaque dampness completely swallowed the village; the mountain breeze blew gently, a storm was brewing.

When the man reached the foot of the mountain, he rested a moment on a huge boulder that jutted out from the roots of a tree. Clouds were slowly piling up on top of each other, making it so dark it was hard to see windows winking in the village nearby.

The man started off again. His climb lasted the whole morning and a good part of the afternoon; and, since he didn't have a watch and couldn't refer to the sun's position, he gradually completely lost his sense of reality thinking it was already far into the night while in fact, in the village where the fog was lifting, the clock of the church bells was only striking eight.

Since the paths were growing narrower and the mountainside steeper, the man had to make his way up by zigzagging! The sky was very low, and soon the man was lost in a cloud. It was only when he'd completely lost his sense of direction, could no longer tell if he was going up or down, and was gripped by the fear of falling or being attacked by an animal, mixed with a wild panic—that survival instinct that makes an animal tremble when it senses its death approaching—and was finally so tired and delirious he could no longer put one foot in front of the other, that he collapsed in the middle of the brambles and fell asleep. At that instant, the howling of wolves was heard...

François stopped his story for a moment. He took out a cigarette and offered one to Victor. They stayed like that for a long while, smoking in silence.

This won't help my investigation, but go on. It's so rare for someone to tell me a story in this damned line of work. Go on!

The man was awakened by the movement of the sky opening up. Bolts of lightning illuminated the horizon, relegating the day that was struggling to rise to twilight regions where it died at every clap of thunder. The wind played with the rain, darting and dancing with the drops in a crazy farandole, blowing bubbles of water into the air that briefly resembled a furtive shadow about to explode.

Come on! Be strong! the man said to himself. It's only a storm. It will peter out eventually. And I'll get through it eventually. In two days it'll all be over. I just have to keep going, keep climbing higher and higher!

He went on climbing. Here and there he grabbed onto whatever twigs he could, and when he glimpsed the dark mass of trees living higher up on the mountain, it gave him a second wind. But, at the curve of a little cloud the man saw the wolves for the first time. There were four of them, and they seemed to be waiting for him because as soon as he was facing them they moved towards him, lowering their heads as if in greeting, then turned and set off along the road, inviting him to follow. They led him higher, crossing through the clouds, winding 'round the rain, avoiding the wind, all the way to the summit of the storm from which they emerged to discover the firmament and the Milky Way spilling out along the sky. The wolves stationed themselves on a boulder that overlooked the valley and howled at the night. The man stood contemplating the cloudy mass of the storm: it formed a dark ocean at his feet and continued to unleash fierce torrents of rain.

It wasn't until the damp dawn that they arrived in front of a cave with a narrow opening. The wolves stood guard on either side of the entrance and lowered their heads once again. The man squeezed through the narrow passage and pressed on until he could only continue by crawling! It was suddenly very cold. There was a smell of dead leaves that grew stronger where it was most damp. If the cave keeps narrowing I won't be able to go any further, he said to himself. Sounds reached him from a distance, from the other side of the rocky walls. He crawled for a good while longer until he reached a cavity where he could almost stand up. Now look where I am! he sighed. Now I'm lost for good.
—I've been waiting for you for a long time.
The gentle wild child with a one-note voice who's never surprised by anything was there, beside him, in the bowels of the earth.
—You're here?
—I've been waiting for you for a long time!
—A long time? The man asked again.
—A long time! Yes!
—How old are you then, you whose voice is so old, so slow, and who people still call the "wild child"?
—Like all children, my age varies according to the day. Sometimes I like to be as old as a tree.
—Can you see me?
—I can imagine you. It's nicer that way.
—Do you know where I come from, wild child, do you know what world I live in?
—Tell me.
—Listen. I come from a strange, lost world. Everything started one morning, when after getting up and walking outside, I saw that all those around me had a terrible despair in their eyes. All of them without exception, were walking and weeping as they walked. And crying out. I'd heard of you. So I came to see if your eyes contained the same terrible despair. But I can't see you. It's too dark!
—I'm a gentle child with a one-note voice and I'm never surprised by anything, since I'm not familiar with the world you describe.
—Does it make you unhappy, little child, not to know the world? Or does it make you happy?
—What do you think?
—It's hard to tell from your voice. But it's possible that you're no happier or unhappier than me.
—Then that doubt is more than enough. Don't you think? Maybe that's what you call hope.

—You're awesome.
—I'm the wild child.
—Farewell.
—Farewell.
In the morning, some shepherds found him dead, frozen, at the foot of the mountain. He was a man of about forty whom no one could identify. Nobody knew him. Some had seen him walk through the village the previous morning, before the storm had struck the mountain.

Victor and François had been finished their cigarettes for a while. Victor rose, and the two men shook hands.

It's a shame the man dies at the end, Victor said.
I shared that same thought with Alphonse. He said no, on the contrary, it was better that way since the man had actually died the moment he fell into the brambles, which meant that the second part of the story, about the storm, the wolves and the cave was his last dream. And a last dream, in Alphonse's opinion, is a beautiful story to tell.

—A last dream! mused the Inspector.

VICTOR'S INVESTIGATION CONTINUES AT SCHOOL
AND IN THE SURROUNDING AREA

Tell me, Walter, what did you two do together when you didn't have school?
On Sundays, we used to go to the museum to laugh at the stuffed horses, Mr. Inspector.
And after that?
We also liked to run around in the big parks and it was always very late by the time we found our way home and said goodbye.
So you two got along very well it seems.
Well… Alphonse ate a lot of cookies. And I lost at marbles pretty much all the time. That was the secret of our friendship.

The children were gathered together in the sunlight of the schoolyard, sitting in a circle around Victor. It felt like one of those days at the end of the school year, when the summer holidays are just around the corner, exams are over and the teachers, having nothing more to teach, just do fun activities with their students. But now, because Victor was so serious, the children weren't the least bit rowdy or unruly. Walter even had his head down and was having trouble hiding his immense sadness. Because Walter knew a thing or two about Alphonse.

—We weren't too sure about Alphonse! In class, he always sat at the back and he never talked. All he did was smile!
—It's true what Leopold says. Even the teacher was afraid of him! Plus, he was a liar!

—Yeah, a big fat liar. I know. My name's Jules, and one day Alphonse tried
to make me believe he was a secret agent hired by the government to spy on
people his age in the schools! He tried to suck me in! But I'm not stupid!
—I believed him a little. My name is Ahmed. One day I figured out that
Alphonse was just telling stories! But me, Ahmed, I said this to Alphonse and
then, Alphonse, he didn't want to talk to me, Ahmed, anymore.
—Mr. Inspector! I'm the most serious one in the class, that is, the top student.
You can ask Mr. Gayaud—he'll tell you "Hubert's the top student"—and I knew
right away that all that talk about the night and sailors and everything was
a bunch of lies. I told Walter and Walter could tell that Alphonse was just
making up stories, so we all told Walter: "You have to watch Alphonse! He's
a real weirdo! He isn't normal!" He tried to make us believe his mother was
dead! He's a liar! He says all kinds of things, Mr. Policeman, all kinds of things!
We don't even know where he comes from! And we told Walter: Alphonse is
gonna fail, he's not a good student at all! You saw for yourself, at recess he sucks
at sports and he whines his head off!
That's not true, Walter replied. At marbles Alphonse is awesome—
—But we don't care about marbles, Walter, we don't give a shit, understand?

The Inspector took Walter aside and let his classmates go.

Does it upset you, what they say about Alphonse?
They're all jerks! Yesterday, when Alphonse had been missing for a week, they all
acted like idiots!! They were saying the most horrible things about him—that he
had choked to death on his own tongue, that he'd fallen off a bridge, and even
worse stuff, but I know why Alphonse left, he was sick of it! Yeah, and now if
he's dead, it's 'cause someone bashed his head in! Alphonse will always be at
the foot of my bed. At night I hear him telling his fantastic stories, I see him
in the mirror, sitting in the armchair, Alphonse is everywhere! He told me such
beautiful stories, I believed every word! How can I be mad at him? For what?
They were so beautiful!

When he reached the gates of Pastryburg, it was raining buckets. Entire clouds
were bursting open one on top of the other. Pierre-Paul-René went up to two
enormous wooden doors without any idea how he was going to go through
them. They were adorned with heavy, solid gold sculptures and capped by
a crown of ice. The keyhole was much too high and far too narrow. There was
also an old man crouched in front of these doors, a hat pulled down over his
eyes, and a beard that went on forever wrapped around him. Pierre-Paul-René
stopped.
Who are you, boy?
Pierre-Paul-René.
Ahhh!!! So it's *you*.
Uh huh.
I'm warning you! If you don't answer my question correctly, I'll turn you into
popcorn like all the others; if you give the right answer, I'll let you in and I'll

grant you any two wishes you like.

Pierre-Paul-René looked around him and saw that he was ankle-deep in popcorn, and that from time to time, the old man would flick a piece into his mouth and crunch it.

So? Are you ready?

Yes.

Suddenly, a wild wind whipped itself around them, sending the popcorn whirling all over the place. The old man's hat hadn't moved at all, something that surprised even Pierre-Paul-René who is however a gentle boy with a one-note voice who's never surprised by anything. Night was starting to nibble away at the day. It was so strange! Pierre-Paul-René and the old man were standing there, at the threshold of night and the kingdom of dreams. The rain wouldn't stop, and the wind seemed to be rising from the earth. Then, as though he were reciting an incantation, the old man asked his question: "Why does a tree grow tall? Why does a man grow old? Why does a river run into the sea? Why does the earth keep turning? My question, Pierre-Paul-René, is the following: These four questions can be contained in a single question. What is that question?"

Still on the road, Alphonse found this sort of situation tricky because he himself—the one making up the story—didn't know the answer. He continued on his way, and pondered.

The imposing fortress facing Pierre-Paul-René seemed to be looking at him tenderly. An owl landed for a moment on the ramparts, hooting "hoo, hoo." The doors certainly looked impenetrable, but he was sure they had a charming side that would let anybody in.

The owl has found one of those sides; now it's up to me to find another. Hoo... hoo... the owl disappeared. Pierre-Paul-René then realized that everything was up to him, that he could decide whether he was happy, worried, or even sad. That he could, if he felt like it, be a good boy and go home to his mother, who must be worried half to death. I don't want to go back home. Then what do I want? To eat, maybe. To sleep, to drink, to live! The day was starting to make itself known. Since nature knows very well what it wants, it doesn't fret or worry. Day exists because we need day, the moon exists because it's beautiful. But me, I'm just a kid, and I don't know how to do anything except keep putting one foot in front of the other, why do I exist? Why do I exist? he cried out loud, which made the old man start and stagger towards him! Bravo, bravo, that's the correct answer! Why do I exist? That's the right answer... now I'll finally be able to shave! Quick my boy, what are your two wishes?

—First of all, I'd like you to let my mother know I'm all right.

—Done.

—With no magic spell??

—You don't need a spell, because spells are only noise. Know, young man, that a tree's branches and the peaks of mountains rise up in the silence of the invisible... and yet what magic is greater than nature's? Abracadabras and other hoopla are nothing more than circumstantial decorations used by people who lack imagination. The man who makes noise is a man who is frightened. Your second wish.

—I'd like to have all the recipes the evil Flupan took away with him.

—Oh no! That would be too easy! Yes, too easy indeed! Pierre-Paul-René, have you really thought about it? When you return what will you tell all the children who are hungry for details? What will you tell them? Children want exciting adventures where danger is synonymous with red roses! That's right! Pierre-Paul-René, if you manage to recover the recipes yourself, and if you manage to get out of Pastryburg alive, you'll become a hero that will inspire future generations.

Pierre-Paul-René felt that the ultimate purpose of his mission had just taken a different turn.

—Can I make another wish then?

—Yes.

—I'd like a kaleidoscope please, sir.

—You'll find one at the entrance to the city. And now, be off.

The doors yawned open slowly, so slowly that Pierre-Paul-René had time to grow up and ponder. When the gap was wide enough for him to slip through, Pierre-Paul-René stood up, said goodbye to the old man, and squeezed through the narrow opening.

That day, Pierre-Paul-René had just turned 14, but he didn't know it.

The school bell rang. The children stood up and left the classroom, since the school day had just ended. As Walter was leaving, he saw the Inspector come towards him. They walked together, slowly, as they talked.

—So tell me, do you have any idea where he might have gone?

—Yes… well, no, not really, because I don't even know if that person really exists or if it was just another one of his stories!

—Who's that?

—A girl! He told me he was living a love story. Yes!

—What's her name?

—Judith. But it was only a story. I realize that now. What he told me was just too crazy.

JUDITH

I introduced myself quickly a while ago, I'm Judith, so there you go! It all started just like that. People thought it was a love story. But generally, people believe anything. They saw us walking hand in hand and rumours have been flying ever since. In the holes in conversations, on street corners, around cafés, on subway trains, on the radio and even in the newspapers, all people talked about was the love that had just blossomed between Alphonse and me.

Yes. I'm Judith. I'm one of the rare truths that Alphonse told Walter, and the only one Walter didn't believe. You can't really blame him, he was starting to

distrust Alphonse. That's partly why they stopped talking. Anyway....
How did the two of you meet?
Very simply, Inspector. Sitting on a bench, in the big park downtown.
Hi, I'm Judith. He looked at me without a trace of surprise: I'm Alphonse. And
that was that. And then, slowly, things started to happen very quickly. A look
and then a smile...

Alphonse was still walking along a country road. At dawn he had come across
an old man.
Gotta bring in firewood for the winter!
Yes, sir.
Where are you going, boy?
Home, sir.
You're a good little boy.
Uh, sure.
And the old man continued on his way.

Alphonse so would have liked for someone to just take him by the hand and tell
him: this is how life is. That it's not important to be successful at what you
undertake, but rather, to undertake what you'd like to succeed at. It seemed to
Alphonse that things were really backwards. Yes, because of course when we
meet those people, those people who can comfort us, we meet them too late.
They always turn up when we're adults. You'd think there was a conspiracy,
Alphonse thought. When we become grown-ups we have furrowed eyebrows
to show how terribly important we are (which is fine). But when we become
grown-ups we don't want anyone to take us by the hand anymore, we wave our
arms and we say, No! Out of my way! Let me by! Don't you see my furrowed
eyebrows? Can't you see how busy I am?

After passing through the gates of the fortress, Pierre-Paul-René expected to
find the city. But instead, there was a forest filled with a bizarre assortment of
fruit trees. "I'm not there yet," he thought. The tree closest to him was an orange
tree. Hanging from one of its branches was the kaleidoscope, which blended
right in with the oranges. Pierre-Paul-René plucked it down. There was the
woods. The forest was shamelessly cavorting with the horizon. Weird, he said.
The wind suddenly encouraged him to enter the very quintessence of the forest.
The sun was snuffed out and, with the forest so dense, Pierre-Paul-René found
himself in utter, uncompromising blackness. He was afraid. Solitude had
turned against him, the trees were suffocating him, the air was whistling in
the dark and the darkness enveloped him in a bottomless night. The owls had
disappeared, turning the forest's wisdom into a whirlwind of cries, creaks and
cracks that Pierre-Paul-René's imagination was magnifying into all sorts of
monstrosities. At dawn, the dampness hammering at him, he collapsed at the
mouth of a cave, convinced he'd be devoured by the monsters of his mind.

The fog rose and so did Alphonse. He kissed me on the lips and said "Goodbye, Judith. Thank you." He handed me a letter and he left. That was the last day anyone saw him.

Can you read me that letter, Miss?
Of course, but you mustn't talk about it. It's better for his parents to believe I'm a lie.
Here is that letter:

Judith,

It's no secret, this is Alphonse writing to Judith. I'm sitting down in an armchair and I'm writing to you. Because I love you very much. This isn't a declaration of love.

Judith, I'm afraid. Because I don't think life will bring us any closer together. I'm writing to you and you aren't answering me, I'm writing to you and you don't know that I'm writing to you. Do you ever think about me? Judith, I'm not happy here where I am, I'm not happy!

I've come to tell you who I am. It isn't easy because I'm young, and at my age you aren't supposed to say such things. I love you, but I'm afraid. I don't want to scare you, frighten you, see you run the way wild horses run. I love you.
How to tell you who I am? My name is Alphonse but that's just a convention. What I love about you isn't your face, because your face isn't you, but something that belongs to you. Just like your smile, your legs and your hands, which are part of you, but not the essence of you. You're much more than a hand or a face and it's you that I love Judith.

Close your eyes. Listen. Listen to the rain on my face. Listen. You told me yesterday your name was Judith. Come. There's a cliff, a cliff, where it's good to jump, where it's good to die. I wish the storm would make three times as much racket.
Come on! A simple leap! Then we'd see life from a bit higher up, we'll fly like migratory birds. I'll show you fragile places, you'll learn to weep the way eagles weep when they fall beneath the storm, come, we'll fly away and we'll see the oceans, we'll see them flow into each other, their blues, their reds, we'll see the oceans make love to each other to give birth to new continents, come with me, let's return to that special cliff. Come. You'll know who I am.

Alphonse

Judith?
Yes, Mr. Inspector?
Where could he be?
I don't know, Mr. Inspector.

Alphonse was still walking straight ahead, determined to follow the road that would lead him north. But since Alphonse had no sense of direction and since he didn't realize he had no sense of direction, he had no idea he was actually walking west, and that if he continued that way he'd be completely lost, and that in fact he was a bit lost already. A car pulls up beside him. The window rolls down. Where are you going, lad? Home. Right. And where might your home be? My home? ...ummm... (Alphonse gestured vaguely) That way! And guess which way the police station is! Let's go! In the car, laddie! Everyone's been looking for you for the past two weeks!

Now Pierre-Paul-René is lying in the belly of the cave. Being a hero to inspire future generations doesn't interest me anymore. The complex architecture of the cave was weighing on his feelings. Not far from him, a stalactite was dripping. Each drop would appear, detach itself slowly, break away from the stone, hang in the air for a moment, then crash onto the rock an instant later. Why are you weeping, cave?

There is the known and the unknown.

Pierre-Paul-René didn't dare to ask any other questions.

I am the cave. I'm the open mouth of mountains and I shelter beings from the rain. And for centuries I've been weeping because I'm growing old, and I weep because I'm growing weak! So much weight rests on me. So I weep and my tears climb, they climb, and, becoming solid, they rise to my ceiling to help me support all that weight; but a day will come when all these columns of tears will fill me. And then I'll disappear.

You weep so you can disappear, cave? That isn't a good idea.

I weep to change.

There must be other ways to change, cave.

This is the only way I know. I'm only a cave.

A while ago, there were monsters who wanted to devour my chest. It hurt so much I wept too.

Changing isn't easy. Ideas, beautiful things change; they know how to change, because to change is to go beyond pain, to change is to disappear one day and then fill the space with yourself! That's the great secret of caves.

AT THE POLICE STATION

When I saw him come in, he looked like every kid who's brought into the police station after being caught. Eyes downcast and worried. They're all like that in the face of power. In the face of authority. But if he only knew how endearing I found him, maybe then he'd have smiled at me. We get so many scumbags parading through here all day long, a boy like Alphonse is a real gem. I'm Victor, the Inspector for the police station. I think I already told you that. Anyway, Alphonse wouldn't look at me. I was happy to know his parents lived so far away, it'd take them a while to come and get him. An hour, maybe. An hour to get him to look at me.

The sister, in her bed, started to cry. Alphonse is coming home, I'll be able to sleep. My mother, in the living room, still hasn't spoken a word to my father who must be waiting by the window as usual, a cigarette in his heartstrings. My other brother has left to get Alphonse at the police station. I'd like to leave too! Go off towards the midnight sun and freeze to death....

She closed her eyes.

Alphonse opened his.

His brother was there, standing beside Victor.

His brother signed the release forms and I watched them leave. I never saw Alphonse again, but they say he's happy now, in some other country.

THE RIDE HOME AND MEMORIES OF DRIVES PAST

It was a long drive. Alphonse's forehead was pressed against the rear window of the taxi. A very long time ago, when Alphonse was still small, every Sunday the whole family would go for a drive.

In the car, they would sleep. It was quiet, it was boring, and it was carefree. They rarely remembered their dreams. Maybe the car was moving too fast, there's no time to figure things out, get oriented. The mountains in the distance were touching down on the earth, clouds were clinging to them. When Alphonse's father drove, no one could tell what was going through his head. But the signs seemed reassuring. A smile, he turned on the radio... he was trying not to worry, today was Sunday.... As for the rain, it spawned more drops on the rear window; on Sundays, when the father took the whole family to a restaurant overlooking a ravine, the sun was often hanging out somewhere behind the rain. The rain too was part of the Sunday ritual.

Alphonse didn't like sitting in the middle of the back seat between his brother on the right and his sister on the left. You couldn't sleep there. You couldn't see into the ravines and you couldn't see the seashore. It was the most insignificant place to sit, and they put him there just because he was the smallest. No one ever seemed to notice these sorts of injustices.

On lonely roads, where no other cars kept them company, roads that wound endlessly above ravines, roads from which the city appeared at their feet even dirtier than before, it seemed to Alphonse that they were alone in the world. At those moments the radio would inevitably be playing a slow song, with long monotonous chants, a song where a single voice recounted the tragic epic of some Persian king. At those moments, everyone was silent. His sister, brother and mother would look out their respective windows; only his father, smiling, would still be staring straight ahead. The wonderful road, twisting and turning, surrounded by cedars and pines with their arms wide open, showed him the path to happiness.

"So, Alphonse," his father would ask, "Are you hungry?"

Sometimes we respond awkwardly to those affectionate questions, and then we think that all is ruined. Things really changed. Yes. His father wasn't sad and unhappy yet, wasn't making compromises, he was trying to be happy. Those drives every Sunday were a recipe for happiness that, years later, proved not to be enough.

Pierre-Paul-René now finds himself in the most hidden, the most intimate, most secret place in the cave. There is rock all around his hunched body and there is a terrible rumbling.
Cave! I'm afraid of this rumbling I hear.
What you hear, boy, is the sound of the universe moving forward, over there, on the other side of the invisible! This sound, the origin of all life, can only be heard in the depths of caves. Listen to it; let it cradle you; let it lull you to sleep, I am the cave! Here, nothing can hurt you!
What some of us have to go through for a little chocolate cake, thought Pierre-Paul-René.

Desserts had always posed a problem. The choice was never made without a few tears, and very often Alphonse lost all appetite, to the great delight of his brother who'd get to eat the dessert their mother would end up choosing.
We always sat at the same table, in the same places, just like at home during the week; even in the restaurant the family wore the same faces as usual. For Alphonse, the setting didn't break the phenomenal silence of his childhood.
Obviously, the drive home was more tedious. It was nighttime, with the whiff of "enough fun and games" floating in the air. The father seemed preoccupied by business at the office, he was no longer smiling, and the sense of the invisible had disappeared.

Pierre-Paul-René, still lying in the belly of the cave, had a dream. He dreamed about Alphonse, walking along his country road. He saw him climb up a tree and turn towards him.
Hello Pierre-Paul-René.
Hello Alphonse.
Recite me a poem, Pierre-Paul-René.
I'll never reach Flupan's castle, Alphonse.
Recite me a poem, then open your eyes and you'll see.
A poem, Alphonse? …All right.
Poem.
We have only one candle left to recognize the world that surrounds us.
We mustn't hide anymore.
Look ahead.
Where is life? It's so often somewhere else.
Beyond our disasters of the heart, we will remain true to each other.
How can I forget you without killing you?
And I'd a thousand times rather kill you than leave you behind on the threshold of my memory.
My friendship for you is so strong that in spite of you, I'll remain your strength.
Your friendship is so clear that I need only say the word to begin the journey.

The boy you call Alphonse doesn't seem to be feeling too hot, eh.... I'm the taxi driver who drove him home from the police station. His brother sat beside me and yakked about the weather the whole time... what it was like today, what it would be like tomorrow and after that.... It's strange—now that I'm telling you all this, something just came back to me. At one point in the night sky there was an amazingly bright lightning bolt and it started to rain.

What the taxi driver didn't know, and what I'm going to tell you, is that the amazingly bright lightning bolt was Pierre-Paul-René entering Flupan's castle. When he opened his eyes, he found himself sitting in the taxi on the back seat beside Alphonse, but neither the taxi driver, nor Alphonse's brother had noticed a thing. Alphonse and Pierre-Paul-René, who were pressed up against each other, whispered in each other's ears so they wouldn't be overheard.
—Hi, Alphonse.
—Hi, Pierre-Paul-René.
—I recited the poem, there was an incredible light and I was inside Flupan's castle.
—You see Pierre-Paul-René? Flupan's castle is the world I live in. Flupan's castle is the school and the traffic lights and the sidewalks and the buildings and the mountains and this taxi and this taxi driver—all of this is Flupan's castle.
—The recipes could be hidden anywhere.
—Yes, Pierre-Paul-René, anywhere at all.
—Oh well. Listen, Alphonse, I promised to bring back those recipes, so I'll have to keep on looking.
—Wait, Pierre-Paul-René, I'll never be able to survive here, in this world. You stay here and I'll go back to your world, where the brontosauri frolic on the grass and the vacuum cleaners speak and are kings.
—You'll comfort my mother for me, answered Pierre-Paul-René.
—And you'll do the same for mine, said Alphonse.
And Alphonse and Pierre-Paul-René, who looked so much alike, parted ways once again. In a splendid flash of lightning, Alphonse went back to Pierre-Paul-René's world, and Pierre-Paul-René remained behind in the taxi.
And, coincidentally, the taxi had just come to a stop in front of Alphonse's apartment building.

ALPHONSE

I am Alphonse.

I'm the one people have said all kinds of things about from the beginning.
I didn't mean to run away, or escape, I wasn't sad or unhappy and I loved my parents very much... in fact what happened is much simpler. I simply went in the wrong direction taking the subway home after school. I didn't get off at the next station. Too tired. So I kept going, right to the end of the line. Everybody knows that in certain situations we don't know how to react. And when the

invisible opens before us, it's terrifying. No one teaches us anything about the invisible. Not a thing. When we're children, no one tells us much. For example, when I was small, no one ever told me that the Earth is in a galaxy and that the stars are formed from a pile of star dust that binds together and forms a mass and grows and grows till it collapses onto itself and dying, creates enough energy to shine, sometimes for millions of years. No one ever said a word to me about that. But had I known, it seems to me that yes, it would have comforted me! Yes, it would have helped me sleep.

When Pierre-Paul-René entered the apartment, I don't know exactly what happened. But I can easily imagine. The front door. The hallway, my mother in the living room knitting, my father not talking, my sister sleeping (she must have been pretending) and my brother walking behind Pierre-Paul-René, all the way to my bed. Pierre-Paul-René lay down, he slept. That must be how things went; but what I'm sure of, is that no one noticed a thing. No one could tell the difference between Pierre-Paul-René and me. And no one will ever see the difference, because no one believes in Pierre-Paul-René. Everyone thinks that Pierre-Paul-René doesn't exist, people think that Pierre-Paul-René is a figment of my imagination! So they smile and look at each other and say: Oh, that Alphonse! Honestly! What an imagination! People only believe in what they can see and touch! In fact, people don't want to believe anymore! They want to know. They don't *believe* that the earth is round, they know it. They don't *believe* that the sky is blue, they know it! And people have trapped what they know about me. What they knew about me. But the rest, everything else that's inside me, and around me, and that belongs to me, that part of me that's so small it has to be *believed in*, that part that's even more real than my flesh and blood can ever be, that part that their tired eyes will never be able to see, they haven't caught that part of me, it's still on the road as free as the colours of the night. That part of me is hidden, tucked away, buried; *that's* the part of me that *truly exists*. At least I want to believe that... I want to believe it, so that life, which is just beginning for me, and death, which could strike me at any moment, will both be easier to accept, more joyful, and more beautiful.

Beuys Buoys Boys

a monologue

Ken Garnhum

Ken Garnhum is a comic raconteur who has created many poignant and bittersweet theatrical moments in shows such as *Beuys Buoys Boys*, *Surrounded By Water* and the Chalmers Award-winning *Pants On Fire*. Ken has been playwright-in-residence at Canadian Stage and is also a designer.

Beuys Buoys Boys was first produced by Tarragon Theatre, Toronto in 1989, and remounted for the DuMaurier World Stage Festival, Toronto in 1990 with the following company:

PERFORMER   Ken Garnhum

Designed by Ken Garnhum
Directed by Andy McKim
Lighting Designed by Kevin Lamotte
Stage Managed by Marta Stothers (Tarragon), Allen Clements (World Stage Festival)

Characters

PERFORMER

Notes on Staging

Beuys Buoys Boys does not require a realistic setting, it does require a visual one; objects and images should play an important role. The performance space is a neutral space—a "found" space that has been claimed, or is in the process of being claimed by the performer. When the performer leaves the space at the end of the piece, he leaves it unaltered, with the singular exception of the monument. The erection of this monument is the central action of *Beuys Buoys Boys*; it is the performer's ultimate gesture; it is the mark he leaves behind. There is an attempt in the body of the text to describe the monument and the process of building/assembling it. Directors and designers should feel free to invent, keeping in mind that the monument should, when it is completed, suggest a buoy on the open sea, and that this resemblance to a buoy should be a visual surprise near the end of the performance. This idea of a visual surprise is an important one. When the text notes say that something "appears," the appearance should be unexpected, or even—occasionally—magical. The act of drawing is essential to *Beuys Buoys Boys*, as is the appearance of projected images to support and enhance particular passages of the spoken text. Placement of drawing and slide sequences are indicated in the text, but are described in such a way as to leave much room for invention. Lighting and sound should also play their part in creating a theatrical atmosphere. But the text, for the most part, leaves it to individual directors and designers to decide where these important tools can best be used.

Playwright's Note

The following version of *Beuys Buoys Boys* is a new edition of the play, revised in 2008. The production edition was originally published by Coach House Press in *Making, Out: Plays by Gay Men*, edited by Robert Wallace.

BEUYS BUOYS BOYS
a monologue

It is dark. The performer enters with a hand-held light and delivers the Prologue.

PERFORMER   Late at night, in the dead of winter, the road would look so black, flanked, as it was, by the high, white banks of snow. The patches of ice on the road would look blacker still, black on black. The telephone wires hummed loud in the cold air, and every once in a while the air itself would seem to crack. And a million stars appear.

Stars appear.

I would be walking home from babysitting at the MacLeans's, a couple that actually stayed up late and went to town on a Saturday night. Everyone else was asleep: the Gays, the Judsons, the Wetherbys, the Garnhums, even the goddamn Jenkinses, all asleep.

But then I would think, maybe they're not asleep, maybe they're all dead—yeah, dead—poisoned quietly and painlessly in their sleep by some insidious gas, and now all of the houses are uninhabitable, but I also instinctively know that I have ten minutes in which to enter the houses and collect what I will need to survive. My mind immediately begins to construct a list. Quilts! I decide to collect as many quilts as possible so that I can build a yurt in the back field, just like the Mongolians in the *National Geographic* at the MacLeans's. A quilt tent. I think about this just about every Saturday night for a whole winter.

Hand-held light out. Stars fade to black slowly during the following voiceover, which is spoken, à la Joseph Beuys, with a German accent.

"I was completely buried in the snow. That's how the Tartars found me days later. I remember voices saying '*voda*' (water), then the felt of their tents, and the dense pungent smell of cheese, fat and milk. They covered my body in fat, to help regenerate warmth, and wrapped it in felt as an insulator to keep the warmth in."

End of the Prologue. Lights up on the performer, who is wearing a Beuysian grey-felt hat and felt boots. He is pacing, laying claim to the performance space. He speaks, as he will more or less throughout the performance, directly to the audience.

What a day—what a heavenly day! This is not mere rhetoric—I really mean it. Today is a happy day, because today is the day I get to put it all together. You see, a while back I got this incredibly strong urge to build. Just that—an urge to build—I had no idea what it was that I was going to build; I just knew that I had to build something period! And I thought, boy, this is just a little abstract.

I mean, usually, I get these burning ideas and I have to go about deciding how best to manifest the ideas, but this was a different kettle of fish. I tried to ignore the urge, but it was strong; it stuck with me, and so I began to concentrate on it. I tried to find the idea behind the urge and I was surprised that my mind kept coming back to monuments. *Monuments*—this seemed strange indeed, because I've always thought that most monuments are a big wank; and there are too damn many of them; and they have very little to do with what I think public art should be about. Most public monuments are diversionary at best—they divert our attention away from the present to the past; and they are demanding—they demand reverence for gods, or heroes, or rulers who often deserve much less. Let's face it—most public monuments are just big, ugly, expensive hulks of metal, paid for with public money, to celebrate wars, and kings, and politicians who acted against the public interest.

Monuments are tricky bloody things, too. They often derive their power with sheer scale. A bronze figure of some wanker the same size as me is nothing compared to one forty, or fifty, or sixty feet high.

> *First slide in a sequence of slides of monuments—some literal, some figurative—appears at this point. It depicts a huge bronze figure.*

Suddenly, we were so diminished that the merely huge becomes powerful. But, I discovered, something doesn't have to look like this *(refers to slide)* to be a monument. Any memorial,

> *Slide of tombstone.*

a tombstone, for example, is a monument. A monument can be a mere indication, something that serves to identify or mark,

> *Slide of a roadside granite marker or a Beuys sculpture.*

something that gives a warning, a portent.

> *Slide of buoy on the ocean.*

There are many monuments to industry,

> *Slide of industrial smokestack.*

and many monuments to capitalism.

> *Slide of a bank skyscraper.*

Monuments can be extremely ugly,

> *Slide of "Gumby Goes to Heaven," a monument on University Avenue in Toronto.*

or profoundly beautiful,

> *Slide of the War Memorial in Ottawa.*

in spite of, or occasionally because of what they commemorate.

Additional slides chosen by the performer.

Anything, that by its survival, commemorates a person or action or time, is a monument. We are monuments; each of us is a monument to those whom we have lost because we are the enduring evidence.

> *End of slide sequence. Beginning of a drawing sequence. Throughout the next section of the text the performer will draw with white and coloured chalk on a chalkboard. There could be a chalkboard on easels, or part of the set or theatre wall could be a big chalkboard. The performer draws to illustrate his text as he speaks.*

In addition to scale, a monument can derive power from its situation, its site. *(drawing)* The site of a classical monument, for example, was always carefully chosen or constructed: in the centre of a square; at the end of a long, tree-lined avenue; or in a front of suitable building, almost as if the building were put there solely to be a backdrop for the monument. The site of a monument is its focal point—it is a theatrical space—it is a trick. The first time I found myself in New York City on my own I headed right for the Guggenheim Museum. *(drawing)* I'd seen photographs of it, and I found its spiraling architecture irresistible, like a kid with a Slinky. When I arrived outside of the museum I almost expected to be sucked up inside it from the street. Ironically, what I hadn't given much thought to at all was Art—what was inside this particular monument to art. I didn't have a clue as to what was being exhibited at the time—and so it was that I had my first encounter with the work of the great German artist Joseph Beuys.

I didn't know a whole helluva lot about Joseph Beuys at this time—just the art-world hype, really. I mean, I knew that he was a pretty interesting guy, a man who believed that one could mix history, and science, and politics, and mysticism together to make art. I knew that Beuys was the man who made sculptures—social sculpture—out of fat and felt. And I knew that because of these and other things about Joseph Beuys and his work, he was regarded by half of the art world as a nut and a charlatan, while the other half revered him as a kind, benevolent *Art God*.

Anyway—the Guggenheim show turned out to be his first American retrospective—so there was lots of fat, piles of felt, and many delicate marks on paper. However, I remember vividly one particular work, it was a sculptural piece called "The Pack": a Volkswagen van stood, open-ended, at the top of the incredible spiral which is the Guggenheim; pouring out the back of this van, and seemingly racing down the slope, were twenty identical wooden sleds; *(drawing)* packed on the back of each sled was a tight roll of felt, a serious chunk of fat, and a large, powerful flashlight. They seemed alive, these sleds, and absolutely determined. One sensed that there was a mission here, and that it was desperate. Not only that, but there seemed also to be a warning in this sculpture, and one felt that this warning was real and important because it was based on something real: it was based on Joseph Beuys's personal history.

The voiceover of Beuys's words at the end of the Prologue is repeated here.

"I was completely buried in the snow. That's how the Tartars found me days later. I remember voices saying '*voda*' (water), then the felt of their tents, and the dense pungent smell of cheese, fat and milk. They covered my body in fat, to help regenerate warmth, and wrapped it in felt as an insulator to keep the warmth in."

End of first drawing sequence. A chair suggesting a tree appears.

In 1961, Joseph Beuys was appointed to the Professional Chair of Monumental Sculpture, at the Düsseldorf Art Academy. *(the performer sits)* The early sixties was a time when, conceptually speaking, some pretty heady ideas were bouncing around the art world. To oversimplify—it was a time when many artists decided that the idea for a work of art was more important than the artwork itself—that "process" would take precedence over "product."

Slide sequence of Beuys's sculpture.

Joseph Beuys was always making ideas manifest. Joseph Beuys was always making monuments. In performing his "Actions," even just in speaking, he created monuments. Sometimes he memorialized ideas themselves; often he memorialized himself and his experiences; but always his works are invested with a relatedness to an idea, or an experience, or a memory, conscious or unconscious, that is transmitted to us as a feeling. We feel the work; and even when the object of his memorializing remains a mystery to us, we feel the mystery. And more than that, we feel the energy inherent in the mystery, and if we cannot feel the energy inherent in a work of art, then why bother?! Words won't help—all of the words, all of the explanations in the world, will not make it meaningful for us.

Words! Boy—there are so many words about Joseph Beuys, and many of them came from Beuys himself. Like many great artists, like Brecht, for example, Beuys often said far too much about his work; but words are important and explanations are irresistible. Joseph Beuys believed that his art could be explained, and should be explained, yet he constantly confronted us, his audience, with works of art whose greatest strength is their mystery. This is what we must confront first, before any words, before intellectualizing.

End of slide sequence of Beuys's sculptures.

So—when I said that this is a happy day because it is the day that I get to put it all together—this is what I meant. I'm building a monument. I've collected and shaped all the pieces, and they are even paid for. It seems that I am forever working at one thing to pay for the materials to create another thing. I remember I had this job once... *(The performer sits. Goes off on a tangent.)*

right after college. I was the assistant display artist in a big department store in Charlottetown, Prince Edward Island. The store was called Holman's of P.E.I.... I did the windows, dressing ancient mannequins which had an average of 2.5 fingers each hand, and wigs like plastic helmets; I made a lot of polyester rosettes in Fabricland, a lot of Styrofoam tin soldiers for Toyland; and I was in charge of Santa Claus—I was truly Santa's helper. From the twelfth of November until the twenty-fourth of December, I brushed the beard, stocked the candy canes, and made copious cups of tea for Mr. MacLean. That was Santa's real name—Mr. MacLean. I was actually quite lucky; previous Santas had been a series of drunks from the hardware department, but my Santa was a piece of cake, a real doll, no trouble at all. No trouble that is, until the day of the "May Your Every Christmas Wish Come True 20% Off Everything In The Store Except Tobacco And Appliances Sale,"—one of those horrible ten-till-midnight-every-lunatic-in-the-province-comes-out-to-shop sales, and Santa and I were expected to be in a dozen different places at the same time, all day long. So, at about four in the afternoon, I noticed that the seventy-five-year-old Mr. MacLean was looking a little the worse for wear, and so I insisted he come up to my fourth-floor cubbyhole office so that I could make him a nice cup of English Breakfast. I made him sit in my chair, which was the only approximately comfortable one in the room, I gave him a stack of lingerie sales flyers to put his feet up on, and I handed him his tea. His prompt response was to fall off my chair and die, right there at my astonished feet, beard askew, red hat rolling, rolling away. And to this day, whenever anyone mourns the figurative death of Santa Claus in their childhood, I have very little sympathy. After all, I have experienced the literal one.

But Holman's was just one of two experiences in retail hell. The second was my stint at a Dominion Playworld in a mall in Stoney Creek, Ontario. I know that doesn't sound too hellish—so let me put it this way—I worked in the doll department of a toy store in a busy, suburban mall at Christmastime the year that the Barbie camper came out. We had waiting lists, we had all female fist-fights, we had attempted bribery, it was a nightmare. I learned my first truly nasty lesson about human nature and consumerism, but I learned something of even more importance—I learned that there is something absolutely irresistible about an accessory for a Barbie doll. This special knowledge stayed with me all these years, resulting in the project I am about to unveil, a project that I hope will pay for many materials in the years to come... Barbie Does Beuys!

Barbie Does Bueys! is a Barbie-sized performance space in which a Barbie doll stages tableaux from the performances/actions of Joseph Beuys. Tableau One—The Felt Room: The space is filled with Beuysian felt. At centre stage sits a grand piano covered neatly and completely in the same grey/brown felt. On the upper stage wall hangs Barbie. She is wearing a perfect replica of the famous Felt Suit, except that her version is pink.

It's The Felt Room. I saw the original at the Anthony D'Offay Gallery in London. Sadly, Joseph Beuys was not there hanging on the wall, wearing his famous felt suit, as Barbie is here. She insisted we use her trademark pink, however, saying that grey would make her look fat.

Beuys said of The Felt Room that "everything is taken away which is genuinely communicative—everything is isolated, and knocking on the walls has no resonance." I remember my footsteps made no sound. I remember I could hear my breathing, and holding that, my pounding heart.

(fast) Barbie Does Beuys! comes with everything you need for hours of High Art Fun! Some restrictions apply. Dolls not included. Audiences not guaranteed.

> *Barbie Does Beuys! disappears.*

So? What do you think? Pretty catchy, eh? It's just a prototype, but we hope to go into production soon. I had some difficulty with the Felt Suit, "I'm not much of a tailor, and this really crazy thing happened…"

> *The performer refers to the jumble of chalkboard drawings he has made.*

Boy—if someone else waltzed in here right now, they'd have an interesting time deciphering all of this, wouldn't they? Whole blackboards on easels, with Joseph Beuys's marks on them, have been preserved and marketed by art dealers. Beuys was highly regarded as a teacher, and he rarely spoke to groups or students without drawing, or writing, or otherwise making marks on a blackboard. Like his view of art in general, Beuys's view of drawing, of just what a drawing is, was quite broad. He defined a drawing as any kind of a notation, whether it reproduces a traditional figure, or whether it merely consists of a verbal explanation, or an idea. I like this definition, because the way we make a mark, our gesture, is of fundamental importance to drawing.

> *Beginning of another sequence of drawing to illustrate the spoken text.*

How we each write is a personal gesture, and that is why some people believe that they can read a personality by analyzing handwriting. In a drawing, the object or idea drawn is important, of course, *(drawing)* but "how" it is drawn, the quality of the line, the gesture, is what invests the drawing with its meaning. For example, *(drawing)* if I were to draw a skull… it would be very different from a skull drawn by Georgia O'Keefe… I can't pretend to represent O'Keefe drawing accurately, although I do find that in attempting to reproduce her style, no matter what the subject, be it flower or skull, if you begin with that old vulva, you will get there eventually… or… if we were lucky enough to have had Joseph Beuys draw a full skull for us *(still drawing)* …anyway, what I am trying to show is that the quality of the lines, even the approach to the chalkboard, is very different in each of these examples. The lines in a Beuys drawing are extremely delicate, somewhat tentative, though not insecure, and always mysterious. Actually, if we had asked Joseph Beuys to draw a skull for us, he might have reacted by trowelling some fat into a corner—you never know.

Leaving behind a line is leaving behind a noticeable trace of an impulse.

End of drawing sequence.

Beuys left many such traces. Beuys was a great teacher because of his need to "show" ideas.

> *The performer exits and quickly reappears pulling a red cart. This cart contains the monument—wooden sections that, when assembled, form a brightly-coloured obelisk which will eventually be topped with a light-emitting pyramid. The entire obelisk will then be placed on the inverted cart, which becomes the base of the monument. The top of the cart should be raked, so that when the cart has been inverted the whole monument sits at a jaunty angle, as if it were a buoy on the sea.*

"You captains tell the guns to slacken
And give the infanteers a break;
It's Mother Courage with her wagon
Full of the finest boots they make..."

Just kidding, it's me!

> *Throughout the next scene, the performer sorts his tools and materials from the cart, in preparation for actual assembly.*

I made a monument once before, a long time ago. It was an angel on wheels. Like many kids, my friends and I used to have funerals for the variety of dead creatures that our community produced, from, say, water beetles, on a slow day, right up to squirrels and occasionally cats that the friggin' Jenkins boys would kill with their BB guns. I saved boxes, any and all boxes, from matchboxes to boot boxes, so that in the event of a death, I would solemnly usher the bereaved into my room to pick out a suitable coffin, which my partner, Hazel Judson, and I would then decorate. After this, we would have an elaborate funeral procession; we'd go up the Pownal Road, and then turn down the Shore Road, proceeding to our cemetery beside Reanney Gay's fishing shack on the beach. Our processions got more and more grand, until one day we decided that we needed a new hearse—Hazel's wagon just wasn't good enough. So... I built this angel on wheels. I built her with these flat, outstretched arms that held the coffin up for all the world to see. In spite of even the angel, we remained unsatisfied; we had become obsessed with our funerals. Then Hazel came to me, all excited because she had read in the *National Geographic* that the early Egyptians had buried valuables with their dead because they believed that the dead would need their earthly goods in the next world. Well—we thought this was pretty fabulous—so, from then on, whenever we had a big funeral coming up, Hazel and I would go up the road to Horne's store, and we would buy candy necklaces and surprise packages, and we'd put all the best stuff in with the corpse. And old Mrs. Horne—she was just great, she'd see us coming a mile away, and we'd walk in, and she'd get this really long look on her face, and say,

"Oh dear, it's not another death, is it? It's been a terrible hard week for you two, now hasn't it? You must accept our deepest condolences," and great shit like that. We just loved her for it.

Before the end of the summer, though, the entire funeral enterprise came crashing to an end when it was discovered that Dilly Cannon was digging up the graves and eating all the candy. Poor Dilly—it's a wonder she didn't die. Now—a child psychologist might say all the ritual interaction with dead creatures was natural, a necessary introduction to death... but I'm here to tell you that burying a rat that Tommy Jenkins killed with a shovel in George Lawton's potato barn was no help at all when it came to people.

The performer sits in his tree-chair to tell the following story.

My mother told me that Keith MacKenzie was dead. Keith was a foster kid and, as a result, he was tormented by every other kid his age in the community, and was old enough to know better. My quiet brother David was an exception. Keith and David were best friends, and on the rare occasions that Keith got off the farm, he would end up hanging around our place. He almost worshipped our mother, and I think that was because she treated him exactly the same way as she treated every other kid we brought home; which is to say, she teased the "bejesus" out of him, and every once in a while she'd wrestle him to the floor and kiss him on the neck.

At that time, I certainly thought that I was far too sophisticated to pay much attention to my little brother's buddies, but I did treat Keith with a respect that he got precious little of. When she told me, she spoke very quietly, and she said that when the tractor flipped over he was most likely killed instantly. I was quiet myself for a long time, but when I started to cry, I couldn't stop. I can remember my mother sitting beside me on my bed with her arm around my shoulder, saying over and over, "It's all right Kenny, it's all right. You were always really nice to Keith; it's all those Mutch kids and Doyle kids who should feel bad not you." Then my father—Mr. Patience—he yells from the kitchen that if I don't stop my goddamn crying soon, they'll have to take me to town for a needle, but I couldn't stop.

Slide with the word "Fear" appears.

Throughout the next scene, the performer tries to re-create, at least in spirit, the Beuysian Action that he is describing, using whatever objects and set pieces are at hand. Among these objects are the performer's Beuysian hat and a large piece of felt. The performer howls like a coyote to start the scene.

A coyote. For the First Nations of North America, the coyote was one of the mightiest of all deities. The coyote could change its state from the physical to the spiritual, and vice versa, at will. The coyote was respected and venerated because of its ingenuity and its adaptability. Upon arrival, however, the white man decided that the coyote was actually low, cunning and untrustworthy—talk about the pot calling the kettle black. Anyway, all of a sudden the coyote was despised and persecuted.

The coyote was of great interest to Joseph Beuys, partly because of his overall interest in the animal world, specifically the connections between the natural world and the world of the spirit, but also because he saw embodied in the coyote what he called "a psychological trauma point of the United States"— and, that is to say—America's trauma with its indigenous peoples.

So—in 1976, when Joseph Beuys was scheduled to exhibit at the Rene Bloch Gallery in New York City, he had himself picked up at the airport, immediately wrapped in felt, and then driven at high speed, in the back of an ambulance, directly to the gallery, where he quickly incarcerated himself in an exhibition space with more felt, a walking-stick, a flashlight, and other small items, fifty copies of that day's *Wall Street Journal* (which were changed daily throughout the exhibition), *and* a live coyote. Mr. Beuys and the coyote lived together in this room for three days, and during this time Mr. Beuys performed a number of repeated ritual actions. At any given moment he might ring a little triangle that he wore around his neck and then wait for coyote's response. There are many photographs documenting this event, photographs of a tall figure shrouded in grey felt, with a long walking-stick projecting upwards, like some great shepherd, and a wild dog with his teeth in the felt, pulling and pulling at the man; the epitome of the tension between nature and culture.

Coyote is about isolation. Isolation and communication, and the possibilities and the impossibilities therein. I wish I could convey it better. Perhaps Barbie can help

> *Barbie Does Beuys! appears. Tableau Two—Coyote: I Like America and America Likes Me. Barbie stands stage left, bending forward, swaddled in a roll of tatttered felt. The crook of a shepherd's staff protrudes where Barbie clasps the felt around her. Stage right, an adult standard poodle, clipped and dyed pink, has one end of the roll of felt grasped in its teeth; the felt stretches taut between them as the dog pulls and Barbie holds on.*

Oh my, this is a gorgeous moment from Coyote. Brava, Barbie. All the tension of the original is here for the sensitive viewer to eke out. I do question the replacement of the coyote with Barbie's poodle Kenny, but safety and animal welfare groups must be considered, and, apparently, the coyotes have since joined IATSE and they just won't pull that hard anymore.

> *Barbie Does Beuys! disappears. A microwave oven appears.*

Breaktime!

> *The performer opens the oven and extracts a metal lunch pail. He opens the lunch pail and takes out a mug of coffee, which he places back in the oven to heat up. He waits.*

I love to cook. When I was a kid I used to watch Madame Benoît cooking on the CBC; I loved everything that woman did and said. I loved her Tenderflake commercials, remember: "I love dat wurd—Tenderflake. To me it say two ting. It say 'tender,' and it say 'flaky.'"

> *Coffee is hot. The performer sits near the audience, eating rice cakes from the lunch pail, sipping coffee, and talking.*

I actually saw her cooking, live, once; it was in a mall in Charlottetown. I was just walking through, and there she was, bigger than life, and in the middle of preparing a cream of turnip. As I sat down, she was saying; "In making de cream of turneep, you can use de budder, because de turneep and de budder, dey are friend, *but,* I use de cream because de turneep and de cream, dey are lovers." How could you not love a woman who spoke like that?! She even made microwaves seem like somehow passionate, spiritual. She was once asked what she would say to people who only use their microwaves to heat coffee and to make popcorn, and she replied: "I would tell dem dat I will say tree Hail Mary for dem every night." You may not believe that I can cook since all I have are these, *(referring to the rice cakes)* but they were the only thing I thought I could eat in front of people without feeling guilty. *(eats, obviously without enjoyment)* I've always thought that there is a correlation between cooking and drawing. I mean, I spoke earlier about how artists must have a particular gesture with which they invest their works with meaning; well, I think that the same goes for good cooks as well. Madame Benoît certainly had a gesture that shaped her works; there is that trace of the cook's impulse in any good food. I even think I know what Madame Benoît's gesture was. In her last interview before her death, she interrupted the CBC radio interviewer mid-question, and she said: "Non— what I really want to talk about is love." *(Performer pauses. Eating, thinking.)*

Anyone been having any housing problems lately? "Does Rose Kennedy have a black dress"—right? In my ten or so years here, I have managed to develop a pretty impressive paranoia about housing. Every renter has at least one good horror story; I have several myself, but even my own stripes seem minuscule when viewed in the larger picture. Not long ago, I was walking down Rosedale Valley Road and I had this uncomfortable feeling that I was being followed. Eventually I became sure that I was, so I slowed down—real bright, eh— thinking the person might pass me. But he slowed down, too. This made me very nervous, so I took off like a bat out of hell. When I finally stopped and turned around, no one was there, not a trace. That was when I realized that whoever had been behind me lived there, in the ravine, and that he simply did not want me to see where; the privacy of homelessness. My mind went immediately back to a time in my childhood when I used to drag cardboard and boards into the woods and build forts, often with Peter Worth, but that's another story, and anyway, then I would beg my mother to let me sleep out there, but she never would. And now—now I'm afraid that I will end up doing just that after all.

End of the break. The performer sits on the tree-chair.

When my aunt Muriel died, we had quite a time of it. It all began at the funeral with poor Maureen—Maureen—she was Aunt Muriel's daughter, my father's first cousin. The trouble really started because of that perverse custom many funeral homes have of ceremoniously closing the lid of the coffin just moments before the actual funeral service begins. You see, at that point, they always ask if any member of the immediate family would like to say a final goodbye to the dearly departed, as it were, and of course Maureen says yes. My father and I stood at opposite ends of the casket, kind of like sentinels, and so we were the ones who had to deal with it. Maureen drags herself up that aisle as if she would surely be the next one to depart this earthly toil, and when she got to the coffin she grabbed a hold of her mother's hand and she would not let go; and howl, holy Christ, I swear you could hear her four blocks away. I'd say that it took my father and me a full two minutes to pry those two hands, the living and the dead, apart. Then, later, at the cemetery, I swear again that if it hadn't been for my father's vigilance, and the fact that her spike heels kept getting caught in all that fresh dirt, she would have managed to throw herself into the goddamn hole after the box was lowered. Poor Maureen, it's a terrible thing.

Slide of the word "Guilt" appears.

Throughout the next scene the performer assembles the obelisk portion of the monument.

"The sea, with such a storm, would have buoyed up and quenched the stilled fires." That is from *King Lear*. If I were quoting that line in the Maritimes, I would say it somewhat differently: "The sea, with such a storm, would have buoyed up and quenched the stellèd fires." "Boo-ee!" On Prince Edward Island you could cause a real panic if you said, "Oh my, look at that 'boy' floating out there in the harbour." You just never know the subtle ways in which the pronunciation of a single word might have an effect. For example, last summer, while wandering on the East Coast, I decided to write some haiku—you know—those lovely, simple Japanese poems that must conform to two strict rules: they must have exactly seventeen syllables, and they can't have any abstract thought. Anyway, I was very upset when I realized that the best one that I had written—"I swim in sea-grey water past marker boo-ees and yellow dories"—wouldn't be a haiku anymore when I got it back to Ontario.

But for me, buoy's richness as a word doesn't just come from its pronunciation, it has all kinds of other meanings and associations. Literally, a buoy is an object anchored as an aid to navigation, or to indicate dangers like hidden wrecks or rocky shoals.

A sequence of slides begins, and continues throughout this section about buoys. That is, until the monument is completed.

Even though a buoy is anchored, it still moves; it sways and bobs and rings its message: "this way, over here, careful, careful, watch your step." As a verb, "buoy" means to rise, or lift, or to cause to rise. There are many kinds of buoys.

Slides of buoys and of the sea continue.

"Can" buoys, "nun" buoys, "spar" buoys, "gong" and "bell" buoys. My father worked with buoys for many years—not the kind most of us are familiar with, little wooden or Styrofoam bubbles—he worked with the giant deep-sea buoys that look like missiles and weigh tons. When my siblings and I were kids we thought it was so fabulous that our father had our mother's name on the back of all his overalls—Dot, D.O.T., Department of Transport. Underneath that was the romantic phrase "Boo-ee Maintenance."

Because buoys took him away for long periods of time to exotic places like Baffin Island and the Arctic Circle, I think we all developed a relationship to the "idea" of buoys. For me, they conjured up images of clanging bells, flashing lights, high, stormy waves and great winches turned by sailors' arms. In later years, I always intended to talk to my father about his years on the sea, but like most other conversations I had ever imagined having with him, I never quite got around to it. Oh, I know how that must sound, you're probably thinking, "Poor baby, couldn't talk to his daddy—how unique." I honestly don't mean to whine, it's just that not being able to talk to my father about buoys somehow came to represent all of the things that I had never been able to talk to him about—boy oh boy—I mean, talk about investing things with meaning. I did eventually broach the subject with him, and I guess I was expecting beautifully constructed metaphors about his life on the high seas; what I got, of course, was a tired man describing a very difficult job that kept him away from his family in order to support them. A different set of meanings to be sure. But I guess I finally clued into the fact that, for me at least, buoys are my father, and that part of my childhood that he represents.

End of monument assembly for now. End of slide sequence.

The performer once again sits in his tree-chair for the following story.

When Louie Herman died, Tina called in a big panic and Dad had to go up the road to help her out. We all knew that something was wrong because Dad actually walked and, like most men in the country, he always drove anywhere further away than the end of our own lane. Now—Tina and Louie, along with their retarded daughter Louise, were just about the most comical trio you'd ever want to meet. Tina and Louie liked to stay up all night with a quart of Captain Morgan's and a pack of well-worn cards, and then, at about four or five in the morning, they'd wake up Louise and the three of them would traipse down to the shore, and they'd all go fishing in Louie's yellow dory. So—this particular morning, Louie pulls on those big fishing boots, and dies, right there in the kitchen; which I personally do not think he would have complained about if he had been in a position to do so. The big problem with arranging Louie's funeral was that they couldn't find a box in town big enough to put him in, or, as it turns out, in the whole damn province. Sinclair Cutcliffe, the cheapest, meanest undertaker in town, offered to cut an end out of a coffin and stick a piece on, but we all agreed that would be pretty friggin' tacky, so Dad says, "It's okay Tina, it's okay. Delmar and I,"—Delmar was Tina's nephew—"Delmar and I will get in the wagon and drive over to Moncton and get a box for Louie," which they did. Tina always loved to tell this story about how Louie was too damn big for any box in Prince Edward Island, and she told it as if she knew how much Louie would have loved the story, too.

Slide of the word "Love" appears.

During the next scene, the set and lights conspire to create an atmosphere of bleak confinement.

"Our block was occupied only by homosexuals, with about two hundred and fifty men in each wing. We would only sleep in nightshirts and we had to keep our hands outside the blankets.... The windows had a centimeter of ice on them. Anyone found with his underclothes on in bed, or his hands under his blankets... was taken outside and had several bowls of water poured over him before being left standing outside for a good hour. Only a few people survived this treatment. The least result was bronchitis, and it was rare for any gay person taken into the sick-bay to come out alive. We who wore the pink triangle were prioritized for medical experiments, and these generally ended in death."

That's a quote from a book called *The Men with the Pink Triangle*, written by a concentration camp survivor by the name of Heinz Hager. Most of us know, I think, that all prisoners in German concentration camps during the Second World War had triangles of coloured cloth sewn onto their uniforms to denote their offence or their origin, which, in some cases, was their only offence. Yellow was for Jews, who got two triangles superimposed to make the Star of David. Red was for politicals, green was for criminals, black for antisocials, purple for Jehovah's Witnesses, blue for immigrants, brown for Gypsies, and pink was for homosexuals. This pink triangle was two or three centimeters larger than all of the others, and the prisoners who were the most tortured and persecuted, according to Heinz Hager, were the Jews, the Gypsies and the homosexuals.

The word "survival" is a word with a great variety of significances. If you were to ask a survivor of a concentration camp about survival, the answer would surely relate to their wartime experiences. "Survival" has one set of meanings in the natural world, and quite a different significance when considered as a cultural term. Since the end of World War II, we have even created a situation where the term "global survival" has a very real and particular meaning.

The atmosphere "lifts" a little, and the performer becomes more relaxed, now sitting near the audience.

It is a difficult thing for most of us to credit that which we perceive as overwhelming with any sense of immediacy; it's easier to say, "Why bother?" I have personally always had a pretty romantic notion of survival; as a child my favourite book was *Robinson Crusoe*; I longed to test my own ingenuity, to make an umbrella that worked, practically and aesthetically. But lately my understanding of survival has undergone a change. For instance, I have not just been ignoring, but I have actually been embracing the oppression that comes with being a gay man in this society. What I mean is—I feel so damn guilty about being a First World, white, able-bodied *male* person, that my oppression as a "faggot" is almost welcome to me. It alleviates my guilt by making me a part of the oppressed masses.

There are many kinds of holocausts, some natural and others man-made, but I think, perhaps, that there are really only two possible reactions to any holocaust. Which is more human—"compassion,"

Slide of the word "Compassion" appears.

or "complicity"?

Slide of the word "Complicity" appears.

Once again, the performer wraps himself in felt.

I'm tired.

It gets darker. He sits.

I could close my eyes. Darkness against the darkness.

He closes his eyes.

Many times one can only anticipate the things that are meant. What are the things that are meant? What are the things to be remembered? I must get up. Rise into the infinite emptiness. A speck in the emptiness. Rise up.

He doesn't move. He opens his eyes. He speaks from his seated position.

Joseph Beuys was a bomber pilot in the German army during the Second World War. He was wounded five times, and the last time, he was shot down on the Russian Steppes, from which, he has said, he was rescued by nomadic Tartars, who wrapped him in fat and rolls of felt. To keep him warm. To help him survive. Real or half-imagined, this experience was the catalyst for a body of work compulsive in its concern with ideas and modes of survival. Beuys spoke openly and eloquently about the war and his experiences in it; he did not believe in hiding history. He spoke often of "healing processes," and for him, the greatest healing process of all was the making of art.

Barbie Does Beuys! appears upstage of the performer. Tableaux Three— How To Explain Pictures To A Dead Hare: Barbie sits in a simple wooden chair. Her head has been shaved and is covered in honey and gold leaf.

She leans forward in her chair, appearing to whisper to the furry bundle held gently in her lap. The lighting is glorious. There is no pink to be seen. Barbie looks remarkably like Joseph Beuys performing How To Explain Pictures To A Dead Hare.

He gets up.

It is November, 1965, and you are in Düsseldorf in West Germany. You have been invited to an opening at the Gallery Schmele, but when you arrive you find yourself barred from entering the gallery. There is only one door into the exhibition space, and one window at street level. There are already a great number of people gathered, and it is difficult to find a place. Finally, you find a little niche from which you can see into the room. Now you see that there is a man in this room, a man whose head is covered in honey and a gold leaf. An iron sole is tied to his right foot, a felt sole to his left. In his arms the man is cradling a dead hare. For the next three hours the man will walk around the gallery whispering explanations of his pictures to his lifeless burden.

And you think, "Is he nuts, or what?" You are slightly offended by your exclusion; you are being kept on the outside. But at the same time you do have to admit that there is something compelling about this man—his gravity, his apparent, almost painful, concern, his dedication to his task. The honey and gold leaf glisten and trickle, and the man's mouth is moving, silent and serious. And suddenly you want to know what this man is telling, and at the same moment you know that you cannot know; it is unknowable. Oh—how we long for explanations.

He sees Barbie.

And now, it seems to me, Barbie is really beautiful. The power of the artist is to create truth, not simply reveal it.

Barbie remains in view.

I will tell you some things I have seen:
A black lacquer vase with willow weeping
One hundred yellow freesia in a clear crystal sphere
A single rose
A burning candle
A candid photograph
Pungent sprays of lilac in the middle of winter.
Faces, whispers, hands hover
The polished granite cubes of ashes
In lofts full of men full of martinis
And a wild, aching desire for living.

Laughing or wailing, public or private, music-filled or silent—a memorial service is a memorial service is a memorial service; and boys will be boys will be dying. The older I get the more I am clinging to the boy in me. It is a wonderfully rich word for one so short—"boy." It is full of a kind of energy, a lightness, vulnerability.

It is said that there are stages to the act of dying: resignation, spirituality, anger, I think. I do not know them all, nor do I know their order. I do not know. I do know that there are stages to watching death, and anger is one of those. This is something else that I have seen: I have seen the valiant and necessary attempts to celebrate life in the face of death begin to have a hollow ring.

The performer sets about returning the stage to its original state in preparation for the final stage of the assembly of the monument.

There are people in this world who believe that they hold the patent on love. They know to whom they have sold franchises, and from whom they have withheld them. These love capitalists are real people, too; they are Real Women and real Prime Ministers and real former figure skaters. But—I know something. I know that "love" is hiding a pair of great, black wings, and when she unfolds them, and flies up and up into our dark and carking atmosphere, she will be abandoning us all—every one; and while she is still with us, nobody holds the exclusive rights.

The performer places Barbie on the seat of the tree-chair. Then he tips the now-empty cart onto its side and removes the wheel unit from its underside. This unit is then fitted under the tree-chair. This new wheeled unit can now be used by the performer to take things away as he exits at the end of the piece.

One of Joseph Beuys's last major works before he died was a project called "7,000 Eichen" ("Seven Thousand Oaks"), an environmental artwork. As you might surmise from the title, there were indeed seven thousand oak trees, but there were also seven thousand roughly-hewn stone columns, each approximately one metre high. The plan was that these would be planted in pairs, an oak and a basalt column, all round the city of Kassel over a period of time. Beuys planted the first tree in March of 1982. In typical Beuysian fashion, he very grandly declared that "7,000 Eichens" was not only important in terms of "matter" and "ecology," but that it would continue to raise ecological consciousness because, in his words, "we will never stop planting." Trees continue to be planted in the name of this project and its architect in cities around the world. Beuys also said that his point in pairing the two elements was that "each would be a monument, consisting of a living part, the live tree, changing all the time; and a crystalline mass, the basalt column, maintaining its shape size and weight; and that by placing these two objects side by side, the proportionality of the monument would never be the same." Never be the same.

The performer stands where the tree-chair had been to deliver this final funeral story.

After arriving like the proverbial ill wind she was, and announcing that Grammy was dead, Aunt Ann said, "And there's enough money in her purse to pay for the flowers." Now Mom and I thought that this was just about the cheapest, most callous thing we had ever heard in our lives, but then, according to Aunt Ann, my mother and I were almost too sensitive to live, anyways. She also told us that Sinclair Cutcliffe had Grammy already. The ceilings of the Cutcliffe funeral home are really low, and they are stuccoed, with glitter dust embedded in every plaster stalactite. The wallpaper is that red, flocked stuff, worn black at elbow level by the leaning of tired men. In Grammy's case, however, the worst thing was not the décor of Slumber Room Number One; it was the casket itself. It was kind of flocked too, and the blue—blue like nothing natural you've ever seen in your life. I was twelve at the time and I remember thinking, "Why isn't it wooden, aren't coffins supposed to be made out of wood?" Then I realized that under the layers and layers of powder, my grandmother was blue too, as blue as the beaverboard box they'd laid her out in.

Crazy Grammy, who wrote to her dead husband every night for nine years; Grammy, who loved oranges and the smell of mothballs, and who hated Catherine MacKinnon more than any other singer in the world. Crazy Grammy, who took every goddamn pill in the house. And I remember thinking, "Boys oh boys, I would have got her a wooden coffin," and I wanted to tell everyone who kept coming up and saying how nice she looked to "shut up, just shut up."

> *At this point, space—oceanic space, or an illusion of it—is created. The performer places the inverted cart in this space, placing the obelisk on top of it, and the pyramid on top of that. Lights begin to fade as the top of the "buoy" begins to light up. The performer prepares to exit. By the time he is gone, the buoy is the only light on stage.*

My grandmother always said that "a full day is a happy day." So—I guess I was right about this one.

> *Pause. The performer begins to exit.*

Luis Buñuel said that "life without memory is no life at all; [memory] is our coherence, our reason, our feeling." In the end, for my grandmother, memory was none of those things. *(pause)* A memory is like a monument, it is a tricky thing; you have to find a place to put it. The site is all-important.

> *Exit.*

> *End.*

Fronteras
Americanas

Guillermo Verdecchia

Guillermo Verdecchia is a playwright, director, translator and actor. Born in Buenos Aires, Argentina, he came to Canada at the age of two. Verdecchia's plays include *i.d.* (1989, Chalmers Award), *Final Decisions (WAR)* (1990), *The Noam Chomsky Lectures* (with Daniel Brooks, 1990, Chalmers Award), *Fronteras Americanas* (1993, Chalmers Award/Governor General's Literary Award), *A Line in the Sand* (with Marcus Youssef, 1995, Chalmers Award), *The Terrible but Incomplete Journals of John D* (1996), *Insomnia* (with Daniel Brooks, 1998), *Ali & Ali and the Axes of Evil* (with Marcus Youssef and Camyar Chai, 2004) and *bloom* (2007).

Verdecchia also wrote and starred in a short film adaptation of *Fronteras Americanas,* called *Crucero/Crossroads,* which played at film festivals around the world and received nine international awards.

His production of Dennis Foon's *War* won Vancouver's Jessie Award in 1994. In the same year he appeared as the Salvadoran refugee, Elias, in Joan MacLeod's *Amigo's Blue Guitar.*

From 1998 to 2003 Verdecchia was Artistic Director of Toronto's Cahoots Theatre Projects.

Verdecchia has also written for radio and film, and has published a collection of short stories entitled *Citizen Suarez* (1998). He has been writer-in-residence at Memorial University and the University of Guelph.

Para mis padres, Elvira y Rafael

Fronteras Americanas was first produced at the Tarragon Theatre in January 1993 with the following company:

VERDECCHIA/
FACUNDO/WIDELOAD   Guillermo Verdecchia

Directed by Jim Warren
Designed by Glenn Davidson
Stage Managed by Season Osborne

Characters

VERDECCHIA
FACUNDO/WIDELOAD

Rights/Permissions

FRONTERAS AMERICANAS

PRE-SHOW

Music: James Blood Ulmer—"Show Me Your Love, America."

• *Slide:*

> It is impossible to say to which human family we belong. We were all born of one mother America, though our fathers had different origins, and we all have differently coloured skins. This dissimilarity is of the greatest significance.
> —Simon Bolivar, 1819

Slides:

> Fronteras. Borders. Americanas. American.

ACTO PRIMERO

Welcome

VERDECCHIA   Here we are. All together. At long last. Very exciting. I'm excited. Very excited.
Here we are.

> *Slide:*
> Here We Are

Now because this is the theatre, when I say we I mean all of us and when I say here I don't just mean at the Tarragon, I mean America.

> *Slide:*
> Let us compare geographies

And when I say AMERICA I don't mean the country I mean the continent. *Somos todos Americanos.* We are all Americans.

Now—I have to make a small confession—I'm lost. Somewhere in my peregrinations on the continent, I lost my way.

Oh sure I can say I'm in Toronto, at 30 Bridgman Avenue—but I don't find that a very satisfactory answer—it seems to me a rather inadequate description of where I am.

Maps have been of no use because I always forget that they are metaphors and not the territory; the compass has never made any sense—it always spins in crazy circles. Even gas station attendants haven't been able to help; I can never remember whether it was a right or a left at the lights and I always miss the exits and have to sleep by the side of the road or in crummy hotels with beds that have magic fingers that go off in the middle of the night.

So, I'm lost and trying to figure out where I took that wrong turn… and I suppose you must be lost too or else you wouldn't have ended up here, tonight.

I suspect we got lost while crossing the border.

> *Slide:*
> Make a run for the Border, Taco Bell's got your order

The Border is a tricky place. Take the Mexico–U.S. border.

> *Slide: Map of Mexico–U.S. border.*

Where and what exactly is the border? Is it this line in the dirt, stretching for some 3,000 kilometres? Is the border more accurately described as a zone which includes the towns of El Paso and Juarez? Or is the border—is the border the whole country, the continent? Where does the U.S. end and Canada begin? Does the U.S. end at the 49th parallel or does the U.S. only end at your living room when you switch on the CBC? After all, as Carlos Fuentes reminds us, a border is more than just the division between two countries; it is also the division between two cultures and two memories. [1]

Atlantic magazine has something to say about the border: "The Border is transient. The border is dangerous. The border is crass. The food is bad, the prices are high and there are no good bookstores. It is not the place to visit on your next vacation." [2]

To minimize our inconvenience, I've hired a translator who will meet us on the other side.

The Border can be difficult to cross. We will have to avoid the border patrol and the trackers who cut for sign. Some of you may wish to put carpet on the soles of your shoes, others may want to attach cow's hooves to your sneakers. I myself will walk backwards so that it looks like I'm heading north.

Before we cross please disable any beepers, cellular phones or fax machines and reset your watches to border time. It is now Zero Hour.

EL BANDITO

> *Music—Aqui Vienen los Mariachis.*
>
> *Slide:*
> Warning: gunshots will be fired in this performance…
>
> *Slide:*
> Now
>
> *Gunshots.*

FACUNDO   Ay! Ayayayay! *Aja. Bienvenidos. Yo soy el mesonero aca en La Casa de La Frontera. Soy el guia. A su servicio. Antes de pasar, por favor, los latinos se pueden identificar? Los "latinoamericanos" por favor que pongan las manos en el aire... (he counts) Que lindo... mucho gusto.... Muy bien. Entonces el resto son... gringos. Lo siguiente es para los gringos:*

Eh, jou en Mejico now. Jou hab crossed de border. Why? What you lookin' for? Taco Bell Nachos wif "salsa sauce," *cabron*? Forget it, gringo. Dere's no *pinche* Taco Bell for thousands of miles. Here jou eat what I eat and I eat raw jalopeño peppers on dirty, burnt tortillas, wif some calopinto peppers to give it some flavour! I drink sewer water and tequila. My breath keells small animals. My shit destroys lakes. Jou come dis far south looking for de authentic Mejico? Jou looking for de real mezcal wit de real worm in it? I'll show you de real worm— I'll show jou de giant Mexican trouser snake. I will show you fear in a handful of dust...

Jou wrinklin' jour nose? Someting stink? Somebody smell aroun here? *Si,* I esmell. I esmell because I doan bathe. Because bad guys doan wash. Never.

Bandito *maldito, independista,* sandinista, Tupamaro, mao mao powpowpow. *(FACUNDO removes bandito outfit.)* Ees an old Hallowe'en costume. Scary huh?

Introduction to Wideload

Mi nombre es Facundo Morales Segundo. Algunos me llaman El Tigre del Barrio. Tambien me dicen El Alacran porque...

Music: "La Cumbia del Facundo"—Steve Jordan.

My name ees Facundo Morales Segundo. Some of you may know me as de Barrio Tiger. I am de guy who told Elton John to grow some funk of his own. I am de heads of Alfredo Garcia and Joaquin Murrieta. I am a direct descendent of Túpac Amaru, Pancho Villa, Doña Flor, Pedro Navaja, Sor Juana and Speedy Gonzalez.

Now when I first got here people would say, "Sorry what's de name? Fuckundoo?"

No mang, Fa – cun – do, Facundo.

"Wow, dat's a new one. Mind if I call you Fac?"

No mang, mind if I call you shithead?

So you know I had to come up with a more Saxonical name. And I looked around for a long time till I found one I liked. And when I found the one I wanted I took it. I estole it actually from a TV show—"Broken Badge" or something like that.

I go by the name Wideload McKennah now and I get a lot more respect, ese.

Slide:
   Wideload.

I live in the border—that's in Parkdale for you people from outta town. Ya, mang, I live in de zone, in de barrio and I gotta move. Is a bad neighbourhood. Dat neighbourhood is going to de dogs. 'Cause dere's a lot of yuppies moving in and dey're wrecking de neighbourhood and making all kinds of noise wif renovating and landscaping, knocking down walls and comparing stained glass. So I gotta move...

But first I gotta make some money. I want to cash in on de Latino boom. Ya, dere's a Latino boom, we are a very hot commodity right now. And what I really want to do is get a big chunk of toxic wasteland up on de Trans-Canada Highway and make like a third world theme park.

You know, you drive up to like big barbed wire gates with guards carrying sub-machine guns and you park your car and den a broken down Mercedes Benz bus comes along and takes you in under guard, of course. And you can buy an International Monetary Fund Credit Card for seventy-five bucks and it gets you on all de rides.

And as soon as you're inside somebody steals your purse and a policeman shows up but he's totally incompetent and you have to bribe him in order to get any action. Den you walk through a slum on the edge of a swamp wif poor people selling tortillas. And maybe like a disappearing rain forest section dat you can actually wander through and search for rare plants and maybe find de cure to cancer and maybe find... Sean Connery... and you rent little golf carts to drive through it and de golf cart is always breaking down and you have to fix it yourself. And while you're fixing de golf cart in de sweltering noonday sun a drug lord comes along in his hydrofoil and offers to take you to his villa where you can have lunch and watch a multi-media presentation on drug processing.

I figure it would do great. You people love dat kinda *shit*. And I can also undercut dose travel agencies dat are selling package tours of Brazilian slums. Dis would be way cheaper, safer and it would generate a lot of jobs—for white people too. And I would make some money and be able to move out of the barrio and into Forest Hill.

Ya, a little house in Forest Hill. Nice neighbourhood. Quiet. Good place to bring up like 15 kids. 'Course dis country is full of nice neighbourhoods—Westmount in Montreal looks good, or Vancouver you know, Point Grey is lovely or Kitsilano. Or de Annex here in Toronto—mang, I love de Annex: you got professionals, you got families, you got professional families. Ya. I could live dere. Hey mang, we could be neighbours—would you like dat? Sure, I'm moving in next door to... you... and I'm going to wash my Mustang every day and overhaul de engine and get some grease on de sidewalk and some friends like about 12 are gonna come and stay with me for a few... years.

You like music? Goood!

Ya, how 'bout a Chicano for a neighbour? Liven up de neighbourhood.

> *Slide:*
> Chicano:
> ❏ person who drives a loud car that sits low to the ground ?
> ❏ a kind of Mexican ?
> ❏ generic term for a working class Latino ?
> ❏ a wetback ?
> ❏ a Mexican born in Saxon America ?

Technically I don't qualify as a Chicano. I wasn't born in East L.A. I wasn't born in de southwest U.S.A. I wasn't even born in Mejico. Does dis make me Hispanic?

> *Slide:*
> Hispanic:
> ❏ someone who speaks Spanish ?
> ❏ a Spaniard ?
> ❏ a Latino ?
> ❏ root of the word spic ?

Dese terms, Latino, Hispanic, are very tricky you know but dey are de only terms we have so we have to use dem wif caution. If you will indulge me for a moment I would like to make this point painfully clear:

De term Hispanic, for example, comes from the Roman word, Hispania, which refers to de Iberian peninsula or eSpain. eSpain is a country in eEurope. Many people who today are referred to as Hispanic have nothin to do wif Hispain. Some of dem don't even speak Hispanish.

De term Latino is also confusing because it lumps a whole lot of different people into one category. Dere is a world of difference between de right wing Cubans living in Miami and exiled Salvadorean leftists living in Canada; between Mexican speakers of Nahuatl and Brazilian speakers of Portuguese; between a Tico and a Nuyorican (dat's a Puerto Rican who lives in New York) and den dere's de Uruguayans. I mean dey're practically European. As for me, let's just say... I'm a pachuco. [3]

> *Music: "Pachuco"—Maldita Vecindad.*

It Starts

VERDECCHIA   Okay, I just want to stop for a second before we get all confused.

I've known that I've been lost for quite some time now—years and years but if I can find the moment that I first discovered I was lost, there might be a clue...

This all starts with Jorge. After I'd been in therapy for a few months, Jorge suggested I go see El Brujo. I wasn't keen on the idea being both skeptical and afraid of things like *curanderos* but Jorge was persuasive and lent me bus fare enough to get me at least as far as the border...

It actually starts before that. It starts in France, Paris, France, The Moveable Feast, The City of Light where I lived for a couple of years. *En France où mes étudiants me disaient que je parlais le français comme une vache catalan. En France où j'étais étranger, un anglais, un Argentin-Canadien, une faux touriste.* Paris, France where I lived and worked illegally, where I would produce my transit pass whenever policemen asked for my papers. In France, where I was undocumented, extralegal, marginal and where for some reason, known perhaps only by Carlos Gardel and Julio Cortazar, I felt almost at home.

Or it starts before The City of Light, in The City of Sludge: Kitchener, Ontario. There in Kitchener, where I learned to drive, where I first had sex, where there was nothing to do but eat doughnuts and dream of elsewhere. There in Kitchener, where I once wrote a letter to the editor and suggested that it was not a good idea to ban books in schools and it was there in Kitchener that a stranger responded to my letter and suggested that I go back to my own country.

No. It starts, in fact, at the airport where my parents and my grandparents and our friends couldn't stop crying and hugged each other continually and said goodbye again and again until the stewardess finally came and took me out of my father's arms and carried me on to the plane—forcing my parents to finally board—

Maybe. Maybe not.

Maybe it starts with Columbus. Maybe it starts with the genius Arab engineer who invented the rudder. Maybe a little history is required to put this all in order.

History

Slide:
An Idiosyncratic History of America

Our History begins approximately 200 million years ago in the Triassic Period of the Mesozoic Era when the original super-continent, Pangaea, broke up and the continents of the earth assumed the shapes we now recognize.

Slide: Map of the world.

5000 B.C.—The first settlements appear in the highlands of Mexico and in the Andes mountains.

1500 B.C.—The pyramid at Teotihuacan is built. *(Slide: Photo of pyramid.)* At the same time, the Pinto build settlements further north.

Early 1400s A.D.—Joan of Arc *(Slide: Statue of Joan.)* is born and shortly thereafter, burned. At the same time, the Incas in Peru develop a highly efficient political system.

1492—Catholic Spain is very busy integrating the Moors. These Moors or Spaniards of Islamic culture who have been in Spain some 700 years suffer the same fate as the Spanish Jews: they are converted, or exiled, their heretical books and bodies burned. *(Slide: Photo of portrait of Columbus.)* Yes, also in 1492— a chubby guy sails the Ocean Blue.

1500—Pedro Cabral stumbles across what we now call Brazil—Portugal, fearing enemy attacks, discourages and suppresses writing about the colony.

1542—The Spanish Crown passes the Laws of the Indies. This law states that the settlers have only temporary concessions to these lands while the real owners are the Native Americans. Curiously, the Spanish Crown does not inform the Natives that the land is legally theirs. An oversight no doubt.

1588—The invincible Spanish Armada is defeated. Spain grows poorer and poorer as gold from the New World is melted down to pay for wars and imported manufactured goods from the developed northern countries. El Greco finishes "The Burial of Count Orgaz." *(Slide: Photo of El Greco's painting.)* Lope de Vega writes *La Dragontea*. Calderon de La Barca and Velasquez are about to be born.

1808—Beethoven writes Symphonies 5 and 6. France invades Spain and in the power vacuum, wars of independence break out all over New Spain. Goya paints *(Slide: Photo of painting.)* "Executions of the Citizens of Madrid."

1812—Beethoven writes Symphonies 7 and 8, and a war breaks out in North America.

1832—Britain occupies the Malvinas Islands and gives them the new silly name of the Falklands.

1846—The U.S. attacks Mexico.

1863—France attacks Mexico and installs an Austrian as emperor.

1867—Mexico's Austrian emperor is executed, Volume 1 of *Das Kapital* is published, and the Dominion of Canada is established.

1902—Gorky writes *The Lower Depths*, the U.S. acquires control over the Panama Canal and Beatrix Potter writes *Peter Rabbit. (Slide: Illustration of Peter Rabbit.)*

1961—Ernest Hemingway kills himself *(Slide: Photo of Hemingway.)*, *West Side Story (Slide: Photo of "Sharks" in mid-dance.)* wins an Academy Award, a 680-pound giant sea-bass is caught off the Florida coast *(Slide: Photo of large fish.)* and the U.S. attacks Cuba. *(Slide: Photo of Fidel Castro.)*

1969—Richard Nixon *(Slide: Photo of Nixon.)* is inaugurated as president of the U.S., Samuel Beckett *(Slide: Photo of Beckett.)* is awarded the Nobel Prize for Literature, the Montreal Canadiens *(Slide: Photo of 1969 Canadiens team.)* win the Stanley Cup for hockey and I attend my first day of classes at Anne Hathaway Public School.

Roll Call

Music: "God Save the Queen."

VERDECCHIA   I am seven years old. The teacher at the front of the green classroom reads names from a list.

Jonathon Kramer?

Jonathon puts his hand up. He is a big boy with short red hair.

Sandy Nemeth?

Sandy puts her hand up. She is a small girl with long hair. When she smiles we can see the gap between her front teeth.

Michael Uffelman?

Michael puts his hand up. He is a tall boy with straight brown hair sitting very neatly in his chair.

My name is next.

Minutes, hours, a century passes as the teacher, Miss Wiseman, forces her mouth into shapes hitherto unknown to the human race as she attempts to pronounce my name.

Gwillyou – ree – moo…. Verdeek – cheea?

I put my hand up. I am a minuscule boy with ungovernable black hair, antennae and gills where everyone else has a mouth.
You can call me Willy I say. The antennae and gills disappear.

It could have been here—but I don't want to talk about myself all night.

Wideload's Terms

WIDELOAD   Thank God.
I mean I doan know about you but I hate it when I go to *El Teatro* to de theatre and I am espectin to see a play and instead I just get some guy up dere talking about himself—deir life story—who cares? *Por favor*…. And whatever happened to plays anyway—anybody remember plays? Like wif a plot and like a central character? Gone de way of modernism I guess and probaly a good thing too.
I mean I doan know if I could stand to see another play about a king dat's been

dead for 400 years—
Anyway—

The Smiths

When I first got to America del Norte I needed a place to live and I diden have
a lot of money so I stayed wif a family. The Smiths—Mr. and Mrs. and deir two
kids, Cindy and John. And it was nice you know. Like it was like my first contact
with an ethnic family and I got a really good look at de way dey live. I mean
sure at times it was a bit exotic for me you know de food for example but
mostly I just realized they were a family like any other wif crazy aunts and
fights and generation gaps and communication problems and two cars, a VCR,
a microwave, a cellular phone and a dog named Buster dat ate my socks.

Dey wanted to know all about me so I told dem stories about my mafioso uncle
El Gato and how he won a tank and his wife in a poker game and stories about
my aunt, the opera singer, Luisa la Sonrisa, and about my cousin, Esperanza,
about her border crossings and how she almost fell in love.

I came here because I wanted some perspective—you know working for
a mafioso gives you a very particular point of view about de world. You know,
we all need a filter to look at de world through. Like standing in Latin America
I get a clear view of Norte America and standing on Latin America while living
in Norf America gives me a new filter, a new perspective. Anyway, it was time to
change my filter so I came here to estudy. *Si,* thanks to *mi tio* El Gato and my
cousin Esperanza who always used to say, "you should learn to use your brain or
somebody else will use it for you," I practically have a doctorate in Chicano
estudies. Dat's right—Chicano estudies…. Well not exactly a doctorate—more
like an MA or most of an MA—cause I got my credits all screwed up and
I diden finish—my professors said I was ungovernable. I lacked discipline. You
know instead of like doing a paper on de historical roots of the oppression of La
Raza I organized an all night Salsa Dance Party Extravaganza. I also organized
de month long "Chico and de Man" Memorial Symposium which I dedicated to
my cousin, Esperanza, back home.

Going Home

VERDECCHIA   I had wanted to go home for many years but the fear of military
service in Argentina kept me from buying that plane ticket. Nobody was certain
but everybody was pretty sure that I had committed treason by not registering
for my military service when I was sixteen, even though I lived in Canada.
Everybody was also reasonably sure that I would be eligible for military service
until I was thirty-five. And everybody was absolutely certain that the minute
I stepped off a plane in Buenos Aires military policemen would spring from the

tarmac, arrest me and guide me to a jail cell where they would laugh at my earrings and give me a proper hair cut.

I phoned the consulate one day to try to get the official perspective on my situation. I gave a false name and I explained that I wanted to go HOME for a visit, that I was now a Canadian citizen and no, I hadn't registered for my military service. The gentleman at the consulate couldn't tell me exactly what my status was but he suggested that I come down to the consulate where they would put me on a plane which would fly me directly to Buenos Aires where I would appear before a military tribunal who could tell me in no uncertain terms what my status actually was.

Well I'll certainly consider that, I said.

And I waited seven years. And in those seven years, the military government is replaced by a civilian one and I decide I can wait no longer; I will risk a return HOME. I set off to discover the Southern Cone.

To minimize my risk I apply for a new Canadian passport which does not list my place of birth

Slide: Passport photos.

and I plan to fly first to Santiago, Chile and then cross the border in a bus that traverses the Andes and goes to Mendoza, Argentina.

After an absence of almost fifteen years I am going home. Going Home I repeat the words softly to myself—my mantra: I am Going Home—all will be resolved, dissolved, revealed, I will claim my place in the universe when I go Home.

Music: "Vuelvo al Sur"—Goyeneche.

I have spent the last fifteen years preparing for this. I bought records and studied the liner notes. I bought "mate" and "dulce de leche." I talked to my friends, questioned my parents and practiced my Spanish with strangers. I befriended former Montonero and Tupamaro guerrillas and people even more dangerous like Jorge: painter, serious smoker, *maître de cafe*. Jorge the Apocryphal, Jorge of the savage hair. Jorge who moved to Italy and left me alone with my memories. I've spent the past fifteen years reading newspapers, novels and every Amnesty International report on South America. I tracked down a Salvador Allende poster, found postcards of Che and Pablo Neruda. I drank Malbec wines and black market Pisco with a Chilean macro-economist whose cheques always bounced. I learned the words and sang along with Cafrune and Goyeneche.

I saw *Missing* three times.

Santiago

Santiago, Chile.
Chile, your Fodor's travel guide will tell you, immediately strikes the visitor as very cosmopolitan and is known for its award-winning wines and excellent seafood. Chileans, Fodor's tells us, are a handsome, stylish people known for their openness and hospitality. My 1989 Fodor's Guide also tells me that under Pinochet, Chile enjoys a more stable political climate than it did in the early '70s but reports persist of government sponsored assassinations, kidnappings and torture. (Tell me about it man, I saw *Missing*.)

Well, it is now 1990 and the horrific Pinochet dictatorship is a thing of the past. I ride a comfortable bus into Santiago and continue reading my Fodor's: Unfortunately, South America's democracies seem to have higher street crime rates than the police states. I guess it all depends on how you define street crime. I look out the window and read the graffiti: *Ojo! La derecha no duerme.* I count all the policemen, one per block it seems. What was it like under Pinochet? A policeman in every house?

Music: "Jingo"—Carlos Santana.

Tired from a ten-hour flight I check into the Hotel de Don Tito, listed on page 302 of your Fodor's as a moderate, small hotel with six suites, eight twins, eight singles, bar, homey atmosphere, and it's located on one of the main streets in Santiago on Huerfanos at Huerfanos 578. (*Huerfanos*—Spanish for orphans.) I shower, shave and take an afternoon nap.

Three blasts from the street wake me up and pull me to the window.

There, three stories below, directly in front of the moderate and homey Hotel de Don Tito, there on the road, directly below my window, there's a man in a suit, his shirt soaked an impossible red, lies writhing as an enormous crowd gathers. I reach for my camera and begin to take photographs. I take photographs with a 135mm telephoto and then change lenses to get a sense of the crowd that has built up. I take photographs of the man who was shot on the first day of my return home after an absence of almost fifteen years, as more policemen arrive pulling weapons from their jean jackets. I take photographs as the man in the suit, his lower body apparently immobilized, reaches wildly for the legs that surround him, as the motorcycle police expertly push the crowd away from the Hotel de Don Tito, moderate in Fodor's, Huerfanos 578, homey, page 302. I take photographs as still more policemen arrive waving things that look like Uzis. I take photographs with a Pentax MX and a 35mm F 2.8 lens as the dying man, one of his shoes lying beside him, his gun on the road, gives up reaching for the legs around him. I take photographs from my room in the Hotel de Don Tito, Huerfanos 578, moderate in Fodor's, as the press arrives and NO AMBULANCE EVER COMES. I take photographs, 64 ASA Kodachromes, as he dies and I take photographs as the policemen (all men) talk to each other and I wonder if anyone has seen me and I take photographs as the policemen smoke cigarettes and cover him up and I take photographs and I realize that I have willed this to happen.

Dancing

WIDELOAD   Oye, you know I do like you Saxons. Really you guys are great. I always have a very good time whenever we get together. Like sometimes, I'll be out with some friends from de Saxonian community and we'll be out at a bar having a few *cervezas*, you know, *vacilando* and some music will be playing and "La Bamba" will come on. And all de Saxons get all excited and start tappin deir toes and dey get all carried away and start doing dis thing with deir heads... and dey get dis look in deir eyes like it's Christmas an dey look at me and say, "Hey Wideload, 'La Bamba.'"

Ya mang, *la puta bamba.*

"Wideload man, do you know de words?"

Do I know de words?
Mang, do I have an *enorme pinga*? Of course I know de words: Pala Pala pala la Bamba.... Who doesn't know de words?

Music: "Navidad Negra"—Ramiro's Latin Orchestra.

Espeaking of music I haf to say dat I love de way you guys dance. I think you Saxons are some of de most interesting dancers on de planet. I lof to go down to the Bamboo when my friend Ramiro is playing and just watch you guys dance because you are so free—like nothing gets in your way: not de beat, not de rhythm, nothing.

What I especially like to watch is like a Saxon guy dancing wif a Latin woman. Like she is out dere and she's smiling and doing a little cu-bop step and she's having a good time and de Saxon guy is like trying really hard to keep up, you know he's making a big effort to move his hips independently of his legs and rib cage and he's flapping his arms like a flamenco dancer. Generally speaking dis applies just to the male Saxon—Saxon women seemed to have learned a move or two...

Of course part of de problem is dat you guys wear very funny shoes for dancing—I mean like dose giant running shoes with built in air compressors and padding and support for de ankles and nuclear laces—I mean you might as well try dancing wif snowshoes on. Your feet have got to be free, so dat your knees are free so dat your hips are free—so dat you can move your *culo* wif impunity.

So dere dey are dancing away: de Saxon guy and de Latin woman or de Saxon woman and de Latin guy and de Saxon, you can see de Saxon thinking:

Wow, he/she can really dance, he/she can really move dose hips, he/she keeps smiling, I think he/she likes me, I bet he/she would be great in bed...

Now dis is important so I'm going to continue talking about it—even though it always gets really quiet whenever I start in on this stuff.

Now dere are two things at work here: the first is the fact that whenever a Latin and a Saxon have sex it is going to be a mind-expanding and culturally enriching experience *porque nosotros sabemos hacer cosas que ni se imaginaron en la Kama Sutra, porque nosotros tenemos un ritmo, un calor un sabor un tumbao de timbale de conga de candomble de kilombo. Una onda, un un dos tres, un dos. Saben...?*

Dat's de first factor at work and for dose of you who want a translation of dat come and see me after de show or ask one of de eSpanish espeakers in de audience at intermission.

De second component is the Exotica Factor. De Latin Lover Fantasy. And I'll let you in on a little secret: Latins are no sexier dan Saxons—well maybe just a little. De difference is dis: we like it. A lot. And we practise. A lot. Like we touch every chance we get.

Now I doan want you to get de impression I'm picking on you Saxons. Nothing could be further from my mind... I have de greatest respect for your culture... and you know, every culture has its own fertility dances, its own dance of sexual joy—you people hab de Morris dance

Slide: Morris Dancers in mid-dance.

and hey, you go to a Morris Dance Festival and it's de Latinos who look silly. You have de Morris dance—very sexy dance—you know a bunch of guys hopping around wif bells on and every once in a while swinging at each other— now, I am not doing de dance justice and I am looking for a Morris dance teacher so if you know of one please pass deir name along... you have de Morris dance and we have de mambo, rumba, cumbia, de son, son-guajiro, son-changui, charanga, de merengue, de guaguanco, de tango, de samba, salsa... shall I continue?

Latin Lover

Latin Lovers.

Slide: Antonio Banderas.

Dis is Antonio Banderas. He is a Spanish actor, a Spaniard from Spain. Dat's in Europe. Some of you may know him from Almodovar films like *Tie Me Up, Tie Me Down* and some of you may know him from de movie De *Mambo Kings* based on de excellent book by Oscar Hijuelos or from de more recent *Evita*

where he plays another *Latino way buff dude: Che Guevara.* Now
according to *Elle* magazine (and dey should know)

> *Slide:* Elle *magazine cover.*

Antonio Banderas is de latest incarnation of de Latin Lover. It says right here:
"Antonio Banderas—A Latin Love-God is Born."

De Latin Lover is always being re-incarnated. Sometimes de Latin Lover is
a woman—Carmen Miranda for example.

> *Slide: Carmen Miranda photo.*

She was Brazilian. Poor Carmen, smiling, sexy even with all dose goddamned
bananas on her head do you know she ended up unemployable, blacklisted
because a certain senator named McCarthy found her obscene?

> *Slide: Delores del Rio photo.*

Dere was also Delores del Rio,

> *Slide: Maria Montez.*

Maria Montez, some of you may remember her as Cobra Woman,

> *Slide: Rita Moreno.*

den Rita Moreno, today we have Sonia Braga…

> *Slide: Rudolph Valentino.*

For de men dere was Rudolph Valentino,

> *Slide: Fernando Lamas photo.*

Fernando Lamas,

> *Slide: Ricardo Montalban.*

Mr. Maxwell House and of course…

> *Slide: Desi Arnaz photo.*

Desi Arnaz whom we all remember as Ricky Ricardo from Ricky and Lucy those
all time great TV lovers. Now Ricky may not exactly live up to de steamy image
of unbridled sexuality we expect from our Latin Lovers but you have to admit
he's a pretty powerful icon. Funny, cute, musical and more often dan not
ridiculous.

Let's see what *Elle* magazine has to say about Latin Lovers:
"He's short, dark and handsome, with lots of black hair from head to chest.
He's wildly emotional, swinging from brooding sulks to raucous laughter and
singing loudly in public. He's relentlessly romantic, with a fixation on love that
looks to be total: he seems to be always about to shout, 'I must have you.'"

Slide:
> I must have you

He is the Latin Lover, an archetype of masculinity built for pleasure.

The article begins by explaining the myth of the Latin Lover and then uses the myth to explain Banderas. Banderas cannot explain himself apparently because his English is too limited.

In *Mirabella,*

> *Slide:* Mirabella *cover.*

another glossy magazine, there is an another article on Banderas and it describes how Banderas pronounces the word LOVE. He pronounces it Looov-aaa. Ooooh isn't dat sweet and sexy and don't you just want to wrap him up in your arms and let him whisper filthy things in your ear in Spanish and broken English? Especially when, as also described in the *Mirabella* article, he wipes his mouth on the tablecloth and asks, "What can I done?" Don't you just want to fuck him? I do. I wonder though if it would be quite so disarming or charming if it was Fidel Castro wiping his mouth on the tablecloth?

> *Slide: Cover of* Gentleman's Quarterly *magazine.*

Dis is Armand Assante.

He plays Banderas' brother in de movie, *Mambo Kings.*

He is an Italo-American.

The subtitle here says De Return of Macho. Did macho go away for a while? I hadn't noticed. Anyway it has returned for dose of you who missed it.

According to dis article in *GQ,* Signor Assante almost did not get de part in de movie because de estudio, Warner Bros. wanted a name—dey wanted a big name A-list actor—like Robin Williams—to play a Cuban. But, according to de article the director of the movie had the "*cajones*"

> *Slide:*
> Cajones

to buck the studio and give the part to Assante.
Cajones...

Now the word I think they want to use is *cojones,*

> *Slide:*
> Cojones

which is a colloquial term for testicles. What they've ended up with in *GQ* magazine is a sentence that means the director had the crates or boxes to buck the studio.

Slide:
> cojones = testicles

Slide:
> cajones = crates

Could be just a typo but you never know.

Now I find it really interesting dat all of the advance publicity for dis movie was concentrated in de fashion magazine trade. When a Hollywood trade magazine and major newspapers tell me de movie feels authentic and when the movie is pre-sold because its stars are sexy Latino love gods and macho and 'cause dey wear great clothes I begin to suspect dat de movie is another attempt to trade on the look, the feel, surface of things Latin.

It goes back to this thing of Latin Lovers being archetypes of men and women built for pleasure. Whose pleasure mang? Your movie-going pleasure? The pleasure of de Fashion-Industrial-Hollywood complex? Think about it—

In dose movies we can't solve our own problems, we can't win a revolution without help from gringos, we can't build the pyramids at Chichenitza without help from space aliens, we don't win the Nobel Prize no, instead we sing, we dance, we fuck like a dream, we die early on, we sleep a lot, we speak funny, we cheat on each other, we get scared easy, we amuse you. And it's not just in de movies—it's in—

Sound: Loud buzzer.

Dere goes de buzzer—indicating dat some forty-five minutes of de show have elapsed and dat less dan fifteen minutes remain till intermission. Unofficial tests indicate dat audiences grow restless at de forty-five-minute mark so we are going to take de briefest of breaks and give you de opportunity to shift around in your seats and scratch your *culo* and whisper to de person next to you.

And during dis break we are gonna see some clips from a mega-musical spectacular dat will be opening here soon. It's called *Miss Tijuana*. Dey are gonna be building a special theatre to house *Miss Tijuana* cause is a very big show wif lots of extras. It's going to be an adobe theatre wif Adobe Sound.

Here's de break.

> *Video: Clips of cartoons and movies featuring, among other things: Latinos, Hispanics, dopey peasants, Anthony Quinn and a certain mouse.*
>
> *Music: "Speedy Gonzales"—Pat Boone.*
>
> *Sound: Loud buzzer.*

Travel Sickness

VERDECCHIA   When I travel I get sick. I've thrown up in most of the major centres of the western world: Paris, Rome, Madrid, New York, London, Venice, Seaforth, Ontario, Calgary.... And it's not just too much to drink or drugs, sometimes it's as simple as the shape of the clouds in the sky or the look on someone's face in the market or the sound my shoes make on the street. These things are enough to leave me shaking and sweating in bed with a churning stomach, no strength in my legs and unsettling dreams.

Well, I'm in Buenos Aires and so far I haven't thrown up. So far, everything's fine.

We meet in Caballito, and Alberto and I have dinner in a bright, noisy restaurant called The Little Pigs and everything's fine. And now we're looking for some place to hear some music, a place in San Telmo to hear some contemporary music, not tango and not folklore. Alberto wants to go see a band called Little Balls of Ricotta and Everything's Fine but first we have to get the flat tire on his Fiat fixed. We stop at a *gomeria*, a word which translated literally would be a "rubbery," it's a place where they fix tires. I'm feeling like I need some air so I get out of the car and everything's fine, I'm looking at Alberto in the *gomeria* there's this weird green light in the shop and I'm leaning over the car and suddenly I feel very hot and awful and just as quickly I suddenly feel better. I wake up and I'm sitting on the road and somebody's thrown up on me, then I realize the vomit is my own and I'm in Buenos Aires and I'm sick and I've thrown up and we're in a tricky part of town and the cops will be passing by any minute and I haven't done my military service—

Alberto puts me in the back of the car. From the *gomeria*, Alberto brings me half a Coke can whose edges have been carefully trimmed and filed down—a cup of water. I lie in the back of Alberto's uncle's Fiat as we pull away. There's a knock at the window and I'm sure it's the police saying "excuse but have you got a young man who hasn't done his military service in there, a degenerate who's vomited all over the street"—but no, it's the guy from the *gomeria*—he wants his Coke can cup back.

We drive back to my apartment, not mine actually, my grandmother's but she's not there for some reason and I'm using it. I'm feeling a little better but weak, can't raise my head, I watch Buenos Aires spin and speed past and around me, through the back window, like a movie I think, ya that's it I'm in a Costa Gavras film.

I'm on the toilet in my grandmother's apartment, I leave tomorrow, back to Canada, and I ruined this last evening by getting sick, I can't fly like this all poisoned and I have to throw up again and the bidet is right there and for some reason I remember Alberto telling me how by the end of the month people are coming to his store on the edge of the *villa* and asking if they can buy one egg or a quarter of a package of butter or a few cigarettes and I think yes, in a few

years we will kill for an apple and I throw up in the bidet and I just want
to go home—but I'm already there—aren't I? Eventually, I crawl into my
grandmother's bed and sleep.

Music: "Asleep"—Astor Piazzolla & Kronos Quartet.

I dream of Mount Aconcagua, of Iguazu, of Ushuaia and condors, of the sierras
yellow and green, of bay, orange, quebracho and ombu trees, of running,
sweating horses, of *café con crema* served with little glasses of soda water, of the
smell of Particulares 30, of the vineyards of Mendoza of barrels full of ruby red
vino tinto, of gardens as beautiful as Andalusia in spring. I dream of thousands
of emerald green parrots flying alongside my airplane—parrots just like the
ones that flew alongside the bus as I travelled through the interior.

The Other

I would like to clear up any possible misimpression. I should state now that
I am something of an impostor. A fake. What I mean is: I sometimes confuse
my tenses in Spanish. I couldn't dance a tango to save my life.

All sides of the border have claimed and rejected me. On all sides I have been
asked: How long have you been…? How old were you when…? When did you
leave? When did you arrive? As if it were somehow possible to locate on a map,
on an airline schedule, on a blueprint the precise coordinates of the spirit, of
the psyche, of memory.

Music: "El Mal Dormido"—Atahualpa Yupanqui.

As if we could somehow count or measure these things.

These things cannot be measured—I know I tried.
I told the doctor: I feel Different. I feel wrong, out of place. I feel not nowhere,
not-neither.
The doctor said, "you're depressed."
I said, "yes I am."
The doctor said, "well…"
I said, "I want to be tested. Sample my blood, scan my brain, search my organs.
Find it."
"Find what?"
"Whatever it is."
"And when we find it?"
"Get rid of it."

Slides: X-rays, brain scans.

They didn't find anything. Everything's absolutely normal, I was told.
Everything's fine. Everything's where it should be. I wasn't fooled. I am a direct
descendant of two people who once ate armadillo—armadillo has a half-life of

two thousand years—you can't tell me that isn't in my bloodstream. Evita Peron once kissed my mother and that night she felt her cheek begin to rot. You can't tell me that hasn't altered my DNA.

El Teatro

WIDELOAD   Okay, let's see who's here, what's everybody wearing, let's see who came to *El Teatro* dis evening. What a good looking bunch of people. What are you doing here tonight? I mean don't think we doan appreciate it, we do. We're glad you've chosen to come here instead of spending an evening in front of the Global Village Idiot Box.

Are you a Group? Do you know each other? No, well, some of you know de person next to you but collectively, you are strangers. Estrangers In De Night. But perhaps by the end of the evening you will no longer be strangers because you will have shared an experience. You will have gone through dis show together and it will have created a common bond among you, a common reference point.

That's the theory anyway. That the theatre is valuable because a bunch of strangers come together and share an experience. But is it true? I mean how can you be sharing an experience when you are all (thankfully) different people? You have different jobs, different lives, different histories, different sexual orientations. You are all watching dis show from a different perspective. Most of you, for example, have been awake.

Maybe the only thing you have in common is dat you are all sitting here right now listening to me speculate about what you have in common and dat you all paid sixteen dollars to hear me do so. But not everybody paid sixteen dollars, my friends get in free. So do theatre critics. Weird huh?

People do end up in the weirdest places. I mean some of you are from Asia, some from *el Caribe,* some from Africa, some of you are from de Annex and you ended up in dis small room with me. And me, I left home to escape poverty and I ended up working in de theatre? Weird. Let's take a break, huh?

It's intermission ladies and gentlemen. Get your hot chocolate and Wideload wine gums outside.

   Music: "La Guacamaya"—Los Lobos.

ACTO SEGUNDO
Living Border

Slides:

Every North American, before this century is over, will find that he
or she has a personal frontier with Latin America.
This is a living frontier, which can be nourished by information,
but above all, by knowledge, by understanding, by the pursuit of
enlightened self-interest on both parts.
Or it can be starved by suspicion, ghost stories, arrogance, scorn
and violence.

—Carlos Fuentes[4]

Music: "Peligro"—Mano Negra.

Call to Arms

Sound: Voiceover.

This play is not a plea for tolerance. This is not a special offer for
free mambo lessons nor an invitation to order discount Paul
Simon albums. This is a citation, a manifesto. This is a summons
to begin negotiations, to claim your place on the continent.

Of Ferrets and Avocado

WIDELOAD   NEVER GIVE A FERRET AVOCADO!

Slide: Ferret.

De ferret ees a Northern European animal—known also as de polecat and
related to de bear and de wolberine. Dey are fierce little creatures, used to kill
pests like rabbits. De ferret can be domesticated. Some of you may have a ferret
of your own which you have affectionately named Blinky or Squiggly or
Beowulf. Ferrets, as you ferret owners will attest, are excellent pets: intelligent,
playful, affectionate, cute as all get-out. It takes four generations to domesticate
a ferret but only one generation for the ferret to revert to a feral state—dat
means to go savage. Interesting huh?

De avocado is a fruit from de Southern hemisphere—known variously as
avocado, aguacate and, for some reason known only to themselves, as palta to
Argentinians. De avocado is a rich, nutritious fruit which can be used in all
sorts of ways—as a mayonnaise, in guacamole, spread some on some pork
tenderloin for a sanwich Cubano. Avocados make lousy pets. Dey are not playful
and do not respond at all to commands.

Never give a ferret avocado.
Because it will blow up. Deir northern constitutions cannot process de rich

southern fruit.
Think about dat.

Music: Fela Kuti's "Shakalaode" performed by Wganda Kenya.

Correction

I want to draw some attention to myself. Some more attention. I want to talk about dat nasty "s" word: esterotype. I would like to set the record straight on dis subject and state dat I am by no means an esterotype. At least I am no more of an esterotype dan dat other person in de show: dat neurotic Argentinian. And I know dere's a lot of confusion on dis subject so let me offer a few pointers.

If I was a real esterotype, I wouldn't be aware of it. I wouldn't be talking to you about being an estereotype. If I was a real esterotype, you would be laughing at me, not with me. And if I was a real esterotype, you wouldn't take me seriously. And you do take me seriously. Don't you?

I'm the real thing. Don't be fooled by imitations.

Border Crossings

VERDECCHIA   Los Angeles. Uh, Los, Las Anngel—Lows Anjelees, uh, L.A.

Two weeks.

Pleasure.

I'm a Canadian citizen.

Pleasure. (Didn't I just answer that question?)

I'm… an… actor actually.

Ever seen *Street Legal?*

Well, I'm mostly in the theatre. I don't think…. Okay uh, the Tarragon uh, Canadian Stage, the—

I'm not surprised.

Yes, that's my book. Well, it's not *mine.* It's a novel. That I'm reading.

(Oh, Jeeezzuz.) A guy, you know, who has a kind of identity problem and uh—

I told you: pleasure. Come on what is this? I'm a Canadian citizen—we're supposed to be friends. You know, Free Trade, the longest undefended border in the world… all that? (I had less trouble getting into Argentina.)

No, I'm not unemployed. I'm an actor. I'm between jobs, I'm on holidays.

Thanks.

Some borders are easier to cross than others. Try starting a conversation in Vancouver with the following statement: I like Toronto.

Some things get across borders easier than others.

Slide: Large, angry bee.

Killer bees for example.

Music: "Muiñeira de Villanova"—Milladoiro.

Music. Music crosses borders.
My grandfather was a gallego, from Galicia, Spain. This music is from Galicia and yes, those are bagpipes. Those of us with an ethnomusicological bent can only ask ourselves, "how did the bagpipes ever end up in... Scotland?"

Ponte guapa que traen el haggis!

The bandoneon, cousin to the concertina and step-brother to the accordion, came to the Rio de la Plata via Germany. Originally intended for organless churches, the bandoneon found its true calling in the whorehouses of Buenos Aires and Montevideo playing the most profane music of all: the Tango.

Banned by Pope Pius X, the tango was, at first, often danced only by men because its postures were considered too crude, too sexual for women—it was, after all, one of the first dances in which men and women embraced.

King Ludwig of Bavaria forbade his officers to dance it and the Duchess of Norfolk explained that the tango was contrary to English character and manners, but the tango, graciously received in the salons of Paris, soon swept London's Hotel Savoy and the rest of Europe. Finally, even polite society in Argentina acknowledged it.

The tango, however, has not been entirely domesticated. It is impossible to shop or aerobicize to tango... *porque el tango es un sentimiento que se baila.*

And what is it about the tango, this national treasure that some say was born of the gaucho's crude attempts to waltz?

Music: "Verano Porteño"—Astor Piazzolla.[5]

It is music for exile, for the preparations, the significations of departure, for the symptoms of migration. It is the languishing music of picking through your belongings and deciding what to take. It is the 2 a.m. music of smelling and caressing books none of which you can carry—books you leave behind with friends who say they'll always be here when you want them when you need them, music for a bowl of apples sitting on your table, apples you have not yet eaten, apples you cannot take—you know they have apples there in that other place but not these apples—not apples like these—you eat your last native apple and stare at what your life is reduced to—all the things you can stick into a sack. It will be cold—you will need boots—you don't own boots except these rubber ones—will they do? You pack them, you pack a letter from a friend so you will not feel too alone.

Music for final goodbyes for one last drink and a quick hug as you cram your cigarettes into your pocket and run to the bus, you run, run, your chest heaves, like the bellows of the bandoneon. You try to watch intently to emblazon in your mind these streets, these corners, those houses, the people the smells even the lurching bus fills you with a kind of stupid happiness and regret—music for the things you left behind in that room—a dress, magazines, some drawings, two pairs of shoes and blouses too old to be worn any more—four perfect apples.

Music for cold nights under incomprehensible stars, for cups of coffee and cigarette smoke, for a long walk by the river where you might be alone or you might meet someone. It is music for encounters in shabby stairways, the music of lovemaking in a narrow bed, the tendernesses, the caress the pull of strong arms and legs.

Music for men and women thin as bones.
Music for your invisibility.

Music for a letter that arrives telling you that he is very sick—music for your arms that ache from longing from wishing he might be standing at the top of the stairs waiting to take the bags and then lean over and kiss you and even his silly stubble scratching your cold face would be welcome and you only discover that you're crying when you try to find your keys—

Music for a day in the fall when you buy a new coat and think perhaps you will live here for the rest of your life, perhaps it will be possible, you have changed so much, would they recognize you, would you recognize your country, would you recognize yourself?

WIDELOAD   Basically, tango is music for fucked up people.

VERDECCHIA   Other things cross borders easily. Diseases and disorders. Like amnesia. Amnesia crosses borders.

Drug War Deconstruction

WIDELOAD   Hey I want to show you a little movie. It's a home movie. It came into my home and I saved it to share with my friends. It's called *The War On Drugs*. Some of you may have seen it already so we're just gonna see some of de highlights.

Video: Edited Drug War TV Movie.

(as we watch video) Dis is de title: It says "De War On Drugs." In Big Block Letters. In English. Dis is another title: The Cocaine Cartel. Dey're talking about de Medellin Cartel in Colombia.

Dis is de hero. He is a Drug Enforcement Agent from de U.S. who is sent to Colombia to take on de Medellin Cartel. He is smiling. He kisses his ex-wife. Oh… he is shy.

Dis woman is a kind of judge—a Colombian judge and she agrees to prosecute de Medellin cartel, to build a case against de drug lords even though her life is being threatened here on de phone even as we watch. *(as character on screen speaks)* "But… I didn't order a pizza."

Dis guy is a journalist, an editor for a big Colombian newspaper. He is outspoken in his criticism of the drug lords. He has written editorial after editorial condemning de Cartel and calling for de arrest of de drug lords. He is a family man as we can tell by his Volvo car and by de presents which he loads into de car to take to his loved ones.

Okay, dis is a long shot so can we fast forward through this part? *(tape speeds up)*

He's going home after a hard day at de office. He is in traffic. He is being followed by two guys on a motorcycle. Dey come to an intersection. *(tape resumes normal speed)*

Dey estop. De light is red. De guy gets off de motorcycle. Dum-dee-bumbe dum. He has a gun! Oooh! and de family man editor is killed and as we can see he is driving one of dose Volvos wif de built in safety feature dat when de driver is killed, de car parks itself automatically. Very good cars Volvos.

Dis is de Medellin Cartel. Dese are de drug lords. Dey are de bad guys. We know dey are bad because dey have manicured hands, expensive jewellery, even more expensive suits and… dark hair. Dere's a lot of dem, dey are at a meeting, talking business. And dis guy, is de kingpin, Pablo Escobar, head of de Medellin Cartel, de baddest of de bad. We know he is bad because he has reptilian eyes.

Okay, lemme put dis on pause for a second—Dis movie shows us a lot of things. It shows us dat drugs wreck families—in dis case de family of de nice white guy who is trying to stop de drug dealers—nobody in his family uses drugs—it's just he spends so much time fighting drugs dat his family falls apart.

De movie shows us dat de drug lords are nasty people who will not hesitate to kill anybody who gets in deir way. And de big guy, de kingpin, Pablo Escobar who is now dead, was, according to the *Economist* magazine, one of the richest men in de world. Now Senor Escobar *was* not only a giant in free-market capitalism, he was also very big in public works, especially public housing. Interesting huh? De movie doesn't show us dat. What else doesn't de movie show us?

It does not show us dat for example dat profits from de sale of cocaine are used to fund wars like de U.S. war on Nicaragua which left some 20,000 Nicaraguans dead. Dis movie does not show us dat right wing Miami-based terrorists, major U.S. drug traffickers, de Medellin Cartel, Syrian drug and arms dealers, de CIA, de State Department and Oliver North all worked together to wage war on Nicaragua. It does not show us that charges against major U.S. drug traffickers—dose are de people who bring de drugs on to dis part of de continent—charges against dose people were dropped once they became involved in the Contra war against Nicaragua.

Some of you are, naturally, skeptical and some of you have heard all dis before because you have read de Kerry Sub-Committee report. Allow me to recommend it to those of you who haven't read it. It is incomplete at 400 pages but it does outline dese things I'm talking about. It makes excellen' bedtime or bathroom reading. I urge you to pick up a copy. And if you have any questions gimme a call.

So de next time a blatant piece of propaganda like dis one comes on, I hope we will watch it skeptically and de next time we stick a straw up our nose I hope we will take a moment to make sure we know exactly where de money we give our dealer is going.[6]

Audition

VERDECCHIA   It's two o'clock on a wintry afternoon and I have an audition for a TV movie.

> *Sound: Dialect tape.*

The office has sliding glass doors, hidden lighting fixtures and extravagant windows. There are four or five people seated behind a table including a guy with very expensive sunglasses.

> *Video camera on VERDECCHIA—direct to monitors.*

Hi, I'm Guillermo Verdecchia. I'm with Noble Talent.

(*off camera*) For those of you who aren't in the business this is called slating. And when I say the business I do mean the industry. Slating is the first thing you do when you audition for a part on a TV show or a movie—you put your face and your name and your agent's name on tape before you read the scene.

(*direct to monitors*) I'm 5'9". On a good day.

(*off camera*) That's called a little joke. Always good to get the producers and director laughing.

(*direct to monitor*) I'm from Argentina actually. My special skills include driving heavy machinery, tango dancing, scuba diving, polo playing and badminton.

I speak three languages including English and I specialize in El Salvadorean refugees, Italian bob-sledders, Arab horse-thieves and Uruguayan rugby players who are forced to cannibalize their friends when their plane crashes in the Andes.

(off camera) Actually, I've never played a horse-thief or a rugby cannibal but I have auditioned for them an awful lot.

(direct to monitor) No. I've never been on *Really-True-Things-That-Actual-Cops-Do-As-Captured-By-Totally-Average-Citizens-With-Only-A-Video-Camera* before. It's a pleasure to be here. I'm reading for the part of Sharko.

(off camera) An overweight Hispanic in a dirty suit it says here. I'm perfect for it.

(direct to monitor) Here we go.

> Music: *"Speedy Gonzalez Meets Two Crows from Tacos"*—*The Carl Stalling Project.*

pop cops

A black Camaro slides into the foreground, the engine throbbing like a hard on from hell. Cut to close on trunk opening to reveal a deadly assault rifle. We hear Sharko's voice. (*GUILLERMO slips on a red bandanna.*) That's me.

SHARKO:
There it is man. Is a thing of great beauty, no?

SHARKO:
Sure man, I got what you ordered: Silencer, bullets. I even got you a little extra cause I like doing business wif you. A shiny new handgun.

SHARKO:
Come on man, it's like brand new. I got it off some old bag who used it to scare away peeping toms.

SHARKO:
Ah man, you take all this stuff for two grand, and I'll throw in the pistol for a couple of hundred. If you don't like it, you can sell it to some school kids for twice the price.

SHARKO:
You already got one hah? It was a present... I see. A present from who?

SHARKO:
From your Uncle Sam. Dat's nice. I diden know you had got an Uncle... (*with dawning horror*) You're a cop????

(off camera) Well that's that. I should've done it differently. I could've been funnier.

Uh, would you like me to do the scene again? I could do it differently. I have a blue bandanna.

Okay. Thanks very much.

Nice to meet you.

> *Slide:*
>> Ay ay ay ay I am the Frito Bandito
>
> *Music: "Cielito Lindo"—Placido Domingo.*

Santiago 2

I went back to Santiago and looked for some sign of the man who had been shot on the first day of my return. I looked for a stain, a scrape, anything, his shoe perhaps had been left behind. Nothing.

I wondered who he might have been. I remembered the redness of his shirt, the brightness of the sun. It was five o'clock.

> *A las cinco de la tarde*
> *Eran las cinco en punto de la tarde.*
> *Un niño trajo la blanca sabana*
> *a las cinco de la tarde*[7]

I saw someone die, I watched him die—that's what it looks like—that's where they end up, gun men, bank robbers, criminals and those brave revolutionaries and guerrillas you dreamed of and imagined you might be, might have been—they end up bleeding in the middle of the street, begging for water.

They end up dying alone on the hot pavement in a cheap suit with only one shoe. People die like that here. Ridiculous, absurd pathetic deaths.

I came for a sign, I came because I had to know and now I know.

> **Slides:** *Santiago shooting.*

> *¡Que no quiero verla!*

> *Que mi recuerdo se quema.*
> *¡Avisad a los jazmines*
> *con su blancura pequeña!*

> *¡Que no quiero verla!*[8]

At the hotel they told me he was a bank robber. The papers said the same thing—a bank robber, died almost immediately in a shootout, name of Fernando Ochoa, nationality unknown, not interested. Case closed, Dead gone erased.

I told them I was a Canadian writer/journalist/filmmaker. They believed me. They let me look at the files, they let me talk, very briefly, to the cops who shot him and since no one had shown up to claim him they let me go through his personal effects. There wasn't much. A Bic lighter, with a tiny screw in the bottom of it so it could be refilled, an empty wallet. A package of cigarettes, with two crumpled Marlboros. There was a letter to someone named Mercedes. It read "*Querida* Mercedes: It is bitterly cold tonight in my little room but I can look out the window and see the stars. I imagine that you are looking at them too. I take comfort in the fact that you and Ines and I share the same sky." There was also a newspaper from August 2nd, the day I arrived, the day he was shot. The headline claimed that former president Pinochet and the former minister of the Interior knew nothing about the bodies that had been found in the Rio Mapocho. I asked about his shoe—the one I saw on the road—no one knew anything about a shoe although they knew he wore size 42 just like me—

Decompression

I'm sitting in the bar at Ezeiza, I'm in the bar at Heathrow, in the bar at Terminal 62 at LAX and I'm decompressing, preparing to surface. I'll arrive at Pearson at Mirabel at Calgary International and I know that nothing will have changed and that everything will be different. I know that I've left some things behind—a sock in a hotel in Mendoza, a ring in a slum in Buenos Aires, a Zippo lighter in a lobby in Chile—a toenail in Ben's studio in Pougnadoresse, a combful of hair in the sink in the washroom at Florian in Venice.

These vestiges, these cells are slowly crawling towards each other. They are crossing oceans and mountains and six-lane expressways. They are calling to each other and arranging to meet in my sleep.

The Therapist

So… I went to see a therapist. He trained in Vienna but his office was in North York. I didn't tell him that I was afraid my toenails were coming after me in my sleep—I told him how I felt, what was happening—I have memories of things that never happened to me—I feel nostalgia for things I never knew—I feel connected to things I have no connection with, responsible, involved, implicated in things that happen thousands of miles away.

My therapist asked about my family. If I'd been breastfed. He asked about my sex life, my habits. He asked me to make a list of recurring dreams, a list of traumatic events including things like automobile accidents. I answered his questions and showed him drawings.

Slide: Drawings.

My therapist told me I was making progress. I believed him. (Who wouldn't believe a therapist trained in Vienna?) At about the same time that I started doing what he called "deep therapy work" or what I privately called reclaiming my inner whale, I began to lose feeling in my extremities. It started as a tingling in the tips of my fingers and then my hands went numb. Eventually, over a period of months, I lost all feeling in my left arm and I could hardly lift it.

My therapist told me to see A Doctor.

The doctor told me to rest and gave me pills.

Jorge made me go see El Brujo.

I said Jorge what do you mean *brujo?* I'm not going to somebody who's gonna make me eat seaweed.

Jorge said, "*No, che loco, por favor, dejate de joder, vamos che, tomate un matecito loco y vamos...*"

Who could argue with that? Where is this Brujo Jorge?

En la frontera.

Where?

Bloor and Madison.

El Brujo

Music: "Mojotorro"—Dino Saluzzi.

Slides:
> The West is no longer west. The old binary models have been replaced by a border dialectic of ongoing flux. We now inhabit a social universe in constant motion, a moving cartography with a floating culture and a fluctuating sense of self.
> —Guillermo Gomez-Peña [9]

Porque los que recien llegaron me sospechan,
porque I speak *mejor* inglish *que* espanish,
porque mis padres no me creen
porque no como tripa porque no como lengua
porque hasta mis dreams are subtitled

I went to see El Brujo at his place on Madison and you know I'd been to see a palm reader before so I sort of knew what to expect. And he's this normal guy who looks sort of like Freddy Prinze except with longer hair. And I told him about my therapist and about the numbness in my body and El Brujo said, "he tried to steal your soul," and I laughed this kind of honking sputtering laugh. I thought maybe he was kidding.

El Brujo asked me, "how do you feel?" and I said, "Okay. My stomach is kind of upset."

And he said, "yes it is" and I thought oh please just let me get back to reclaiming my inner whale.

El Brujo said, "you have a very bad border wound."

I do?

"Yes," he said, "and here in Mexico any border wounds or afflictions are easily aggravated."

I didn't have the heart to tell him that we were at Bloor and Madison in Toronto. El Brujo brought out a bottle and thinking this would be one way to get my money's worth, I started to drink.

El Brujo said, "I remember the night Bolivar burned with fever and realized there was no way back to the capital; the night he burned his medals and cried, 'whosoever works for the revolution plows the seas.'"

You *remember* that do you? I said. That was what 1830 or something? And I laughed and had another drink. And El Brujo laughed too and we had another drink and another drink and another.

El Brujo said, "I remember the Zoot Suit Riots. We were beat up for our pointy shoes and fancy clothes. I still have the scar." And he lifted up his shirt and showed me a gash. It was ugly and ragged and spotted with freshly dried blood. And that's when I first suspected that maybe we weren't at Bloor and Madison. You see, the Zoot Suit Riots were in 1943.

What do you remember? he asked.

Not much.

Try.

I remember the Alamo?

No you don't.

No, you're right I don't.

El Brujo said, "your head aches."

Yes it does.

Because your left shoe is too tight. Why don't we burn it? And maybe because I was drunk already or maybe because I really thought that burning my shoe would help my headache we threw it in the bathtub, doused it in lighter fluid and watched it burn this wild yellow and a weird green when the plastic caught on.

"What do you remember now?" he asked.

I remember the French Invasion of Mexico; I remember the Pastry War.

I remember a bar of soap I had when I was little and it was shaped like a bear or a bunny and when it got wet, it grew hair, it got all fuzzy.

I remember a little boy in a red snowsuit who ran away whenever anyone spoke to me in English. I remember *la machine queso.*

I remember a gang of boys who wanted to steal my leather jacket even though we all spoke Spanish, a gang of boys who taught me I could be a long lost son one minute and a tourist the next.

I remember an audition where I was asked to betray and insult everything I claim to believe in and I remember that I did as I was asked.

I remember practising tai chi in the park and being interrupted by a guy who wanted to start a fight and I remember thinking, "stupid drunken Mexican." I remember my fear, I taste and smell my fear, my fear of young men who speak Spanish in the darkness of the park and I know that somewhere in my traitorous heart I can't stand people I claim are my brothers. I don't know who did this to me. I remember feeling sick, I remember howling in the face of my fear...

I remember that I had dreamt I was playing an accordion, playing something improvised, which my grandmother recognized after only three notes as a tango from her childhood, playing a tango I had never learned, playing something improvised not knowing where my fingers were going, playing an accordion, a tango which left me shaking and sweating.

And I remember that I dreamt that dream one night after a party with some Spaniards who kept asking me where I was from and why my Spanish was so funny and I remember that I remembered that dream the first time one afternoon in Paris while staring at an accordion in a stall at the flea market and then found 100 francs on the street.

As I passed out El Brujo said, "the border is your..."

> *Music: "Nocturno A Mi Barrio"—Anibal Troilo.*

> *Slide:*
> Cuando, cuando me fui?

The Other America

The airport is clean clean clean. And big big big. The car that takes me back into the city is big and clean. We drive through big clean empty land under a big, fairly clean sky. I'm back in Canada. It's nice. I'm back in Canada... oh well...

Why did I come back here?

This is where I work, I tell myself—this is where I make the most sense—in this Noah's ark of a nation.

I reach into my pocket expecting to find my Zippo lighter and my last package of Particulares but instead I find a Bic lighter with a tiny screw in the bottom of it so it can be refilled and a package of Marlboros with two crumpled cigarettes in it. And written on the package is a note, a quote I hadn't noticed before. It says:

> *No estoy en el crucero*
> *elegir*
> *es equivocarse*[10]

> *Slide:*
> I am not at the cross roads;
> to choose
> is to go wrong.
> —Octavio Paz

And then I remember, I remember what El Brujo said, he said, "The Border is your Home."

I'm not in Canada; I'm not in Argentina.
I'm on the Border.
I am Home.

Mais zooot alors, je comprends maintenant, mais oui, merde! Je suis Argentin-Canadien! I am a post-Porteño neo-Latino Canadian! I am the Pan American Highway!

Latin Invasion

WIDELOAD   It's okay, mang. Everybody relax. I'm back. Ya, I been lying low in dis act but let me tell you I'm here to stay.

And it's quiz time. Please cast your memories way back and tell me who remembers Jose Imanez?
Ah-ha.
Who remembers de Frito Bandito? Who remembers Cheech and Chong?
Who remembers de U.S. invasion of Panama?

Dat's okay, dat was a trick question.

Who remembers de musical *De Kiss of de Spider Woman*? I do because I paid forty-two bucks to see it: a glamorous, musical celebration of the torture and repression of poor people in a far away place called Latin America where, just over the walls of the prison there are Gypsies and bullfights, women with big busts and all sorts of exotic, hot-blooded delights. Dat's one of de hit songs from de show—"Big Busted Women," some of you may recall...

Who remembers de ad dat McDonald's had for deir fajitas not too long ago—
featuring a guy called Pedro or Juan and he says dat he's up here to get some
Mac Fajitas because *(reciting with supreme nasality)* "dese are de most *gueno*
Fajitas I eber ate." What de fuck ees dat?

Can you imagine an ad dat went like: Hey Sambo, what are you doing here?
Well, Mistah, I come up here to get some o' yo' pow'ful good Macgrits.
Mmmmm-mmm. Wif a watahmelon slice fo' deesert. Yassee.

I mean, we would be offended.

So, what is it with you people? Who do you think you are? Who do you think
we are?

Yes, I am calling you you—I am generalizing, I am reducing you all to de lowest
common denominator, I am painting you all with the same brush. Is it starting
to bug you yet?

Of course, it is possible dat it doesn't really matter what I say. Because it's all
been kind of funny dis evening.

Dat has been my mistake. I have wanted you to like me so I've been a funny guy.

>   *Silence.*

Esto, en serio ahora—
Señoras y señores, we are re-drawing the map of America because economics,
I'm told, knows no borders.

>   *Slide:*
>   Somehow the word "foreign" seems foreign these days. The world
>   is smaller, so people are thinking bigger, beyond borders.
>   —IBM advertisement

Free Trade wif Mejico—dis is a big deal and I want to say dat it is a very
complicated thing and it is only the beginning. And I wish to remind you, at
this crucial juncture in our shared geographies, dat under dose funny voices and
under dose funny images of de Frito Bandito and under all this talk of Money
and Markets there are living, breathing, dreaming men, women and children.

I want to ask you please to throw out the metaphor of Latin America as North
America's "backyard" because your backyard is now a border and the metaphor
is now made flesh. Mira, I am in your backyard. I live next door, I live upstairs,
I live across de street. It's me, your neighbour, your dance partner.

>   *Slide:*
>   Towards un futuro post-Columbian

Consider

WIDELOAD & GUILLERMO   Consider those come from the plains, del litoral, from the steppes, from the desert, from the savannah, from the fens, from the sertao, from the rain forest, from the sierras, from the hills and high places.

Consider those come from the many corners of the globe to Fort MacMurray, to Montreal, to St. John's to build, to teach, to navigate ships, to weave, to stay, to remember, to dream.

Consider those here first. Consider those I have not considered. Consider your parents, consider your grandparents.

Consider the country. Consider the continent. Consider the border.

Going Forward

I am learning to live the border. I have called off the border patrol. I am a hyphenated person but I am not falling apart, I am putting together. I am building a house on the border.

And you? Did you change your name somewhere along the way? Does a part of you live hundreds or thousands of kilometres away? Do you have two countries, two memories? Do you have a border zone?

Will you call off the border patrol?

Ladies and gentlemen, please reset your watches. It is now almost 10 o'clock on a (Friday) night—we still have time. We can go forward. Towards the centre, toward the border.

WIDELOAD   And let the dancing begin!

Music: "Bacalao Con Pan"—Irakere.

Notes

1   Carlos Fuentes, *Latin America: At War with the Past* (Toronto: CBC Enterprises, 1985), 8. This 1984 Massey Lecture elegantly explores, in great detail, the divisions expressed by the Mexico–North America border. Although Fuentes focuses almost exclusively on the U.S., his analysis and insights provide a useful perspective for Canadians.

2   William Langewiesche, "The Border," *Atlantic* vol. 269, no. 5 (May 1992): 56. This excellent article deals specifically with the Mexico–U.S. border: border crossings, the Border Patrol, drug traffic, economics, etc.

3   The term Latino has its shortcomings but seems to me more inclusive than the term Hispanic. Hispanic —which comes from Hispania, the Roman word for the Iberian peninsula—is a term used in the U.S. for bureaucratic, demographic, ideological and commercial purposes. Chicano refers to something else again. Chicano identity, if I may be so bold, is based in the tension of the border. Neither Mexicans nor U.S. Americans, Chicanos synthesize to varying degrees Mexican culture and language—including its Indigenous roots—and Anglo-American culture and language. Originally springing from the southwest U.S., Chicanos can be found all over, in Texas, in California, in New Mexico (!), in Detroit, maybe even in Canada. Chicanos speak a variety of regional tongues, including formal or standard English and Spanish, North Mexican Spanish, Tex-Mex or Spanglish and even some caló or pachuco slang. See Gloria Anzaldúa's essay "Hot To Tame A Wild Tongue," in *Out There: Marginalization and Contemporary Culture* (New York and Cambridge, MA: The New Museum of Contemporary Art and M.I.T. Press, 1990), 203–11. Also of interest are the writings of Ron Arias, the poetry of Juan Felipe Herrera and the conjunto grooves of Steve Jordan.

4   Carlos Fuentes, *Latin America: At War with the Past* (Toronto: CBC Enterprises, 1985), 8.

5   Strictly speaking, Piazzolla's music is not tango with a capital T. Many Purists would hotly contest my choice of music here, arguing that Piazzolla destroyed the tango. I would respond that Piazzolla re-invented and thereby rescued the tango from obsolescence. There is no foreseeable end to this argument.

6   For a thorough analysis of the actual parameters of the war on drugs, see Peter Dale Scott and Jonathan Marshall, *Cocaine Politics* (Berkeley: University of California Press, 1991). See also Noam Chomsky, *Deterring Democracy* (London: Verso, 1991).

7   Federico García Lorca, "La sangre derramada," in *Poema del cante jondo/Llanto por Ignacio Sánchez Mejías* (Buenos Aires: Editorial Losada, 1948), 145.

8   Federico García Lorca, "La sangre derramada," in *Poema del cante jondo/Llanto por Ignacio Sánchez Mejías* (Buenos Aires: Editorial Losada, 1948), 148.

9   Guillermo Gómez-Peña, "The World According to Guillermo Gómez-Peña," *High Performance* vol. 14, no. 3 (Fall 1991): 20. A MacArthur Fellow, Gómez-Peña has

been a vital contributor to the U.S. debate on "multiculturalism," urging a rigorous appraisal of terms such as assimilation, hybridization, border-culture, pluralism and coexistence. A former member of Border Arts Workshop, he continues to explore notions of identify and otherness in his writings, and in performances such as *Border Brujo* and *The Year of the White Bear*, a collaboration with Coco Fusco.

10 Octavio Paz, "A la mitad de esta frase," in *A Draft of Shadows*, edited and translated by Eliot Weinberger (New York: New Directions, 1979), 72.

Here Lies Henry

written by Daniel MacIvor

dramaturged by Daniel Brooks

Daniel MacIvor has been creating new theatre since 1986 and was for twenty years artistic director of da da kamera, an international tourng company based in Toronto which he ran with Sherrie Johnson. His published work includes *See Bob Run, Never Swim Alone, You Are Here, In On It, How It Works, I Still Love You*—a collection of five plays which won the Governor General's Literary Award for Drama in 2006—and *His Greatness*, which won Best New Play at the 2008 Jessie Richardson Awards in Vancouver.

With Daniel Brooks he created the solo shows *House, Monster, Cul-de-sac* and *This is What Happens Next*. He received an Obie and a GLAAD Award for his play *In On It* which was presented in New York at PS122 in September 2001. Also a filmmaker, he has written and directed the feature films *Past Perfect* and *Wilby Wonderful*, and co-wrote and starred in *Whole New Thing*. He was the inaugural senior playwright-in-residence at the Banff Playwright's Colony where he was developing his play *Communion* as part of a trilogy: *Confession*, produced by Mulgrave Road Theatre in Nova Scotia and *Redemption*, which he is developing at the National Theatre School. Currently he is writer-in-residence at the University of Guelph and lives in Toronto. He is represented by Thomas Pearson at ICM Talent. Check out Daniel's web log at danielmacivor.com.

Daniel Brooks has worked as a director writer, actor, producer, and teacher. One of his earliest outings was as a director in a theatrical adaptation of the movie *All About Eve* called *Evening* (1981). He played the lead in the Ken Gass production of *Hamlet* (1981).

Since then, he has become a mainstay of this country's theatre, working with a network of Ontario-based writers, playwrights and directors (Guillermo Verdecchia, Daniel MacIvor and John Mighton, among them). He has been co-director of The Augusta Company and da da kamera, and playwright-in-residence at Tarragon Theatre. He is currently Artistic Director of Necessary Angel Theatre Company.

Among his works as a writer are *The Return of Pokey Jones* (1985), *The Noam Chomsky Lectures* (with Verdecchia, 1992), *The Lorca Play* (with MacIvor, 1992), *Here Lies Henry* (with MacIvor, 1996) and *Insomnia* (with Verdecchia, 1997).

He has also directed and acted in several works other than his own, winning several awards, including the Chalmers (for *Noam Chomsky, Here Lies Henry, House*); the Dora Mavor Moore Award three times for directing, the Edinburgh Fringe First Award (*Here Lies Henry*); and has been nominated for the Governor General's Award (*Noam Chomsky*). In October, 2000, he won the Capital Critics Circle Award for his direction of *Possible Worlds*. In October, 2001, he received the first Elinore and Lou Siminovitch Prize in Theatre for his work as a director.

His highly innovative work has travelled across Canada and around the world. He is married to Jennifer Ross. They have two daughters, and live in Toronto.

Here Lies Henry was developed in a workshop, and first produced by da da kamera and Festival Antigonish, Nova Scotia in 1994 with the following company:

HENRY   Daniel MacIvor

Directed by Daniel Brooks
Technical Direction by Ian Pygott
Produced by Sherrie Johnson for da da kamera
Produced by Addy Doucette for Festival Antigonish

• • •

Here Lies Henry was first produced by da da kamera as part of the Six Stages Festival at Buddies in Bad Times Theatre, Toronto in 1996 with the following company:

HENRY   Daniel MacIvor

Directed by Daniel Brooks
Lighting Designed by Andrea Lundy, Jan Komarek and Andy Moro
Sound Designed by Richard Feren
Produced by Sherrie Johnson for Six Stages and da da kamera

Characters

HENRY

Notes to Future Productions:

Music and Sound: In the original productions Henry wore a microphone through which his voice was at times affected. Sound and music was also used often throughout the performance as an indication of a level of reality outside Henry's control. These moments are not notated in this text. Use your imagination.

Light: The lighting in the original production consisted of a series of boxes that grew increasingly smaller until only Henry's face was lit. I have notated lighting changes in this text.

Costume: Henry is dressed up, looking his best.

Set: A bare stage. In the front row of the audience is a chair which is clearly marked as reserved for a local dignitary. Perhaps the mayor. Someone whose presence is possible.

Performance: Henry is talking to this audience, tonight, in this space. Everything is happening now.

Text: There is a level of improvisation which happens with the audience, I have notated these moments and given suggestions in stage directions. Contemporary and local references should be altered and added to keep the production current and inside the local community. I have notated where these alterations and additions might occur. Also, it would be out of character for Henry not to say "Bless You" if someone in the audience should sneeze. And if a cell phone should ring he would certainly respond with an "I'm not here." or "Is that for me?".

Marketing: In presenting a production it might be in your best interests to downplay the role of the outside writer (me). If the audience is overtly conscious of a "writer" then it makes it difficult to look at the show as happening tonight. Perhaps keep mention of the writer off the posters and promo and only give credit in the show's program. Also, in the program Daniel Brooks must receive credit as dramaturg.

HERE LIES HENRY

A dark stage. Now.
Ominous music.
HENRY enters through a dim tunnel of light.
HENRY coughs. Music out, light up bright.
HENRY regards the audience fearfully.
He smiles weakly.
More fear.
He nods hello to a couple of individuals.
HENRY knows he has to do something but he's not sure what.
HENRY has an idea.

HENRY *(singing, tentative)* "Grab your coat and get your hat, leave your worries on the doorstep, life could be so sweet *(getting into it)* on the sunny side of the street!" *(He hits a bad note on the last word; he tries to find the right note.)* "...street." "...street." No. "... street." *(He can't find the note, he gives up.)*

He regards the audience fearfully.
He checks his fly.
He mimes a bird with his hands, it flies and lands on his shoulder.

An uncomfortable pause.

You don't want to get me started talking, I might never shut up.
I took a public slpeak...
I took a public speaking course.
One: Don't say "um."
Two: Never apologize.
Three: Don't say "anyway."
Four: ...Um...?
Sorry.
Anyway. Ahhh!
It's hard.
I'm not prepared. Not that I didn't have time to prepare but... well you know how these things are. Or maybe you don't, I don't know.
Ah but what's preparation anyway? Just the mortal enemy of spontaneity. I've always had a problem being spontaneous—
No, that's a lie.
All right then, let's get Spontaneous!

He does a little dance.
After a moment he gives up.
He regards the audience.
He tries to think of something to say.

Oh… kay. A tourist in New York and the tourist walks up to a cab driver, and the tourist asks the cab driver: "Do you know where Carnegie Hall is?" and the cab driver says…
Oh.
That's wrong.
Or!
Why are fire engines red?
Because…!
Actually, my grandma told me that. It's kind of for kids. It's silly.
Or….
A podiatrist walks into a bar…. No a proctologist…. Or….
Usually I'm pretty good with…. But when you need one you just can't think of…

> *An uncomfortable pause.*

I've got a place if you're looking. And who isn't? Everybody's always looking for a better…. Two bedrooms, hardwood floors, fireplace, view of the park, nine-fifty all-inclusive. It's a very good deal. Of course if you take it you'll have to contend with the body in the next room. Oooo, what's this suddenly? A mystery! *CSI: Me* suddenly.

> *NOTE: The price of the apartment should support current market and local trends as "a good deal." Also, the television program should be a current mystery-type program.*

No.
I had the strangest dream.

> *Music and light shift: deeply eerie.*

It wasn't that strange.

> *Music out and light restore.*

> *An uncomfortable pause.*

What ever happened to Nigel Kennedy? Remember him. With the violin? He was really… good. Edgy. I'm a little edgy. I'm doing a cold turkey thing. Tried Nicorettes, tried the patch, nothing works for me—just cold turkey. It takes time but—
Time! Oh you'll like this.
"A Brief Moment With Time."
(in a funny voice) Hi I'm Time!
(a different funny voice) Hi I'm Time!
(searching for the voice) Hi I'm Time!
I can't find the right…. I need a few drinks for that one. It's more of a party thing.

> *An uncomfortable pause.*

See *CSI*?
You get *CSI* here?
The one with the girl? I hate that show. That girl's too thin. She's probably
a vegetarian—

> *NOTE: This should be the same television program mentioned earlier.*
> *We can safely assume any television program of this ilk will feature*
> *a too-thin female.*

OH! Okay, this is good:
I'm in the salad bar, upstairs there's some vegetarian symposium or something
going on. Have you ever been in an all you can eat salad bar with a room full of
vegetarians? No wonder they don't eat pigs, they are pigs!

> *A moment as he takes in the audience reaction.*

I didn't mean to offend any vegetarians.
But you should have seen when they brought out the nutloaf!
"Oooo the nutloaf. Have you tried the nutloaf? The nutloaf is gorgeous! Oh the
nutloaf! Forget the bean dip try the nutloaf! Come on everybody gather 'round
the nutloaf!"
Do I have to listen to this much longer?

> *An uncomfortable pause.*
> *He regards the audience fearfully.*

Is this right?
Is this what you expected?
Is this what I'm supposed to do?
Is this what you wanted?
Is this why I came all this way?
Would you love me… if I let you?
Does it matter
Does anything?

> *An uncomfortable pause.*

Good evening.
I am here to tell you something you don't already know. Maybe you knew that
already, I don't know.
I am here—good—to tell you something—yes—that you don't already know—
Exactly!
My name is…. My name! Well some of you may know my name but for those
of you who don't—is Henry "Tom" Gallery. Gallery yes gallery like gallery yes.
Gallery.

Big deal so what. What's in a name?
Ten and a half shoe.

Fifteen and a half neck.

Thirty-one inch waist—thirty-two—thirty three.

NOTE: *The above sizes should suit the actor.*

And I would consider myself, if I was supposed to consider myself, at knifepoint or gunpoint or some point something, I would consider myself a *bon viv*— No. A man of the— No.

A lousy— No.

A... An optimist!

I would consider myself an optimist.

Of course to say that one is an optimist is just to say that one is a liar. I mean just look around. The more of an optimist one tries to be the bigger the liar one must become. I mean just look around.

Although I was probably a liar before I was an optimist. You see my father *(cough)* sorry. My father *(short cough)* sorry. My father *(cough)* my father *(cough)* my father *(cough)*. Sorry. My father *(cough)*'s name was Henry. But everyone called him Tom. Because his father's name was Tom and everyone thought he should have been named after his father so everyone called him Tom even though his name was Henry. I was named after my father *(cough)* sorry. Henry. But since no one called him Henry and everyone called him Tom everybody called me Tom even though my name was—is *(singing)* Ta dah! Henry. And I came to understand at a very early age that not only was my name a lie but I was a liar.

Nietzsche said: *(sneeze)* "Lies are necessary to life and this is part and parcel of the questionable and horrible nature of existence." Honey!

An uncomfortable pause.

It's very easy to be a liar when—when one is a—one is a small child because then one is just said to have an "overactive imagination"—which is to say that if one were to... oh, I don't know say... lock the babysitter in the bathroom and run around the house yelling "Fire!" well, that wouldn't really be a lie, that would just be an overactive imagination. But of course it's a lie. You can't hide a lie like fire, I know I've been there, there's evidence: singed shingles, bits of melted plastic, ashen diaries, burnt words, smoking three-string violins, so on. Of course... out of guilt out of having lied about the fire one might... set a fire. But then one would be an arsonist. And once one is an arsonist that pretty much overrides whether or not one is a liar. Or even an optimist for that matter.

My mother *(short laugh)* was an optimist. "Grab your coat and get your hat".... Even when the house burnt down.... "Leave your worries on the doorstep".... The first thing she said was.... "Life could be so sweet".... Well at least now we can move to.... "The sunny side of the street".... That was her favourite song. My mother *(laugh)*. She was a nurse... ran a restaurant on the side. And my father *(cough)* sorry, was an army man. I was conceived on the evening of June the fourth. I was an only child. This disturbed my sister quite a bit. And I had a dog named Betty. Betty. With a 'y.' Not an 'e.' That would be Bette. Betty with a 'y.' There was a girl on our street named Betty, she thought the dog was named after her but it wasn't it was just named after... nothing, it was just named after... itself. Betty. "Betty, Betty, come for dinner!" That's... what we'd call... when it was... time for... the... dog to... come to dinner.... Sometimes the girl would come.... She might get a sandwich.... Or a bowl of cereal maybe. And other than that.... Just more of the... you know... regular stuff.... Yup.

And that about does it. Me in a nutshell. Yup. *(singing)* Ta dah. *(He looks at a spot on the inside of his forearm.)* Gawd!

> *He regards the audience fearfully. He might cry. He pulls it together.*

I love Scrabble!
And I don't cheat.
Unless someone else is cheating. But then that's not cheating is it, that's just changing the rules.
And I asked for a Scrabble dictionary every Christmas for the past ten years and do you think I got one?
"Nice sweater."
"Thanks for the pen."

> *A moment. HENRY becomes defiant.*

And I don't believe in God.

> *He has second thoughts about being defiant.*

Well I used to—I did when—I don't now...

Should I?

Why am I asking you? Let's just say I'm conflicted. I read his book. I didn't really "get it." I liked that Noah thing—that was good, but that first story. This is something I've thought about. The Garden? I mean really. Ladies. A rib? Do you want fries with that rib? I mean, what does it mean? I mean, they say it means something about knowledge and good and evil but, I mean, to me it seems to mean: the truth will make you naked. I mean, look at it. What have you got? You've got Adam and Evelyn in the garden. Birds, trees, flowers, the silver moon, the blue lagoon, bliss. Ah Bliss! And then along comes the guy in the green suit and the snakeskin boots and the oh-oh tree and "Oh-oh it's the apple." And a nibble nibble later and there stands Truth in the once-blissful now raging, now thundering garden. And what does Truth say? Truth does not say "Goodtaseeya!" Truth does not say "That, sir, is a very nice shirt." Truth says: "You people are naked!"

You people are naked.

So if now is now and this: *(covers his genitals with his hands)* is Truth well, what was then and Bliss? You see? If on one hand you've got Truth and then on the other hand you've got Bliss—and if that's the choice, hey, I'll take Bliss. Hey I'll take two!
That's my thesis thank you.
Whatever.

> *He loosens up. He dances a bit. The Swim. The Hitchhiker.*

Let's have some music, let's have some fun!

> *Nothing happens.*

Perhaps now's not the time.

> *He boldly regards the audience.*

Good evening!
My name is Henry "Tom" Gallery. The second.
And I am a liar.
And if we're going to talk about me—and that seems to be the point—then we are going to talk about lies, and if we're going to talk about lies then you are in very good hands.
All right!
Now it is very important to understand the Art of Lying. There are many— there are uncountab— there are eight types of lies, and the first type of lie is… the Just Kidding Lie.
Now, in order to demonstrate the Just Kidding Lie I am going to need a volunteer.

> *He approaches a member of the audience. He speaks to this person directly.*

Just kidding.

> *He returns to the stage.*

Just Kidding!

Now the second type of lie is… the White Lie. Now, the White Lie is told to keep another from harm or deep embarrassment, or to ingratiate one's self. For example: "No, I don't mind putting my dog down." Well, that's a bit obscure. How about: "What a beautiful baby."

The next type of lie is the Lie Lie or The Excuse. Now the Lie Lie is very easy to perceive because it is accompanied by sweaty palms, darting eyes and incomplete sentences such as: "I-was-just-I-was-just-I-don't-know-why-the-house-burnt-down-Gawd!" The Lie Lie is used on parents, teachers, bosses, creditors. The success of the Lie Lie depends entirely on the Lie-ee's desire to believe the Lie-er. Works almost never in the case of creditors almost always in the case of parents.

The next type of lie is the Pathological Lie. Now the Pathological Lie is a very interesting type of lie, tied up with problems with self-esteem—messy things like that. Advantages of pathological lying include: fame and fortune, great at a party, fabulous resume! Disadvantages of pathological lying include: bad credit rating, time in the slammer, madness.

He laughs a ridiculous mad laugh. The audience reaction throws him.

The next type of lie is the…

He stops having lost his thought. (The "you" following can be the audience as a whole or an individual.)

Oh look now you've got me lost….
I'm not angry I'm just disappointed.
OH. Right. Lucky for you. The Professional Lie. Now the Professional Lie is best left to be explained by those who practice this lie: politicians, lawyers, general contractors, dental hygienists, botanists, urban planners, farmers, tailors, podiatrists, psychics, engineers, members of the clergy, the military and the royal family.

The next type of lie is the Survival Lie or the Lie To Survive. Now this is a complex and anti-mathematical condition where deep belief in the lie manifests the desired outcome. Deep belief in the lie manifests the desired outcome. Such as "I love you." Or "It Will Be Better In The Morning."

And the next type of lie—the final type of lie—is the Universal Lie. Now the Universal Lie is almost impossible to talk about because we all share it. The Universal Lie is also known as Time.

Silence as he looks at the audience.
He turns away, his back to the audience.
Sound: building rain and then a thunderstorm.
Light: slow fade to near black.
(This sound and light should take at least thirty seconds.)
He turns back to the audience suddenly.
Sound and light restore.

You know…. I have a feeling. And I have a feeling that: we're a lot alike. It's simple… it's obvious… it's just the nature of existence. 1, 2, 3.
One, you're born.
Two, you assume… yes… a series of—I don't know—experiences.
Three, you die.
One, you're born: dark passage into a bright room.
Two, you assume… yes… a series of—I don't know—experiences:
You learn to walk
You learn to talk.
You have your first day of school.
You get a dog, or a cat, or a gerbil, or a turtle: it runs away or dies.

You can't wait for Christmas, or Hanukkah, or Ramadan or what have you.
You collect things: matchbooks, Boy Scout badges, cardboard.
You enter puberty and spend two fabulous years in your bedroom with James
Taylor.... Or Carly Simon or whatever the case may be.

> *NOTE: These musicians should reflect a time period similar to that of the
> adolescence of the actor playing HENRY.*

You get your driver's license.
You leave home.
You never write, but you call!
You think about going to college and you don't, or you do.
You lose your ideals and drift aimlessly toward the void.
Until! You meet your love in a Laundromat or at a party. You take that
wonderful walk you make that perfect promise. Or! You convince yourself that
some people just weren't meant to couple.
But either way you seize the day, you change your mind, you make a plan, you
resolve to stop, to start, to seize the day to change your mind to make a plan.
You, in short, experience. Three, you die: bright passage into a dark room.
(*Stretching out his arm toward the audience and making a circle which grows
faster and faster and smaller and smaller.*) Dark passage into a bright room,
experience, experience, experience, bright passage into a dark room. Dark
passage into a bright room, bright passage into a dark room, dark passage into
a bright room, bright passage into a dark room, bright into a dark, dark into
a bright into a dark into bright into dark into bright.
And that's the hook and here's the catch and the catch of the day is sole. And
the bone that runs down the middle, from which grows the fillet, the spine of
the soul, is Hope.
And of course there's always hope.
Of course, there's always hope!
Of course, there's always hope?
And of course you have hope.
But that is where we differ.

> *He smiles weakly. He wipes sweat from his forehead.*

Let's have some music, let's have some fun!

> *Music: "Finally" by CeCe Peniston.*

> *NOTE: In the original production we used "Finally" by CeCe Peniston—
> but whatever the choice, it should be the song he refers to in the final
> segment when HENRY tells us his favourite song.*

Whoo!

> *Light: a dance club.*
> *He dances with mad delight.*

Whoo!

Sound and light restore.

I understand there's a lot of vegetarians in the room tonight. The only thing better than a room full of vegetarians is a room full of vegetarians at an all-you-can-eat salad bar. "Ooooo that nutloaf, oooo that nutloaf, gimme that nutloaf, gimme that nutloaf, gimme that nutloaf." Do I have to listen to you people fuck that nutloaf much longer?
Whoo!

Music and light: nightclub.
He dances with mad delight.

Whoo!

Sound and light restore.

Why are fire engines red?
Because two and two is four and four and four are eight and eight and four is twelve and twelve inches is a ruler and a ruler could be queen and the queen's name could be Mary and *Queen Mary* is the name of a ship and ships sail over the ocean and fishes swim in the ocean and fishes have fins and the Finns fought the Russians and Russians are always red and fire engines are always rushin'.
Oh that's silly, Russians aren't even Russian anymore.
Whoo!

Music and light: nightclub.
He dances with mad delight.

Whoo!

Sound and light restore.

How do I get to Carnegie Hall?
Practice!
What a shitty mood I'm in tonight you lucky fuckers!
Whoo!

Music and light: nightclub.
He dances with mad delight.

Whoo!

Sound and light restore.

Did I mention the body in the next room?
Who thought "poofter"? Who thought "poofter"?
Oh, that was me!
Whoo!

Music and light: nightclub.
He dances with mad delight.
Sound and light slowly restore.

Remember that fire I said I set before? Oh, I didn't say I set it did I? Never mind.

A small jeté.

This is fun.
Okay I talked about the Garden, should I talk about the Flood?

He bows deeply.

Thank you.
So what else about me?
Let's see! Well my father *(cough)* sorry, was a pack of Benson and Hedges Special Lights and my mother *(laugh)* was a fried egg sandwich. I was conceived on the evening of June the fourth, I remember it well. It was a rainy evening, and she with her legs pressed tightly together, but not tightly enough, and he pries them apart and a couple of drunken pumps later and the sperm hits the egg and Ta dah! Oh if only every night could be like that.
I was an only child, as I said this disturbed my sister quite a bit, but as it turned out she wasn't really my sister she was really my mother *(laugh)*. But I bet nobody wants to talk about that though do they? And I had a dog named Betty, for dinner, she was delicious. Ba dum bum!
At the age of nine I had a religious vision which turned out to be not a religious vision at all just something I ate. This disappointed my mother *(laugh)* quite a bit because she always wanted to have a visionary son and instead she just got a comment on her cooking. Which it was. She only had one dish. Fried egg sandwiches. Not that they weren't stupendous fried egg sandwiches. I'm sure it's the only reason my father *(cough)* stayed with my mother. *(laugh)* Unfortunately 1600 fried egg sandwiches later he died. Heart attack. We found him on the floor of the billiards room—no the conservatory—or the library? He didn't have a clue! Didn't help that he was an alka-alka-alcoholic. He started his own group actually, Happy Alcoholics. H.A. HA! Group worked out quite well at first although I don't think they should have met in a bar. BA DUM BUM! At the age of eleven I had to make an important life-changing decision between playing either the violin or rugby. Being a homosexual—

He regards the audience.

And I bet you knew that already, bet you could tell, my father *(cough)* sorry, certainly could. Or perhaps you don't care, my mother *(laugh)* certainly did. Or perhaps you're thinking: "Gee I wish I could take him downtown to a cheap hotel and drown him in sloppy kisses and make long, hot, horny love to him until the sun is high in the afternoon sky!" … Perhaps not. My lover certainly didn't. *(Weeps a moment then pulls himself out of it.)* But! Being a homosexual and having to choose between either rugby or the violin I did what any good young homosexual would do and I chose... Rugby!

I played often to the delight of many.

The next year I was diagnosed as being dyslexic but it turned out I wasn't really dyslexic at all I was really ambidextrous. Which is a good thing. The left hand knows what the right hand does. I'm good with my hands. See? *(He mimes a bird.)* I'm good with birds.

Oh stop that!

Lived in a house. Indeed. Watched it burn to the ground. Very traumatic. And, as I said, my mother *(laugh)* was a podiatrist and my father *(cough)* worked— managed a brewery—or.... And other than that, it was just a sort of idyllic sort of miserable sort of storybook sort of nightmarish sort of remarkable sort of regular sort of existence. One thing was I managed to graduate from high school by the age of thirteen, but what's that really though just intelligence, not even intelligence really, there was a nine-year-old in my graduating class, speaks more about the program than it does about my intelligence, but what's intelligence anyway huh? Can't pay the rent with it. Can't date it. *(Weeps for a moment and then quickly pulls himself out of it.)* And I told you about the thing I had with James Taylor. *(NOTE: Same musician as puberty obsession.)*

Well

I also had a thing with Elizabeth Taylor and I also had a thing with Karen Black, remember her? And I was the guy who blew coke up Stevie Nicks's ass.

> NOTE: It is important that HENRY remain a contemporary with the
> audience and so if there should come a time when Elizabeth Taylor, Karen
> Black or Stevie Nicks would not have been alive during HENRY's lifetime,
> the Elizabeth Taylor comment can be altered to any aging screen goddess
> who might have a perfume (re: the final segment), the Karen Black
> comment can be altered to any Hollywood actress who performed an
> amazing feat in an action movie while wearing a skirt and the Stevie
> Nicks comment can be altered to any off-colour rock and roll myth.

Sorry.

Anyway.

Sorry.

Sorry. Um. Sorry. Anyway. Um. Anyway. Um. Sorry. Sorry. Sorry. Um. Anyway.

> This continues for at least twenty seconds. HENRY gets caught in not
> being able to say anything but these three words in various successions.
> He stops himself and he does a little yoga to try and relax. He relaxes. He
> takes a breath.

Anyway. AHHHHHH!

And I'm a Prince! Sounds far-fetched—not really, went to Spain, ran with some royals, bit of a scandal, had to leave, can't talk about it. And I was in the crash upon which *Airport 75* was based. Well, I wasn't actually *in* the crash but I had reservations which I cancelled at the very last second.

> NOTE: *The* Airport 75 *comment can be altered to the name of the action movie in which the above Hollywood actress replacing Karen Black appeared. For example, one might replace Karen Black in the early segment with Sigourney Weaver. In that case the line above would be "And I was on the spaceship upon which* Aliens *was shot. Well I wasn't actually on the spaceship, but I had reservations, which I cancelled at the very last second." Use your imagination. The point is that HENRY shouldn't be reaching for past events or personalities outside the lifetime of the actor playing HENRY.*

And I become a commercial pilot but I couldn't take the job because it turned out that I was too tall. Then I ran for public office, and I won! But I couldn't take that job either because I'm allergic to air conditioning. So I went to California and got involved in the porn industry under the name Prince McLaine. Perhaps you've seen one of my tapes? The most successful was called "Oh Yeah, Oh Yeah, Oh I'm A Bad Boy, Oh I'm A Bad Boy, Oh That's A Big One, Oh That's A Big One, Give The Bad Boy The Big One, Give The Bad Boy The Big One, Oh Yeah, Oh Yeah, Oh No, Oh No, Oh Yeah, Oh Yeah, HOOOOLLLLLEEEEE!" Google that you'll be up all night. Then I went to prison and I wrote a book based on my experience there which you've probably read because it was a bestseller but I had to use a pseudonym because I'm part of the witness protection program— Oh shit! Forget I said that!

Then I suffered—ha—studied years with the Ernst-Phelps-Greens, famous for their seminal work "The Doors of Deception." Ta dah! And it is from this work whence I take my axiom, which is: "When the rose smells sweet the rose smells sweet, when the rose is dead THE ROSE SMELLS SWEET!" Words to live by. I'm a little edgy. I'm doing a cold turkey thing. Tried Nicorettes tried the patch nothing works for me—just cold turkey. It takes time but—TIME! Time, there's one! Time! You'll love this! "Hi how ya doin. Time." A brief moment with Time! "Hey how ya doin I'm Time. Nice shirt. I like to go go go I don't want any of this stop and smell the roses bullshit. If I wanted patience I would have been a dentist." Beeeeeautiful teeth. Beauty, there's another one. Time and Beauty. They share a place together you know. Oh yes they do. Two bedrooms, hardwood floors, fireplace, view of the park, nine-fifty all-inclusive. It's a very good deal. But Beauty just doesn't "get" Time. And Time loathes Beauty because she's so smug! All she does is sit around all day and drink decaffeinated cappuccino after decaffeinated cappuccino and plan the colours for the sunset. So Time decides he's going to kill Beauty but he realizes he has to be very clever about it so he sets her on fire. But it is a very special fire that burns very slowly and doesn't have a flame. But Beauty realizes "sumthin's up" so she goes to see Hope but all Hope can do is give her a placebo and that's really too bad because a placebo only works if you believe in it and sweetheart, Beauty don't believe in nuthin but herself. Oh yeah! Been there!

After a moment.

And then I suffered—ha—studied for many years with the Ernst-Phelps-Greens famous for their seminal work "The Doors of Deception." Ta dah. Oh I said that already.

And I wrote a paper for them! Yes I did! A radical scholastic revisionism of the flood. The Noah thing? Perhaps you've heard of my paper? "The Water Is Wide I Cannot Cross O'r"? No? Good!

All right. It's the flood. And you're on the ark. The rain was over long, you know, ago, and you're on the ark. You and two of every living animal. The ark's not that big and it's probably leaking, but nobody wants to talk about that I bet do they? And you're wandering on the deck one day and you see that stupid goat chewing on a branch and you think, "Oh that stupid goat, always—" and you think, "Wait a minute, duh, where did the goat get the branch?" It's the flood right? And then you see that stupid bird on the rail and you think, "Oh the goat just took the branch from the stupid bird—" And they you think, "Wait a minute, duh, where did the bird get the branch?" It's the flood, right? So you go and you take the branch from the stupid goat... "Gimme that." And you take the branch to your father *(cough)* sorry, and he recognizes the significance of the branch. And of course he takes credit for the whole fucking thing himself. But who's to judge right? And then he calls a branch symposium down in the common room and we're all gathered down in the common room and up pops Pop on the table and he holds the branch up over his head, just like this, like so, nothing too dramatic, just like this, over his head.

And we all look at the branch and we think: "Well if there's a branch then there must be a tree, and if there's a tree there must be soil, and if there's soil there must be a hole, and if there's a hole there must be a foundation, and if there's a foundation there must be a house, and if there's a house there must be rooms, and if there are rooms there must be closets and drawers and cupboards and boxes and stores and three daily newspapers and all the stuff that goes in 'em, and the body in the next room and me in my comfortable chair in front of my HDTV surrounded by a limitless, boundless, endless sea of the most profound... inertia."

So much for hope.

Downer.

I wish I had my violin. I'd play it. I bet you didn't think I could play the violin but not only was I a star on the rugby field and a member of the Olympic Bowling Team but I was also a *(name of local music festival)* winner.
Runner up.
Worked the coat check.
I couldn't play it anyway though it only has three strings.
(burp) Ooo. Nutloaf.

We could talk about television but I don't watch television. Very much. Well, CBC of course who doesn't. And PBS—for arty stuff. And CNN to keep informed. And once in awhile CTV, or Global. In a pinch maybe ABC. And

NBC for fun. And CBS for "CSI." And now and then MSNBC or TLN or TLC or CMT—but not for the music. And for movies sometimes Showcase or Bravo and HBO but that's not really TV it's HBO. And who can live without Home Shopping? And if it's really late and the cable's out snow can be calming.

> NOTE: Obviously the above should be current and all of the stations mentioned should be recognizable to the audience. Use your imagination.

That's a very nice shirt.
I noticed that before.
You're welcome.
That's a very nice shirt too.
Perhaps you two should have a Shirt-Off.
That's a very nice shirt too.
Thanks for making an effort.

> NOTE: HENRY is speaking to individuals in the audience, but please do not feel a need to light the audience in order for the actor playing HENRY to be able to see them. The actor can use his imagination. The actor may not be able to see the individuals but HENRY can.

Of course there's always love.

> MUSIC: a soft samba.
> He dances, oblivious to the audience.
> Suddenly he notices them watching him.

What?

> He continues to dance.
> He notices the audience once again.

What?! Stop it.

> He continues to dance.
> He notices the audience.
> He teasingly flirts and then stops, smiling mischievously.

Stop it.
What are you thinking?

> He begins to dance openly with the audience.
> He raises his hand over his head and brings it down in a stabbing motion which he repeats over and over with increasing, grinning rage.
> The music cuts in and out with the stabbing until it disappears completely.

> Light has shifted since the beginning of music so that we are now in a smaller playing space.

Ah love.
Love is lovely. Yes it is. Well you should know. So should I. Because we're in love.
Yes we are. You and Me. I'm me, obviously. You're you. You have an overbite,
which I find cute. You have a love of crossword puzzles, which I am willing to
overlook. You have an allergy to my dog, so I put her down. Why? Because this
is love. This is something real something yes something now something true
something oh my God something beyond you and me.
The only thing is, we haven't met yet. It's inevitable that we shall meet, it's just
the method that needs to be settled upon. So, I decide what I'm going to do to
meet you is I'm going to have a Parade!
But have you ever tried to have a parade? The red tape, I must have made
eighty-six phone calls, and all the pressure I just would have started drinking
again and that would have been a book of rejection.
So, I decide what I'm going to do to meet you is rent a hall, get an outfit, invite
some people. But try getting that together. Everybody's got their schedule
everybody's got their favourite caterer.
So, I decide what I'm going to do to meet you is I'm going to dig a hole and I'm
going to climb in and I'm going to sit there and I'm going to wait for you to
walk by. And so I do. And I wait and I wait and I wait, and of course you don't
walk by and of course it rains and of course I don't have a change of clothes and
I have to go and sit in a laundromat in my underwear and wait for my clothes
to dry… and as Fate would have it: you walk in. And of course you don't look
at me because you're trained not to look at people in laundromats in their
underwear. But I look at you. And not only do I look at you but I see you: and
your overbite and your chewed up pencil and your cute little mm mm mm
mm mmmmm and the stupid look on your face when your sock hits the floor
and I think, "It might be" and your reaction when the hot zipper hits your
forearm… *(He looks at a spot on the inside of his forearm.)* Gawd! …and I think:
It is.
And then you look at me, but you don't see me, and then you leave and
I promise that I will meet you again. And I do. At a party. And at first it's a little
uncomfortable, but then we take that wonderful walk, through the garden. And
the trees are green with envy because we're so perfect. And the moon is blue
with sadness because now we're taken. And we make our vow. Our promise:
I promise… I swear on my empty heart and my overworked liver, on my fallen
arches and my bashful kidney, that I may fall and I may stumble and I may take
you down with me. I may drink until I'm numb and spend entire nights with
my head in the toilet. I may give you many many days of despair. I may hate
your family. I may miss your birthday. I may forget to call be late for dinner and
not show up until sometime the next afternoon. I may betray you. With your
friends. Publicly. I may degrade myself in order to win an argument. I may
become only more sour and only more cynical and only more stubborn and
when I die you may wish me one more moment of feeling if only but to slap
me in the face. But I swear on my empty heart and my overworked liver, on my

failing, flailing, falling body, that it is only ever—has only ever been, will only ever be: me for you and you for me.

Now, that's love.

But then of course there's life to contend with. And Reality with her alarm clock earrings. And that weekend in Niagara Falls when we meet Doubt in the bar. And that night we invite Reason to stay over. And that day we discover that all along our landlord had been Compromise…. But poor old Compromise given the bad rap of meaning failure when in fact Compromise is Love's best friend.

But of course Time passes and Beauty unaware burns and what was once the perfect match, the perfect spark, the perfect flame, the perfect match of…? White and white. Now becomes, sugar and salt. So that from a distance: white and white. But try one in soup and the other in tea and you will see how different white from white can be. So where does that leave us?
I'll tell you where.
I'm in the kitchen. You're in the living room. You call out, "Where are you?" and I call out, "I'm in the kitchen." But you can't hear me so you call out, "Where are you?" and I call out, "I'm in the kitchen." But you can't hear me so you call out, "Where are you?" and I call out, "I'm in the kitchen." But you can't hear me and I think: "Yes you can, yes you can so hear me. You just want me to come, you just want me to come like a dog. Well you're allergic to dogs—why do you want me to act like one." And you call out, "Where are you?" and I call out, "I'M IN THE FUCKING KITCHEN YOU FUCK!!"
You come into the kitchen, you say, "What was all that about?"
I say: "I, am, in, the, kitchen!"
You say: "Well why didn't you just tell me?"
I say: "I did!"
You say: "Well you didn't have to yell."
Now. What can I do then?
Well, I can do two things: 'A' or 'B.'

'A':
I can stab you twenty-seven times with a bread knife. Twenty-eight counting zero.
And when I do I think three things, and the first thing I think is: "I guess that psychic was right when she told me to stay away from sharp objects." And the second thing I think is, "That was sooooo easy." And the third thing I think is, "Well, I guess I can't argue now when people say I've got a temper." But isn't that a good thing to be able to admit you've got a temper?
Of course I do think other things but they're all "psychological" and I h-h-hate psychology because psychology says that people were meant to be understood and if people were meant to be understood you'd come with a tag behind your ear, they'd run credits at funerals.

Or 'B':
I can go into the living room, sit in my comfortable chair in front of my HDTV and continue to hate you.
And when I do, I reach down, deep down inside myself and I take out that tiny sharp-edged shrapnel of hope, that we all have lodged within us from the big explosion, and I press it, hard, between my index fingers, until the warm red is running down my arms, dripping off my elbows, and staining the carpet on either side of the chair.

But either way, 'A' or 'B,' it's a bucket of blood, and where does that leave us with our love reduced to being nothing but… "the body in the next room."

And of course it has to be somebody's fault, it always does. And of course it's my fault, it always is. It always comes down to me. Yes that's right, I lost your keys, on purpose. I came home early from holiday, intentionally, so I could catch you in bed with that idiot, how uncomfortable was that, I'm so sorry. You give and you give and you give and you give and you give and I take take take take take take take take take. Because I am the monster. That's right. I'm the monster. I did it all. I take responsibility for everything. All of it. I rang your doorbell and ran away. That was me. I farted and said it was you, Grandpa! I did that too! And I charged you extra for that work I did on your house because I saw you had a nice car. And I told your husband that you were not in fact having lunch with your sister, and I was happy when I heard about the divorce. And when you got that new job and moved away I wished you the worst because I was jealous. And I pointed out the way to Anne Frank's hiding place because she made fun of me at school. And I started a war just so you could warm up your car on those cold winter mornings. And I put the phosphates in detergent so you could get your whites whiter than white. You're welcome. And I told Karen Carpenter she was fat because she said I couldn't sing. And I invented economics just to fuck you up. And I gave Karla and Paul the video camera for Christmas because they seemed so sweet. And I got JonBenet into pageants because you had to have something to watch on TV. And I taught Mohammed Atta how to fly a plane because New York thinks it's so fucking great!

> NOTE: After "*economics*" please feel free to add more or other atrocities. "*Karla and Paul*" were notorious Canadian serial killers—a bounty of those locally known to your audience are unfortunately available, I'm sure. The final atrocity should be recent and possibly just over the line of good taste.

Well… that's enough about me.
How about you?

> He regards the audience until they are silent.

You're so quiet.

NOTE: If the audience does not become silent—perhaps they are laughing, or one person might say something disparaging, then HENRY would say "Exactly."

Well.
So much for love.

He looks away. He rubs his face.

Let's have some music. Let's have some fun!

Sound: ominous.

That's not exactly what I had in mind.

I don't know what the rules are but I think I'm just gonna have to break 'em.

He squints past the lights regarding the audience carefully.

You know what I could really use about now?
Starts with a "C."
Ends with an "igarette."

He leaves the stage and approaches the audience.
He improvises something like:

Could I please have a cigarette? Hello? I'm not going to smoke it, I quit. I'm just going to hold it. It's just a comfort type thing. I couldn't smoke it anyway, that would be against the law! I know nobody actually smokes but sometimes people carry them just to be nice. I won't make you do anything I just want to borrow a cigarette.

When someone gives him a cigarette.

Could you do one thing? Could you light it for me too? Just for the burning ember feeling. I'm not going to smoke it, I quit. I wouldn't light it myself, it's like when you see an old lover, you might shake hands but you wouldn't hug.

When someone lights the cigarette for him he thanks them and takes the cigarette. As he returns to the stage he notices the chair reserved for the local dignitary.

Who's that reserved for? That fucker's not showing up.

He takes the chair and the cigarette and returns to the stage.
He places the chair carefully on two spike marks on the stage.

I wondered what these little marks were for. I could have been sitting down the whole fucking time.

He stands in front of the chair.
If he is wearing a jacket he takes it off and throws it theatrically aside.

Don't get your hopes up Mister *(or Miss)* Just Kidding.

If he is wearing a tie he takes it off.
He regards the cigarette.

That is so tempting.

He takes a long hard drag of the cigarette, inhaling deeply.

I didn't inhale.

He exhales into his shirt.
He speaks to the audience member who gave him a cigarette.

It's all your fault.

NOTE: If cigarette smoking becomes illegal in public to the point of being a criminal offence and you don't want to take the risk of a fine or imprisonment the above can be performed as the following:

I don't know what the rules are but I think I'm just gonna have to break 'em.

He squints past the lights regarding the audience carefully.
He notices the chair reserved for the local dignitary.
He approaches the chair.

Who's that reserved for? That fucker's not showing up.

He takes the chair and returns to the stage.
He places the chair carefully on two spike marks on the stage.

I wondered what these little marks were for. I could have been sitting down the whole fucking time.

He stands in front of the chair.
If he is wearing a jacket he takes it off and throws it theatrically aside.

Don't get your hopes up, Mister. *(or Miss)* Just Kidding.

If he is wearing a tie he takes it off.

After a moment.

Let's get preposterous.

Light: a much smaller playing area.

Say the trees had eyes instead of leaves. Preposterous.
Say the sky was red red red and shut out all the sun. Preposterous.
Say cats had fangs and flew. Say the ocean boiled. Preposterous.
Say you had two little men, one on each shoulder and each one was yelling into your ear in a different language that you didn't understand. Preposterous.
Say they sold you something at the corner store that would kill you but they

wouldn't let you take your own life. Preposterous.

Say every time you went to take a step the ground opened up in front of you. Preposterous.

Say you're in a dark room, a wet room, a tight room, ahead of you is a tunnel, at the end of the tunnel a light, suddenly you are forced through the tunnel into the light, you're surrounded by people in green, little white masks, there's a woman there she's screaming, she's crying, she's laughing, you're covered in blood, lifted by the ankles, slapped on the bottom.

How can we get any more preposterous than the way we came to be?

He sits.

Say you wake up, you have a bite, you watch some TV, you go out, you sit in front of a computer or you stand behind a counter, you go home, you watch some TV, you have a bite, you go to sleep.

Say you have the strangest dream…

You are lying in the remains of a burnt-out house in a field surrounded by singed shingles, bits of melted plastic, ashen diaries, burnt words, smoking three-string violins, so on, and beside you is a telephone and it is ringing but you can't answer it because you can't move. Then at the edge of the field a woman appears. She's dressed as a nurse, she's not a nurse but she's dressed as a nurse, and slowly she crosses the field and approaches the ringing telephone. Then she lifts the receiver and holds it to your ear and a man's voice on the other end says "Water boils. Ice melts. Birds fly south."

Water boils. Ice melts. Birds fly south.

Well, tell me something I don't already know!

Say you wake up, you watch some TV, you have a bite, you try to go out, but you can't, you have a bite, you watch some TV, you go to sleep.

Say you wake up, you try to go out, but you can't, you try to have a bite, but you can't, you try to watch some TV, but you can't, you try to go to sleep, but you can't. So you lie there and look out the window at the rain, at the rain, at the rain. And then finally, very tired, you fall into what might be called a sleep, and then quite unremarkably unsuddenly and after much hanging on and many false alarms say… you die.

I'm a little edgy. I'm doing a cold turkey thing. I tried Nicorettes, I tried the patch. Nuthin works for me just cold turkey. It takes time but…. Time—there's one, our old friend time….

Why are fire engines red?

Because: two and two is four. And four and four is eight. And eight and four are twelve. And twelve inches is… a ruler. And a ruler could be a queen. And the queen's name could be Mary. And *Queen Mary* is the name of a ship. And ships sail over the ocean. And fishes swim in the ocean. And fishes have fins. And Finns fought the Russians. And Russians are always red. And fire engines are always rushin. Ba dum bum.

I like that.

Because it's a perfect little, endless little world.

Well it's not endless, it has a punch line. Or no… not a punch line. It's a riddle.

Jokes have punch lines. Riddles have… something else… reasons.

But everything ends. Jokes end. Riddles end.

Everything ends.

And you can always see it coming.

In your face in the mirror, in a feeling in your stomach, in the strangest dream.

And because we can see it coming that is why we run. We do. I did. Running and running and running and I'm not so so many years old and I feel poisoned and I'm running and I'm running and I'm running and I'm running and I try to take a breath but the air is so thick that when I do I have to chew on it and it tastes sharp and sour. And running and running, and I try to think about tomorrow but tomorrow seems as far away as the sound of a marble rolling down a hill in an oil drum. And I'm running and I'm running and I trip over Time lying drunk on the sidewalk and I crash into Beauty begging for quarters beside a broken telephone booth a piece of glass in her arm. *(He looks at a spot on the inside of his forearm; if he is smoking he would drop the cigarette now.)* Gawd!

And running and running and running and I look up at a second floor window and I see Reason and Compromise toasting Doubt and I'm running and I'm running and the cats are flying and crashing into the eyeball leaves of trees and the wind is spinning up fishbone tornadoes and the sky is red red red over the boiling ocean and the volcanoes are popping up like blackheads on a Boy Scout's back and the ground opens up in front of me and I fall through and as I fall I shatter into a million pieces but the pieces will not separate they are held together by the tiny magnet of my mind—crashing crashing crashing—and I land in the centre of my soul just in time to see all my houses burning burning burning and the walls collapse and the roofs cave in and the smoke pours out into the sky as full and easy as drunken promises, and I stand there and I wait and I watch until there is nothing left, not a single singed shingle not an ashen diary not a burnt word not a three-string violin not a nice shirt not a sunny day not a bad night not a good reason not a wish not a hope not a fear not a tear not a whisper not a whimper not a nothing not a nothing not a nothing not a nothing whimper not a nothing not a nothing not a nothing not a nothing whimper not a nothing not a nothing not a nothing not a nothing nothing nothing nothing…

Of course one might choose to stop running. And if one did then one would look down the dark and one might choose to go. And if one did, choose to go, then one would take you with them. One would. Take you. Everyone does, grandmothers, teenagers, movie stars, soldiers. Whenever anyone goes they take you with them. Say… I… were to go. Then I would take you with me.

Because I know you. I do.

I know you.

You have dreams. Dreams about flying, dreams about falling, dreams that you don't understand. You have landscapes in your mind that you call your own. You try to be humble. You try to be honest. You know that it's better to keep your mouth shut and your eyes open, but it's very hard to do. You look for some small way to have some small way to have some small measure of immortality, but you're concerned that there will be nobody left to care. You hope that one day you'll understand something, but worry that maybe that's not the point. You wonder what's the big deal about sex anyway. And then suddenly, brilliantly remember. You go to movies, you think some of them are good and some of them are bad. You go to plays, even though you hate to be bored. Some nights you look up into the sky and remember what it felt like before everything felt so poisoned. And you think that love is a good thing.
See. I know you.

And so, say you die.
...and I know that's a scary thing but only because you don't know what happens, so I'm going to tell you.
When you die you float up to the ceiling and then you hit the ceiling and when you hit the ceiling you open your eyes and you find yourself in a white room in a kind of uncomfortable chair. And every time you close your eyes your life plays itself out from the beginning, in real time. And so you decide to close your eyes and watch. And then when your life is over a woman comes into the room, she's your maternal grandmother when she was eighteen years old and you don't really recognize her because you didn't know her then. And she takes you by the arm and leads you out of the room, through a wheat field, across a beach and over what looks like it might be the surface of the moon, to a room that is filled with photographs of every person whose eyes ever met yours. And then your grandma sits with you and goes through the pictures and she tells you a little bit about each person. And then you feel tired. So she leads you to an attic that is filled with mattresses from every bed you ever slept in. And in the centre of the room is the mattress from the bed in which you were conceived, and she tells you to lie down there, and you do, and you fall into a deep and restful sleep. And then you are woken up by the person you always felt you should have spent your life with but didn't. And then you get to spend a month together. And at the end of the month your dad comes to pick you up. And he drives you through every storm you ever slept through to a room with a table in it and three chairs. And he leaves you there standing before the table and three people enter the room: the first person you kissed, the first person you cursed, and the last person you saw dead. And they explain many many things to you, that you don't understand. And then they let you go through your best friend's closet and wear all your favourite stuff. And then they tell you that you must enter a room filled with people and you must tell these people something that they don't already know.
And before you can ask why you find yourself in a room full of people.
People you know. People you don't know. People you love. People you wished

loved you. Strangers. Mostly strangers. And you try to tell these people
something that they don't already know.

And then you realize that that is quite impossible. Because how can I tell you
what you don't know when I don't even know what I know.

> NOTE: *In the above section it would be great if this audience, this
> evening, could be clearly included before the line "Strangers. Mostly
> strangers." For example if a phone had rung during the show HENRY
> would say "People who forgot to turn off their cell phones." Or if someone
> had left to go to the washroom he would say "People with small bladders."
> Or if someone had been sneezing "People with colds." The actor must be
> alive and aware in the space on the evening. He must be HENRY, or
> HENRY must be him. Also, in the following section, adjustments
> regarding* Airport 75 *or the music played for HENRY's dance or Elizabeth
> Taylor must be continued. And "The Bay" is a Canadian department
> store—not unlike Saks or Macy's or H&M.*

Well, I guess I know a few things.

My father had his moments.

My mother was a waitress, but she dressed like a nurse.

My sister was really my sister but I thought it would be more interesting if I said
she was my mother.

And I can play the violin. It's just that some people don't call it a violin, some
people call it a ukulele.

And I worked at The Bay for twenty-two years. In skin care. Gawd.

And my favourite song is "Finally" by CeCe Peniston.

And my favourite movie is *Airport 75* because Karen Black landed a plane in
a skirt.

And my best day, if I had a best day, would be the day Elizabeth Taylor came to
The Bay to sell her perfume and I got to hold her dog while Elizabeth Taylor
went to the bathroom.

And I don't have a problem being a homosexual I just have a problem with
other people's problem with my not having a problem, maybe that's a problem
I don't know.

And I never meant to be mean, I was just trying to be funny.

And I did write a book, it just hasn't been published. There's always hope.

And no I didn't set the fire, there was never any fire, I just wanted there to have
been a fire because I wanted something to end.

And I think that love is a very good thing.

> *He waits for the end to happen.*

And it still doesn't feel complete. It's like it's not over until the lights come up
bright bright and then slowly slowly slowly fade to black and then Henry "Tom"
Gallery, the Second, were to turn and walk away, singing a little song, and

disappear forever.

But I can assure you, that is not going to happen.

> *He leaps out of his chair, tossing it aside.*
> *Light: up bright, bright.*
> *He regards the audience*
> *Light: slow slow slow fade as:*

I am such a liar.

> *Slow slow slow fade to total black as HENRY turns and walks away, quietly singing a little song, and disappears forever.*
>
> *End.*

Property

based on Marc Diamond's novel *Property*

adapted for the stage by DD Kugler
and Marc Diamond

DD Kugler, a Vancouver-based freelance dramaturg/director in theatre and dance, was the first Canadian president of Literary Managers and Dramaturgs of the Americas (LMDA, 2000–2002). He served eight seasons as Production Dramaturg with Toronto's Necessary Angel Theatre (1985–1993), five seasons as Artistic Director of Edmonton's Northern Light Theatre (1993–1998), and since then has taught for the past ten years in the Theatre Area at Simon Fraser University's School for the Contemporary Arts. Kugler (in collaboration with Richard Rose) co-authored *Newhouse*, as well as the adaptations of Michael Ondaatje's *Coming Through Slaughter* and Timothy Findley's *Not Wanted on the Voyage*.

Marc Diamond (1944–2005), a theatre Professor in the School for the Contemporary Arts at Simon Fraser University for twenty-five years, was an active interdisciplinary artist with a freelance career both as writer and as director. Marc wrote in a wide variety of forms—many short stories, texts for dance (*The Brutal Telling*), opera libretti (Underhill's *Star Catalogues*), several plays (*The Ziggy Effect, Eulogy for Lois L.*), stage adaptations (Sophocles's *Oedipus* and *Antigone*, Frisch's *Firebugs*), and two novels (*Momentum* and *Property*). Marc's direction included numerous contemporary operas (Satie's *Genevieve de Brabant*, Stravinsky's *The Soldier's Tale*, Komorous's *Nonomiya*, Nyman's *The Man Who Mistook His Wife for Hat*) and plays (Kafka's *Report to the Academy*, Witkiewicz's *The Madman and the Nun*, Handke's *Self-Accusations*, Kaufman's *Gross Indecency: The Three Trials of Oscar Wilde*).

Property premiered in a production by Necessary Angel Theatre at Theatre Passe Muraille (Main Space), Toronto on March 3, 1992 with the following company:

ALL ROLES   Stephen Ouimette

Directed by Richard Rose
Set and Lighting Designed by Graeme S. Thomson
Costumes Designed by Charlotte Dean
Sound Designed by Evan Turner
Stage Managed by Maria Popoff
Production Managed by Aidan Cosgrove
Publicity by Dianne Weinrib
Photography by Cylla von Tiedemann
Graphics by Dreadnaught Design
Board Operated by Steve March
Running Crew by Joel McLean

Characters

ACTOR
M____
LONDON ONTARIO
MOM
BRILLIANT COUSIN
BEAVER WINSLOW
ARIADNE
ROBERT CROW
TIBOR LUMEX
K
CLEIGH McNABB
NURSE
FRANCO HERMES
MAGGIE KLUE
BEN SCHAM
RICHIE OREX
CONRAD SHADOW
ASSISTANT
LAWYER

PROPERTY

Enters holding envelope.

ACTOR   The envelope containing the letter came through the slot, floated down, hit the wood floor with a muffled slap—*(throws envelope to floor)*—the sound of a gloved hand striking a face. I observed this descent, this unwelcome confirmation of the inevitable laws of gravity.

Sits motionless on wood floor, hands grasp bent knees.

I happened to be staring at the front door of my house in Vancouver, a house that is not my house, it really belongs to the bank, most of it, but I live there, I pay the bank for the privilege of living there, and I am grateful.

Stands, walks to envelope, looks down, reads.

M____   Robert Crow, 97 Blackpool Drive, London Ontario.

This disturbs me.

ACTOR   In fact it ruined my day. Anything to do with London Ontario ruins my day, for once it is in my mind there is no escape from London Ontario, from those twisting streets. It is better if I do not think of London Ontario, the town in which I grew up, the town which I abandoned, the town which I loathe—yet I am always thinking of London Ontario, the town where my mother still lives on the graceful curving street known as Blackpool Drive. More or less.

But the letter wasn't from my mother, the letter was from Robert Crow of 97 Blackpool Drive—the next-door neighbour. My mother lives at 99 Blackpool Drive.

She doesn't actually live there. To tell the truth I don't know where she lives. But legally she lives there. I own the house. I own the house in London Ontario. The bank is not involved with that house. I truly own it. There are some who claim that I do not own it. But I do. I have the papers. And they are clear.

My mother has what is known as a life interest in the property. This is stipulated in my grandmother's will. The truth is it is set down in a codicil which states: *My daughter shall have a life interest in my said residential property known as 99 Blackpool Drive.* This sentence made my mother the life tenant of my house when my grandmother died, although my mother does not now occupy my house and I don't know where she is.

When my grandmother, in her wisdom, wrote the first version of the will, before the addition of the codicil, she gave the property on Blackpool Drive to my brother and me. I remember Grandma's very words: "Now I have taken care of the boys." Meaning my poor brother, now dead, and myself, still alive. She was proud of this will. And she was relieved. My father was dead; my brother, despite unusual ability, had determinedly flunked out of school; I was lazy and sullen. My grandmother was concerned about us. She wanted us to have a stake, a chance. With this will, she had, in her mind, secured our future. But when Grandma, in her wisdom, blabbed about the will, my mother began the shrieking ruckus which led in the end to the addition of the codicil now pinned to the back of the baby blue cardboard binder containing the will.

My grandmother added the codicil on the advice of my cousin, a truly brilliant guy who was often consulted in family matters, and still is. In this way my mother was appeased. It was only a slight revision. The boys got the property as before *and* my mother got a life interest in the property. My mother didn't trust her boys to put her up in her old age. So she got it in writing in the codicil that was added to Grandma's will 29 years before the letter took a nosedive through the mail slot and belly-flopped onto the gleaming floorboards of my front hall, the letter from Robert Crow, the neighbour living in the house next to my house in London Ontario, the house legally occupied by my mother.

I had met Robert Crow once.

M____   I vaguely remember him as a decent fellow. And yet now, for some reason, he feels compelled to send me a letter. It shows how wrong first impressions can be.

ACTOR   I did not open the letter. I did, of course, open the letter. But I did not open it immediately. I was in no hurry to open it.

       Plugs in phone, dials.

M____   You should have gone with Ariadne to Arizona. You could have gone with her to the desert. You could have had a sexual experience in the desert. Ariadne might have gone along with something like that. But no. You stayed in Vancouver, you stayed to work—rewrite a few sentences, work up an audition, house-sit.

ACTOR   This speculation was cut short by a man's voice on the telephone.

M____   It's Ariadne's father in Arizona.

ACTOR   He said that Ariadne had gone to see the rodeo. Or maybe she had gone to see the big cats at the Wild Kingdom in the desert. One or the other, but probably not both. He asked me how things were.

M____   Oooooo, fine.

ACTOR   It was the first lie of the day. My day was already ruined by the letter that had crash-landed in the front hall, the letter from London Ontario, and now to compound matters I was lying.

It disgusts me to lie. I am confused when I lie. I am paralyzed when I lie. I am strangled by my lies. I often lie. When I am asked the simplest question, such as that asked by Ariadne's father in Arizona, I lie. My first impulse is to lie.

I learned this as a child. My mother taught me this lesson. She had no interest in the truth. I don't recall her ever telling the truth about anything. I admire her consistency in this, the way she lied to the lawyers, the tax collectors, the door-to-door salesmen, the milkman, the meter reader, the cleaning lady, the psychiatrists, the family, her brothers sisters parents children. My mother had lies enough for all. And I'm sure that wherever she is at this very moment, and I don't know where that is, she is in all probability lying to someone.

I don't know where she learned to lie. Not from her mother. Grandma was not a liar. She was a notorious teller of the truth. If only she had been a liar, she could have lied to my mother about the will and there would have been no ruckus, no codicil, no life interest and, 29 years later, no letter spurting through the door.

I know how to tell the truth. Despite my natal inclination, I am able to choke down the lie, and cough up the truth. But many times I have regretted telling the truth. I have wounded someone with the truth, when to lie would have been the correct procedure. "How did you like my performance of Lady Macbeth?" an actress once asked me. I didn't understand a word of it, I replied. This was the truth. She never spoke to me again.

And what if I had told Ariadne's father in Arizona the truth. That:

M____ A letter launched by some anonymous postal person whapped down on the floor and ruined my day because this letter has…

ACTOR I assume.

M____ Something to do with my mother.

ACTOR That:

M____ I don't even know where my mother is.

ACTOR Nor:

M____ Am I attempting to find out where she is.

ACTOR Although:

M____ I would like to know where she is.

ACTOR What if I said that? What would he think of the truthful man who lives with his daughter, the monster who is breaking the Fifth Commandment given to Moses which states that one should:

LONDON ONTARIO Honour one's parents so that thy days may be prolonged, and it may go well with thee—

ACTOR Now there's an unveiled threat.

And I know one thing: to honour your mother you have to know where she is. And I don't.

What would he think, the father of Ariadne, a nice guy, a family man? The truth is he would find it inconceivable, inexplicable, that I don't know where my mother is. The truth is he would think I was lying. He would think that his daughter was living with a liar. And she is. And yet I would be telling him the truth. I do not know where my mother is. And so when I got Ariadne's father on the telephone, I naturally lied to him in order to avoid the deleterious consequences of the truth. I think it was a good move.

I routinely lie on the telephone. I think most people lie on the telephone. This is one of the many reasons why I detest the telephone. The ringing of the telephone invariably fills me with horror. This is why I leave the telephone unplugged. To lie is a well-known verb, but where is the verb to truth? The truth is that the verb to truth is not needed—not in this world. There is not enough truth in this world to even justify a verb!

All telephone users are liars. The authorities should consider this when they tap telephones. And if callers don't literally lie on the phone, they nevertheless use the telephone to lie in other ways. Most sexual infidelities, for instance, are arranged on the phone. The furtive lovers get on the phone and make arrangements behind their husband's and wife's back. That's how I got together with Ariadne, and I am grateful to the inventor of the telephone for it. Telephones have their uses. They're not all bad. They come in attractive colours. When you want a pizza it's nice to have a phone. And the truth is that I have never once lied to the pizza man, an individual whom I don't care about in the least. On the other hand, I did lie to Ariadne's father whom I quite like. Perhaps he lied to me as well.

Hangs up, looks at phone, toward envelope, at phone.

I thought about unplugging the telephone. But I did not.

M____   Give the callers their chance.

ACTOR   The truth is I wanted to be interrupted.

M____   No caller is going to rescue you, no caller is going to take you to a movie or to some pleasant eatery or to Joe's Café for espresso. No. No caller is going to do that. And do you know why no caller is going to do that? They all think you've unplugged and they've given up trying to call! That's why.

Returns to hall, picks up envelope.

ACTOR   The stamp bore a photograph of the Queen of England, who in turn bore an uncanny resemblance to my mother: the same forced smile, the same maniacal look in her eyes as if she might throw a screaming fit at any moment—even the dress looked familiar, a white brocade with little white flowers embroidered along the neckline—only the diamond-studded crown distinguished this woman, the Queen of England, from my mother, at least in my mind.

Gets large butcher knife, prepares to stab envelope.

Nine rings—he counts.

M_____   Some caller wants something from me.

Rushes to answer phone.

No one on.

My callers are not patient people. My callers are in a hurry. If you are not hovering by the phone when they call, if you are not poised to pounce, if you do not jerk into action at the bell like some Pavlovian trainee, if you do not drop everything and sprint for the phone, even if you are in the bath or otherwise engaged, if you do not get there lickety split, my callers close off, moving on, no doubt, to other calls.

ACTOR   Of course there are occasional callers who hold and wait through as many as 20 rings. Those are the real nuts. When the phone rings 20 times you must never, never pick it up.

M_____   Never. It can only be trouble, it can only be a caller who is desperate, psychotic or bored, it can only be some maniac some malcontent some bush-whacker scouring the telephone directory for a victim foolish enough to pick up after 20 rings. Now if a caller rings nine times, as my previous caller had, that caller is civilized, impatient but civilized, the kind of caller one would like to be with on the telephone.

Too bad I missed that caller.

Slits envelope, withdraws and unfolds single sheet, gags.

ACTOR   I became aware of a nauseous sensation in my solar plexus. This was not unfamiliar. I am frequently disgusted by my mail. How different from the old days when as a child I enjoyed receiving, opening and reading mail from my friends, those days long ago when I had friends.

M_____   All your friends will become enemies if you wait long enough.

ACTOR   A poet said that. And he is right.

M_____   My friends have either become enemies, or have died before they had the chance. Neither group sends me letters. And I don't blame them.

ACTOR   I reflected as I held the letter, the letter from Robert Crow, the vaguely sociable neighbour whom I had met in the late summer during a visit, *the disastrous visit*, to London Ontario one year before.

I tried to picture Robert Crow—but I could not. I could only remember an air of boyish congeniality. I remembered the impression created by Robert Crow, but I could not remember Robert Crow. There was, now that I think of it, something negative lurking in my memory, something that had disturbed me about my meeting with Robert Crow, but I did not remember the details. I have a good memory, but at the time I made the acquaintance of Robert Crow I was in an agitated frame of mind due to certain *things* that occurred during my travels through the twisting streets of London Ontario, and in consequence I don't remember him as well as I normally might.

To be brief: back at the beginning of the summer I had gone to London Ontario to explore the possibility of selling my property. That doesn't sound too bad, does it? People sell their property every day. Of course there was the small matter of my mother, the legal occupant of my house, but that small matter had been settled. At least in my mind.

My family, aunts, uncles in-law along with certain members of the psychiatric community frequented by my mother, had been urging me to sell my property on Blackpool Drive for some time. Even my cousin, a truly brilliant guy, the financial doyen of the family, a wise and reliable entrepreneur who dealt in jewels and real estate and advice, informed me that it was time to sell my property. I had been reluctant to sell because my mother loved her garden, cherished her own peculiar independence, was afraid of old persons' homes, seniors' apartment buildings, retirement havens, and so on—and I don't blame her. But now, I somewhat grudgingly agreed, the time had come to take action.

And so at the beginning of the summer I went to London Ontario to talk to my mother about selling my property. At the time, I even knew where she was. She was in the London Psychiatric Hospital on Highbury Avenue—the crazy house.

She frequently spends time in psychiatric institutions and has since the middle of the century. They did the usual things to her: psychotherapy group therapy drug therapy shock therapy aversion therapy dance therapy whatever therapy or combination of therapies happened to be in fashion that year; and some things worked for a while, but nothing worked permanently. She would go home, have another episode, as they say, and return to some psychiatric hospital.

I entered the unending corridors of the London Psychiatric Hospital, and asked my mother what she thought about selling the property. She told me to stop smiling.

MOM   There's nothing to smile about. I hate your smile.

ACTOR   I stopped smiling. I asked her again about the property.

MOM   The police are going to arrest me because I've killed a cat.

ACTOR   She was preoccupied with this cat murder. I thought, based on past experience, that she was lying about this cat killing, this felicide, and she was. And yet, as I discovered later, she was not, not entirely.

I asked her again about the property. She said she thought it was a good idea to sell.

MOM   I can't keep up the house anymore. Just get rid of it.

ACTOR   So at last I had her permission to sell the property. And it was the perfect time to do it. Not only were prices at an all-time high, but it so happened that last summer I was flying from Vancouver every other week in order to attend The Collaborative Vision, a series of workshops for television writers at the CBC in Toronto, just a few hours up the road from London Ontario. It was, I reasoned, a favourable and convenient time for action—decisive action. After each three-day session I would simply rent a car, drive to London Ontario, stay over at my brilliant cousin's house in the suburbs, where I was always welcome, and lay the groundwork for the sale of my property.

My dream was simple: I would sell my property on Blackpool Drive, give a chunk of the proceeds directly to my mother, apply the remainder to pay off the mortgage on the property in Vancouver, and use the savings on the mortgage to pay my mother a decent monthly salary. Instead of paying the bank every month, I would pay my mother.

M____   I would just as soon pay my mother as the bank.

ACTOR   I told my brilliant cousin. He chuckled at that. My dream was clean. It was rational. It was easy.

BRILLIANT COUSIN   *By the way—*

ACTOR   My brilliant cousin told me—the same cousin who twenty years before advised my grandmother to add the codicil now pinned to the back of the baby blue cardboard binder of my grandmother's will, the codicil that gave my mother a life interest in my property on Blackpool Drive, the property I inherited with my poor dead brother.

BRILLIANT COUSIN   *—in order to sell your property—*two things need to be accomplished: *first,* you need to get your mother to sign a power of attorney; *second,* you need to clean the place up a little to make it saleable.

ACTOR   How I admired my brilliant and wise cousin, twenty years my senior, who knew about real estate, and powers of attorney, and money, who had spent his adult life in the real world buying and selling and getting rich.

I did not, however, admire him without limitation. I remembered that in the '60s, a few years after my grandmother wrote her will, he had staunchly supported the U.S. action in Vietnam, and even subscribed to the domino theory, a comical world view that had virtually nothing to do with the game of dominos and even less to do with reality. That had bothered me, a brilliant guy like that, but what the heck, he's entitled to his opinion, right?

My brilliant cousin scored sensational grades when he went to school. He wrote perfect exams. He was in *Time* magazine. He was one of the few guys, they said, who understood the theory of relativity. He went off to Princeton for a doctorate, married a girl from Bryn Mawr, and did some flashy research on black holes. My grandmother, in her wisdom, pleaded with him to stick with the sciences—make a contribution. Instead he returned to the convoluted streets of London Ontario where he had inherited some property. He sold the property and founded a chain of jewellery stores that proved lucrative. He got into stocks and bonds and real estate. He went into business for himself. He preferred to be independent, to do things his own way. And who can blame him?

And when he went into business for himself, my grandmother was bitterly disappointed in him, and she wrote him off, although he never figured this out, despite his brilliance. And who can blame her?

When I was a kid, two or three decades back, this brilliant cousin took me camping and taught me how to sail and gave me tips on the stock market, tips that eventually paid my tuition in university. He was a perfect being, this brilliant cousin. When my mother got into legal trouble, financial trouble, psychiatric trouble, he was there to lead her out. He was generous with his time and energy, this brilliant cousin. He was a good guy.

And so, last summer, when he told me how straightforward it was to sell the property, when he sanctioned my dream that would enable me to support my mother and pay off the property in Vancouver, I knew it was a good dream.

I believed him. I had no reason not to believe. That he was reputed to be a shrewd guy in a business deal, even a dangerous guy, did not concern me. This wasn't, after all, a business deal, this was *family*.

BRILLIANT COUSIN   By the way. Let's you and I share the power of attorney. Then, when you're out there in Vancouver, I'll be in a position to expedite matters here in London.

M____   Sounds like a sensible plan to me.

ACTOR   I opted for it. I was grateful. Even flattered. The truth is I knew that he was tired of my mother and her problems that had gone on for decades, and still he offered to share the power of attorney. What a guy! What a great and brilliant guy! And when my mother signed the power of attorney, which she did with surprisingly little hesitation, she stated that she was delighted by the inclusion of my brilliant cousin's name on the document.

M____   She signed the power of attorney! Things are moving right along.

ACTOR   The second thing that had to be taken care of, according to my brilliant and clever cousin, was to clean up the house and make it saleable.

M____   No problem.

ACTOR   Although I had not seen the house for some time, I suspected that the house, my house, needed a bit of work, and so I went over to the winding street called Blackpool Drive, in the rather desirable neighbourhood known as Old South, to size up the job.

I pushed open the front door and entered the topography of my mother's imagination: where mounds of newspapers, hillocks of junk mail, drifts of soiled rags, and swellings of clothing all combined to obscure the floor of the front hall; where walls were covered with mysterious maps and cryptic messages were written in pen pencil crayon and lipstick; where unwashed dishes, glasses and cups lay heaped in and around the sink; where black and brown scorch marks scarred the grimy white floor; where every knob on every cupboard was missing; where cat shit and cat food lay atrophied at every point of the compass; where the refrigerator still contained vegetables and bottles of milk and fruit juice that had been stashed there in biblical times; where a profusion of crud-covered knives forks and spoons fossilized on the counters; where the electric stove had somehow been dismantled with elements hanging here and there and the oven door suspended from its hinges at an odd angle; where the air was rancid; where the yellow wall clock hummed pathetically without moving its hands.

M____   Mom's never been much of a housekeeper.

> *Gags, escapes house.*

(*sings*) Baa, baa, black sheep…

Things aren't too bad. My house had once been a beautiful house. It has changed. It has been changed by the legal occupant of my house, who doesn't occupy my house, but resides in the psychiatric hospital on Highbury Avenue. But all in all things aren't too bad.

> *Repeats final sentence till convinced.*

ACTOR   That's how you think when you think you've got it all figured out. You head for the Promised Land, but you wind up in hell.

Take The Collaborative Vision, my series of workshops in TV writing with the CBC: I thought I knew what that was about, because they told me what it was about; but I didn't know what it was about because what they said it was about, was not what it was about.

They said they wanted new writers, they wanted fresh blood, they wanted new ideas, they wanted to shake things up, they wanted me. They chose only 15 writers from across the country. I was honoured. I didn't have a big track record. A novel, a few plays, a short story or two, one letter to the editor. I was surprised. Not that surprised, however, for the truth is a friend of mine was on the selection committee—a fact that probably increased my chance of being selected. And this didn't bother me.

M____   For in show biz, a friend is always on the selection committee. That is show biz. That is life. Without a friend in the right place: *(tap-dance)* show biz is no biz.

ACTOR   The CBC began flying me into Toronto, giving me a room in the Delta Inn and teaching me TV. Famous TV guys from around the world came in and taught me. Producers and story editors and buyers and sellers and directors and execs. Even writers.

Beaver Winslow, a producer from the popular series "Scary Dinner Party," was the very first teacher. Beaver was a pro.

BEAVER WINSLOW   The writer does the first draft. I tell him what to fix. Then he does the second draft. Then I take the script and I tell the writer to shove off. His work is over.

ACTOR   Beaver said the main thing the writer has to do was to make sure the viewer stayed there in front of the tube.

BEAVER WINSLOW   The main thing is to make sure the viewer stays in front of the tube right through the commercials. TV is a business. It's gotta be fast, it's gotta make sense, it's gotta have three acts. It's gotta be 22 minutes long. That's the formula. A half hour is 22 minutes long. The act breaks are the main thing. The commercials. You hook the audience with your story just before the act breaks. You gotta keep the audience in their seats through the act breaks. Television is a business and the main business of the writer is to kiss my ass.

ACTOR   He didn't really say this. And yet he did. I had a suspicion at that point about the true nature of The Collaborative Vision. But it passed.

Surely, the CBC, the national television network of our country, the communication lifeline of Canada, wouldn't spend a half a million taxpayer dollars in these hard times, the same CBC that was purportedly being bled dry by a hostile federal government, the same CBC that was being murdered in the ratings by the American networks, the private networks, the public network, the sports network, the feature film network, the rock video network, the home-shopping network, the Christian network, the porn network, the Christian-porn network, by almost everybody, in fact, who knew how to plug in a video camera; surely, the CBC wouldn't spend a cool five hundred thou to give fifteen handpicked writers, the cream of the crop, as they kept telling us, a very special elite group, as they kept repeating, the hope of the future, as they were enamoured of saying; surely, the CBC wouldn't blow all that cash just to let us know that our job as writers was to kiss Beaver Winslow's ass.

And, I reflected one year later holding in my hands the letter from Robert Crow, my enchanting neighbour in London Ontario, I was right. Sort of. It was not that simple.

M___   Nothing is this world is simple. And yet I keep searching for the simple. The hope, the longing, the quest for the holy simple.

ACTOR   That was my quest last summer as I drove my rent-a-car out of Toronto, with my power of attorney in hand, with Ariadne in hand, with my hopes in hand, to begin the big cleanup, the final three-week onslaught, the cure.

My brilliant cousin and his wife insisted that we stay with them in the distant suburbs. And we agreed. My brilliant cousin wanted the company. He wanted someone to talk to. He loves to talk. He is a great talker. He leaned back in his La-Z-Boy and spoke about his real estate deals, about how he had finessed business rivals.

BRILLIANT COUSIN   You create diversions. You wear them out by arguing about trivial details, you soften them up with complications, you mystify them until they lose their sense of direction and aimlessly turn this way and that, until, finally—exhausted, stupefied, scarcely conscious—they wander into the trap. And timing is everything, timing is everything.

ACTOR   He was brilliant.

BRILLIANT COUSIN   By the way. *(laughs)* There is some problem about a cat associated with your mother, some cat in a cat hotel, *(laughs)* some cat running up a monstrous tab at a cat hotel.

ACTOR   We all laughed about that one.

BRILLIANT COUSIN   Crazy things happen around your mother, that's for sure. *(laughs)*

ACTOR   We all laughed.

He leaned back in his La-Z-Boy and told us about the economic consequences of world events. I sat on the edge of my seat. My brilliant cousin was a financial eagle flying above it all, analyzing, waiting for his chance. His wife went to bed. He leaned back in his La-Z-Boy and described how the Hunt brothers from Texas once tried to corner the world silver market; he was able to narrate the whole labyrinthine story from beginning to end, masterfully negotiating every twist and turn leading to the startling downfall of the Hunt boys.

Later, in bed, I said to Ariadne.

M___   My cousin, a brilliant guy.

ARIADNE   He's a very good storyteller.

ACTOR   Ariadne replied.

And now one year later holding the letter from Robert Crow in my hands, the letter that had entered my house and ruined my day, I was unable to recall what had happened during those three weeks of cleaning up. In my memory there was only a dismal whirl: papers and dirt and shit and trucks and a real estate agent and a hotel room and garbage bags and a trip to the lawyer and garbage dumps and spent tears and unspent tears and visits to the London Psychiatric Hospital and my mother—brittle and small—sitting in her chair. Three weeks without beginning, without end—nothing but middle, nothing but muddle, nothing but misery.

My brilliant cousin was able to remember every detail of the Hunt's struggle to get a stranglehold on the silver market, an event that had occurred more than a decade before, an event he had not participated in; but I was unable to remember the three-week cleanup in London Ontario, an event, to the best of my knowledge, I had participated in just last summer.

M____   With a mind like his, it's no wonder he can outsmart an opponent in a business deal—a feint here, a phrase there, a deke or two. That's how it is with business. That's the way business is done, you've got to be sharp, like a knife, you can't miss a trick. It's just like life. And life, for my brilliant cousin, is business, and business, for my brilliant cousin, is life.

ACTOR   And business, let's face it folks, is right at the centre of things, business is what put this country where it is today. And what is the business of business? Wrong. It is not about making money. The cult of the bottom line is only a symptom of the disease. *The true business of business is murder.* If people could just get this into their heads, that the business of business is murder, then we could all lean back in our La-Z-Boys and really get a handle on the miserable blood bath taken by people all over the world in the twentieth century—the rivers of blood leaking out through bullet wounds and shrapnel wounds and whatever wounds you get when a smart bomb lands on dumb you; we could all lean back in our La-Z-Boys and relax as arms legs bones and minds are broken in torture chambers around the world. The business of America, a politician once said, is business. He meant murder. And it's the same here in Canada, a business-like country that in the '60s and '70s just happened to be the world's largest per capita war exporter—quietly enriching itself from the destruction of Vietnam while publicly deploring American brutality. It's the same pretty well anywhere. Riding our La-Z-Boys into the slaughter.

M____   If Ariadne were here—

ACTOR   I reflected holding the letter that had ruined my day.

M____   —she would help me bring order to that grim mazy time in London Ontario.

ACTOR   But Ariadne was in Arizona, at the rodeo or at the Wild Kingdom in the desert with the big cats.

M____   If only Ariadne were here—

ACTOR   But she was not.

　　　Begins reading letter.

ROBERT CROW   "I am the next door neighbour to your mother's property."

M_____   Stop right there, Bob! You think you live next door to my mother's property. But you do not. It is not my mother's property. My mother has no property. It is my property! She is the legal occupant of my property. It says so in the codicil pinned to the back of the baby blue cardboard binder containing the will!

Bob, you poor guy, you don't even know where you live. What if you invited someone over to your place for smart drinks, and you told them that you lived next door to my mother's property? Your guests would go to city hall to search Mom's title and it would not be there and they would miss the whole party. Like many people in London Ontario, you are lost and you do not even know it.

ACTOR   And who can blame him? People smarter than Misguided Bob have gotten lost in London Ontario. My brilliant cousin got lost in London Ontario. My poor dead brother lost his way, not to mention his life, in London Ontario. Many of my friends got lost in London Ontario. My mother is currently lost in London Ontario. I still get lost in London Ontario. When I cross the city limits and enter the serpentine thoroughfares of London Ontario I feel my inner compass whirling. The only thing one should do in London Ontario, a friend once told me, is leave. He did not take his own advice. That friend is now dead. He got lost in London Ontario. I, on the other hand, took his advice. And I am grateful.

M_____   Something is wrong in the brain of London Ontario. Something is lurking within the gnarled heart of London Ontario that takes the liveliest part of a person and turns it into the deadliest, something in those complacent twisting avenues that makes a person smug and mean and trivial, something embedded deep within the very molecular structure of London Ontario that pervades a person and crushes the spirit.

That's how it is with these provincial towns, these little fiefdoms of money, snobbery, fear and good taste.

On the other hand, London Ontario has a minor league baseball team, a plethora of psychiatric hospitals, and many beautiful churches. Everybody says it's a terrific place to raise a family. I even heard my mother say this once, years ago.

    Shudders.

ACTOR   In point of fact, I ran away from home at the age of twelve because I knew that:

M_____   I was dying in my mother's house.

ACTOR   My hard-working father, a respected physician, had already died in my mother's house. My poor brother would only last a few more years before his fatal "accident." I doubt I ever said to myself, you are dying in your mother's house, and yet I knew I was. And so, at the age of twelve, I made a run for it.

I realize now, thirty-five years later, with the teen suicide rate swelling exponentially, with psychotic and abused kids crammed into hospitals and half-way houses, with pre-pubescent dope addicts falling down stoned in school yards at recess, that her parenting methods have finally been embraced by moms and dads everywhere. And, like mother like son, I was also ahead of my time, a new kind of child, a new kind of casualty; for in those days, in the early 50s, twelve-year-olds did not run away from home. Of course now in the 90s it is not unusual for kids to run away from home. Many have no other choice.

M_____   Run and live. Remain and die.

ACTOR   The streets are full of these casualties. Entrepreneurial types cruise the streets in their vehicles and pick them up and pay them for a quick fuck or blow job in order to relieve the tension and stress of another hard day on the job; they talk to their wives and their own children on cellular phones while casualties are sucking them dry in parking lots and alleys across the nation.

M_____   Why did my mother, of all people—

ACTOR   A woman with no aptitude for the delicate, complex and exhausting task of shaping a human life, a spoiled self-indulgent selfish erratic woman, a woman who should have been an artist of some kind regurgitating her insides onto paper or canvas, a woman who should have entered a convent and shut out forever the world that was driving her mad—

M_____   —have children?

ACTOR   The truth is she lacked alternatives. She was the wrong gender in the wrong place at the wrong time. *She was a woman in London Ontario in the middle of the twentieth century.* She was genetically geographically and chronologically doomed.

A man as crazy as this difficult brilliant woman would have found a wife to support him and protect him and enable him to go into the world.

M_____   My mother needed a wife! A sacrifice, a sacrificial lamb.

ACTOR   Instead, she found my father, a respected physician, and she married him and gave birth to me and my brother.

M_____   My father was no lamb. He was tough and aggressive and dominated those around him.

ACTOR   He was not unlike my brilliant cousin in this regard. And yet for reasons of his own he made the sacrifice when asked. And my mother was not shy about asking. In a few years, my hard working physician father was up to three packs a day and almost 300 pounds. And he didn't mind.

M____   The truth is he loved it!

ACTOR   He was addicted to guilt responsibility and exhaustion.

M___   That's why he chose my mother. She was his worthy adversary. She was his fix.

ACTOR   But in the end he overreached himself. He underestimated the burden and overestimated his own resources. In the end, he was crushed by the weight of his chosen responsibility. He did not protest, nor did he reproach her, he simply dropped dead. In this he was a modern man. In this he was, at least for me, a tragic hero.

M____   He took care of her, he took care of his patients, he took care of the boys, he took care of everyone. But himself. She took care of that.

ACTOR   It was her first killing. I was next on the list.

M____   But I made a run for it.

ACTOR   So she went on to my poor brother. And he is now dead.

The night I made my run I was twelve years old. Without warning my mother burst into my room.

MOM   It is all going to come down on us!

M____   What?

MOM   All of it! You'll see, you'll see.

ACTOR   She dragged me into the kitchen to watch as she methodically smashed every dish, cup and glass in our possession. This performance, which went on for an eternity, filled me with terror. When she had finished off the last dish she turned and gave me a murderous look. I took off to the bathroom and locked myself in. She began to pound at the door with a hammer. I remember the head of the hammer splintering through the wood panels of the door. I knew if she got though that door she was going to kill me. Without thinking I unlocked the door, ripped it open, and sprinted past her and ran out of the house—

M____   Ran into the night ran through the twisting streets of London Ontario ran for my life.

LONDON ONTARIO   You must not do this, you must not run, something horrible will happen if you run, something even more horrible than death.

ACTOR   I was afraid of this voice. I almost stopped. But then I thought about my mother and the dishes exploding on the kitchen floor and I kept running. And nothing horrible happened. The voice was lying. The voice, I now know, was the voice of London Ontario. I learned a lesson that night:

M____   You can always make a run for it.

ACTOR   I am forever amazed when people in despair don't make a run for it. You just rip open the door and run for it.

I remember back around the time of my particular run, there was an abundance of suicides in London Ontario. These were the years before teen suicides, but it seemed like a fad nevertheless. Not a month went by without a high-rise leap, a monoxide job in the garage, a bullet in the brain, an overdose of sleeping pills, or a hanging.

My uncle Theodore did it during lunch hour. He used the belt off his pants. Nobody could understand it. Theodore was a nice guy, well-liked and unusually quiet. He was famous for his silences.

Uncle Theodore was survived by a son who also committed suicide. This son got totally lost in London Ontario. After he flunked out of school, he couldn't or wouldn't find a job. He began to do community work. He joined something called the Volunteer Traffic Patrol. He would drive around town looking for people who needed assistance with their vehicles and then he would change a tire, or radio for help, or simply give them directions—he knew intuitively that people were getting lost in London Ontario. A few years later he too was dead.

Uncle Theodore had a good-looking wife. She used to stroll around at family gatherings poking and squeezing tits. I remember her poking the tits of my aunts and female cousins, she even poked my mother's tits. She was greatly concerned about the way all these tits looked. She preferred a pointy look for tits and would recommend certain brassieres that gave tits a pointy look. She was listened to with horror and respect. Appearances are important to the people of London Ontario.

Decades later I discovered that the old tit-squeezer had moved to Alaska and opened a boutique featuring foundation garments. The wife of Uncle Theodore had made a run for it.

Life's chock full of surprises.

Uncle Theodore could have made a run for it. He had money, he had a car, he knew how to drive. But he didn't know the way out. He was lost in London Ontario. And he wanted to leave. So he put his belt around his neck and took the emergency exit out of London Ontario.

Running for it is a simple act—as simple as telling the truth. There are those who would call running for it an act of cowardice, I suppose, but I call it an act of courage, and act of survival. And as I sat in Vancouver holding the letter from London Ontario in my hands, I thought:

M____   I am lucky to be alive.

Returns to letter.

ROBERT CROW   "I am writing to ask you to take care of the grounds."

M____   Bob wants me to cut the lawn! My mother, wherever she is, is 2,077 miles closer to the lawn than I, but Bob wants me to hustle down to the airport, buy a ticket, fasten my seatbelt, hail a cab, motor on over to the looping swerves of Blackpool Drive and shove the lawn mower up and down a few times.

ACTOR   And the worst thing about it is that I had a raging desire to do just that. Swoop into London Ontario and solve something, anything, nail it down, fix it, kill it off, get it right for Mom. Simple as that.

M____   *(laughs)* You devise your simple plan to sell your property and give your mother an income for the rest of her life. You thought that would work. And now you dare to imagine that you can simply make your way into London Ontario and cut the lawn.

Only a madman would have ever returned to London Ontario! Once you make a run for it, and get out alive, you should stay out.

ACTOR   But I was so busy cleaning out the Augean stables that I didn't notice I was mad. The double-cross was right there in front of my face, but I was too deranged to see it. Like many madmen I chose instead to see what was not there. I chose the dream.

And although I blame my brilliant cousin who engineered the charming little betrayal which led to the ultimate failure of my dream, and although I blame myself for having hope for telling the truth for naïveté stupidity blindness, and although I blame London Ontario for almost everything—I place the real blame for the disaster on the Canadian Broadcasting Corporation!

M____   It was the CBC that sucked me back into the mess in London Ontario.

ACTOR   I reflected as I held the partially-read letter that had ruined my day.

Canada is a country that provides for certain geographical strategies. When I moved to Vancouver some time ago, I did so in order to put some distance between myself and London Ontario. The dark mountains provide a certain psychic protection that I find comforting. When one lives in Vancouver, there is only so much one can do to alleviate a problem that might arise in London Ontario—a lawn or something. But when the CBC chose me as a participant in The Collaborative Vision, and began flying me to Toronto every other week or so, I found myself drawn once again into the entanglements of London Ontario, just down the highway from Toronto, just a rent-a-car away.

M____   I was swooping into Toronto every other week to save the world of television from itself, so I figured I might as well save Mom too.

ACTOR   There is something about people who swoop down from the heavens. Sometimes they try to save everybody, sometimes they drop bombs. The results are frequently similar. This is typical MFF, mad-from-flight behaviour, commonly known as "muff" behaviour. Ariadne, who flew through the air to Arizona, and was watching the rodeo or the big cats at the Wild Kingdom in the desert, has a theory about Muffs. Your soul, she says, can't keep up with your body when you fly. If you fly across the country it takes a week for your soul to catch up. When you fly all the time, your soul gets left so far behind that it never catches up. It gets lost forever. And you become a Muff. Muffs like to call themselves frequent flyers.

Only Muffs could have conceived the scheme of blowing 500,000 dollars on a frolic such as The Collaborative Vision. Tibor Lumex, a head Muff at the CBC, came in and gave us an overview of the industry. They introduced him as a badly needed and inspiring omnipresence. Tibor Lumex wore a beautiful grey suit but looked puffy and uncomfortable inside it.

TIBOR LUMEX   I am not a conformer, I was kicked out of all the best schools. I am a child of television. I understand the medium. I grew up with the medium. I understand the responsibility of being a public broadcaster. I understand that we must reflect our cultures, our history, and languages. I mean there's nothing wrong with respecting your heritage and traditions. I'm Hungarian in origin myself.

But it has to be popular. That's the nature of television. It has to be popular. I believe in Canada. I believe in the star system. We need stars in this country. I believe in major talent. We need to woo major talent back to this country, people like Anne Murray and Toller Cranston. I was in Hollywood, I was at NBC with Hector Kodak, a genius. It was a real learning experience, a chance to compete with the best in the world, to push yourself. It makes you do better. It makes you go harder. The best in the world. I came back to Canada. Sure I could have stayed in L.A. for a lot more money. But Canada is my home. I came back here to contribute something meaningful, to make a difference. And remember there is one thing you have to understand to write for television.

    Pause.

Kids—

ACTOR   The writers leaned forward in their chairs.

TIBOR LUMEX   —control the set between seven and nine. If you understand that you understand everything. And you must care about what you do. You have to have passion, you have to have integrity. There is nothing we have here at the CBC that can induce you to become whores.

ACTOR   Said Tibor Lumex.

TIBOR LUMEX   The money is not good enough. Do it because you enjoy it. Because you believe in it. Whores don't enjoy it, whores don't have passion. You must have passion, I want you to enjoy it. And remember, the secret to writing for television—

ACTOR   We leaned forward again.

TIBOR LUMEX   —is to look at the schedule in the TV guide and figure out where the hole is. Then you develop your property to plug that hole. That is the here we are in.

ACTOR   At that moment a man entered the room and whispered something in the ear of Tibor Lumex.

TIBOR LUMEX   I have to go, there's a big story breaking in Ottawa, someone has hijacked a bus and driven it to the House of Commons.

ACTOR   And without another word, Tibor Lumex, a head Muff at the CBC, walked out of the room and was never again seen at The Collaborative Vision.

Beaver Winslow took over.

BEAVER WINSLOW   The message of a television show is never contained in the script. The message is contained in the commercials. The message in a commercial is simple: if you buy, your life will be better. The goal of the TV writer is simple: he must not contradict this message.

ACTOR   As Scary Beaver spoke I got out a newspaper and looked at the Toronto theatre listings. After a day of watching television at The Collaborative Vision I often would go to the theatre. Nothing about the theatre indicated that if I bought something my life would be better. That in itself was a relief. Hope is a detestable commodity.

At first I asked my fellow television writers to come along. They regarded me as if I were a pervert. Some of them, I discovered, had never been to a play in their lives. They knew TV. They learned to write for TV by watching TV. They formulated their ideas of acting by watching TV. They learned about culture, history, and the human heart by watching TV.

And so I would go to the theatre by myself, or with K, a Toronto theatre director—one of the few friends from my youth who was not missing, alienated or dead. Afterward, over drinks, I would update K on my experiences at the CBC.

M____   The whole Collaborative Vision is devoted to repression. The message is: nothing is possible. The message is: do it the way it has always been done or fuck off. The message is: if you are a complete hack in addition to being a whore you might get a job once in a while but don't count on it. The message is: writers are shit in this industry, scum. The message is: mediocrities will censor and re-shape your work and you better be grateful for that. The message is: kiss my corporate ass.

K   What did you expect?

ACTOR   Asked K.

M____   When they publicized this thing, they made it sound different. So I applied. They said they were looking for new ideas, a change of direction, new talent, a fresh approach, a saviour.

K   And you believed them? You believed the advertisements sent out by the people in the television business?

M____   Well. Yeah, sort of?

ACTOR   This made K laugh and laugh. And who can blame him?

After a particularly grim morning at the CBC, during which we analyzed the dramatic values of *Night Heat, M*A*S*H, 21 Jump Street, Street Legal,* and *L.A. Law*, we, the selected writers of Canada, formed groups, or quality circles as they are called. Each quality circle had a professional story editor— a personage who massages your script into shape. Cleigh McNabb, a gangly bearded redhead from Moose Factory, was our story editor. He led us into a room where our quality circle circled a table. He asked us to pitch our ideas one by one. It was a bit like Alcoholics Anonymous.

When my turn came *(tap-dance)* I pitched a comedy science fiction series about a family of the future who have an android butler and live in a giant high-rise city.

Cleigh McNabb said:

CLEIGH McNABB   I hate this idea.

ACTOR   And I didn't blame him. I had written it as a play several years before, there had been an invisible production of it in Seattle, and as far as I was concerned, it was now a dead property.

Later that day Cleigh came over to me and said he would help me develop my idea and we would go 50/50 on the profits.

M____   I thought you hated it.

CLEIGH McNABB   I told them about it, and they loved it, I realized I love it too. Everybody loves it. We'll be partners. I'll tell you how to clean it up and make it saleable. Then we'll pitch it to the network. It needs some work, but I love it.

M____   Sounds good, Cleigh.

ACTOR   The truth is I didn't have much interest in it. I pitched the idea just for the sake of hearing my own well-trained voice. But now, to my mortification, my new partner Cleigh and I were resurrecting it as a saleable property. I was about to undertake work on a property that did not interest me, a property from the past that I did not care for, a property that I knew, in my heart, was bereft of life.

M____   I was becoming a Muff, a soulless Muff.

ACTOR   I reflected one year later holding the letter from Bobby Crow, the letter about my thriving lawn.

ROBERT CROW   "When your mother was in her house, I often cut the grass and my wife trimmed the bushes and helped her in the garden. Because this gave her pleasure to sit in her yard and enjoy the garden, we didn't mind doing it. But now that she is no longer resident in her house we do not feel it is our responsibility."

M____   A disturbing passage, a mendacious passage, a bullshit passage!

ACTOR   The mind works in mysterious ways. I finally remembered that Benign Bob, when I had met him briefly last summer during my mad and frenzied journey through the maze that is called London Ontario, uttered the same words:

ROBERT CROW   Pleasure. Helped. Bushes. Enjoy. Trimmed. Yard. Responsibility.

ACTOR   Then, and this was the thing that was not in the letter, Bob had gone on to say that he would be:

ROBERT CROW   Very interested in buying the property.

ACTOR   It was a creepy moment, one that I comprehended on the spot.

M____   Vague Bob and his evasive better-half thought my mother might be willing to forfeit fifty or sixty thou in return for a little help in the backyard.

ACTOR   The truth is I would be delighted to sell my property to any devoted cutter-of-lawns and trimmer-of-bushes who made a decent offer. But I cannot sell. I own the property but I cannot sell it. The law states that:

LONDON ONTARIO   "A grantor in a will may grant an interest in the lands to someone for a time period. That interest will cease at the death of the named individual, e.g. 'to A for his life' or 'to A until B dies.'"

   Shudder.

ACTOR   In other words Mom has the final say. Last summer, however, I did not think this was a problem.

M____   After all, I had the power of attorney.

ACTOR   That is to say, I had the power of attorney along with my brilliant cousin.

M____   And my mother said she wanted me to sell the house—she told me so when I visited London Psychiatric Hospital!

   Violently wads letter, throws it into the wet garbage.

   I didn't do that. It just happened.

ACTOR   And I immediately regretted it for I was curious about the remainder of Bob's letter.

Hesitates, retrieves letter from garbage, brushes it off.

I conveyed the letter that had ruined my day to the front hall and then out through the front door, and onto the front porch where I gave my body completely to a sturdy Adirondack chair. I placed the letter from Robert Crow, the letter that had once entered but had now left my house, on the wide arm of the sturdy Adirondack chair so that it might dry.

Seventeen rings—counts.

M____   Clearly not a person I wish to talk with.

ACTOR   My mother, the one time she visited Vancouver, had complained:

MOM   A house without comfortable seating is not a house it's just a place to stay out of the rain.

ACTOR   She had come to Vancouver in 1986. She had come for the purpose of seeing Expo '86. Her visit unfortunately occurred before Ariadne purchased the Adirondack chair in 1989. I think my mother would not have complained so much if the Adirondack chair had been there for her.

When my mother phoned me from London Ontario and said she wanted to see Expo '86, I believed her and I invited her. I believed the woman who practically invented the art of lying.

She was going to be with us for ten days. Each morning I would offer to take her to Expo '86. But she would only shake her head, mutter about—

MOM   Tomorrow...

ACTOR   —and go back to sleep.

After six days of sleeping and complaining about the lack of comfortable seating, my mother announced that:

MOM   Yes I suppose I can go to Expo '86 today if you insist.

ACTOR   And so on the seventh day of her trip to Vancouver I bought the three $20 tickets and entered the west gate of Expo '86. I was disgusted to be there.

M____   This so-called world exposition is nothing more than a hyped-up trade show. It represents everything I detest about our civilization. It's all machine-worship, and blinking lights, and metal tubes, and lineups, and bad food, and tasteless pavilions, and sleazy fast buck operators, and Christian businessmen. The whole city has gone mad.

ACTOR   The message of Expo '86 was simple:

LONDON ONTARIO   We are whores in B.C. Come and fuck us in the bum.

ACTOR   And that, in the end, is just what happened, but on a scale that surprised even me, for in the end Expo '86 turned out to be one of the great property scams of all time. It was saleable, and they sold it, but they are still cleaning it up.

And as I stood there in the west entrance before a silver dome that reminded me of the eye of an insect, I said to myself:

M_____   You will be a good boy. She has not had a happy life, this woman, but today she will have a brief interlude of happiness. You are an actor, a trained actor, a trained liar, a professional liar, and you are capable of making this a day to remember.

ACTOR   And as I made these resolutions I noticed that my mother was no longer standing beside me. I looked down and discovered that she was lying flat on her back on the concrete. Her face was white and she was still. I knelt down and held my mother in my arms.

M_____   Mother, Mother.

ACTOR   She was stiff in my arms.

    Shudders.

M_____   I have killed my mother at Expo '86. She wanted to stay home and sleep but I forced her to come to Expo '86 and die.

ACTOR   Her body interrupted my thoughts, emitting a long shivering moan.

M_____   She's alive!

ACTOR   Paramedics loaded my mother into a little electric car and we all went down a ramp to an exceedingly well-equipped and well-staffed infirmary hidden deep within the bowels of Expo '86. My mother regained consciousness and looked around calmly. I thought she had died, but she hadn't. Nevertheless she went straight to heaven. Hospital heaven.

The nurse said:

NURSE   Are you taking medications?

MOM   *(little girl voice)* I don't know.

NURSE   Did you have any medications?

MOM   I'm not sure.

NURSE   Did you have any medications today?

MOM   Well maybe I did.

NURSE   What medications?

MOM   Just a little nitroglycerin for my heart.

NURSE   How much did you take?

MOM   Oooooo, maybe a little extra just to get me through the day.

ACTOR   My mother had OD'd on nitro in order to help her through the day at Expo '86, and now she was in the hospital, and she was happy.

On the morning of her scheduled return to London Ontario, I peeped into her room and discovered that she had not yet packed. My mother was standing at her dressing table pushing, from one place to another, small articles of recently acquired booty, mostly air travel plethora: toothpicks, napkins, plastic cutlery, minute packages of salt and pepper, peanuts, little rosettes of used Kleenex, a vomit bag, and a brochure which explained where the emergency exits were located. Mom was right at home. I went back into my room sat on the bed and stared at the floor. Her plane was leaving in less than two hours.

M____   She is not ready. She will miss her plane. She will never leave. I will soon be dead.

ACTOR   Ariadne talked with my mother. My mother explained that it was—

MOM   Time for a bath.

ACTOR   —went into the bathroom and slammed the door. Ariadne, however, threw my mother's possessions clothes newspapers litter into her suitcases. When my mother finally emerged from the bath, Ariadne managed to get her dressed and into the car. We pulled up in front of the terminal.

MOM   You'll have to get me a wheelchair.

ACTOR   During the ride to the airport my mother had apparently lost the use of her legs. The plane was leaving in ten minutes. I sprinted over to a red cap, gave him all my money—about $80.

M____   Get that woman on her plane!

ACTOR   The red cap rolled her through security at high speed and she was gone.

She did not say goodbye.

It took several days before we realized that my mother had not come to Vancouver to see Expo '86. She had in fact lied about that. She had no interest at all in Expo '86. The real objective of her trip was to move in with us. Permanently. She had decided to relocate. Ariadne and I were young and strong and would serve her well. The frightening thing is that without Ariadne's iron will, it would have happened! And I would now be dead.

M____   What a lucky guy I am. At least I have escaped.

ACTOR   I reflected looking at the soggy letter on the arm of the Adirondack chair, the soggy letter that ruined my day.

M____   Yes, I have escaped. I am still alive and I have escaped. I am alive. I have escaped.

Repeats final sentence till convinced.

ACTOR   The truth is that I had not escaped. If I had truly escaped I would not feel this oneiric urge to fly to London Ontario and mow the lawn.

M___   No, you have not escaped. You still have your property and as long as you have your property there is no escape. You made a run for it, but you have not escaped. You have not really escaped.

ACTOR   It is difficult to really escape.

When I finished The Collaborative Vision at the CBC, for example, I thought that I had really escaped. But I had not. Of course, I did not go into The Collaborative Vision thinking about escape. I was a good boy at The Collaborative Vision. I did what I was supposed to do. I cleaned up my property and made it saleable—for the big buyers. *(ching-ching)*

The organizers of The Collaborative Vision had talked interminably about the coming of these big buyers *(ching-ching)*—powerful people in the industry, decision-making people who knew the business inside out, real creative types, the best, with a whole lot of marketing savvy. We, the chosen writers of Canada, were going to pitch our newly developed properties; and they, the big buyers, were going to sagely critique our properties. And maybe even buy them. *(ching-ching)* And so when the big buyers arrived on the final day of The Collaborative Vision there sure was a heck of a lot of excitement around.

And who were the big buyers? Well, there was Franco Hermes, the co-creator of a sitcom that had run in the late '60s. Then there was Maggie Klue, who worked somewhere in production at the CBC. There was Ben Scham, a marketing exec for a rival network. And finally, there was Richie Orex, who worked as a story editor for "Fish Farm"—one of the most stupid and inept shows ever conceived.

The first writer pitched her property—a sitcom about a member of parliament.

FRANCO HERMES   It doesn't have enough jeopardy.

ACTOR   Said Franco Hermes.

MAGGIE KLUE   It's too "public affairs."

ACTOR   Said Maggie Klue.

BEN SCHAM   From a marketing point of view demographics are skewed.

ACTOR   Said Ben Scham.

RICHIE OREX   I agree with the others.

ACTOR   Said Richie Orex. So much for the first writer.

The second writer pitched his property—a dramatic series about a Canadian soldier fighting in World War I.

FRANCO HERMES   World War I is not a draw anymore, all that gas and slogging through the mud, no one wants to see that, World War I is too low-tech.

MAGGIE KLUE   The trouble with just setting a single character in World War I is that there's not enough room for dramatic conflict.

BEN SCHAM   Your low concept is good but your high concept is bad.

ACTOR   What do you mean asked the writer.

BEN SCHAM   Your low concept is the thing your show is about. That has merit. But the high concept, that is to say, what other show it is like, is your real problem. It isn't like anything. If I can't say to a producer, it's like *Hogan's Heroes* or it's like *M*A*S*H*, how the hell do you expect me to sell it?

RICHIE OREX   I agree with the others in everything they've said, also I think there is some kind of jeopardy problem.

ACTOR   *(tap-dance)* I stood before the big buyers and pitched my science fiction series.

FRANCO HERMES   I'm sorry I just don't like this kind of thing.

ACTOR   Said Franco Hermes, who once had a series in the '60s.

MAGGIE KLUE   I think there's a jeopardy problem.

ACTOR   Said Maggie Klue, who worked somewhere in production at CBC.

BEN SCHAM   TV is not a pioneering medium.

ACTOR   Said Ben Scham from the rival network.

BEN SCHAM   Do you think we're crazy? Science fiction sitcom? This is TV! This is business! If you want to write a poem, keep it at home in the drawer!

ACTOR   Richie Orex of *Fish Farm* added:

RICHIE OREX   I have to agree with what the others have said.

ACTOR   I sat down. Cleigh McNabb, my good pal and partner, leaned over and whispered:

CLEIGH McNABB   The big buyers are right, I don't like your property, I never liked your property.

ACTOR   So that was that. I was finished with the CBC. I was humiliated. I was relieved. The Collaborative Vision was over, and I had escaped television forever. And I rejoiced.

But I had not escaped. A few weeks later…

   One ring, picks up.

M____   Conrad Shadow. The Head of Something at CBC.

CONRAD SHADOW   I've just read your proposal for a new science fiction series. I love it.

M____   Great.

CONRAD SHADOW   So if you can just prove to me that you can write, I could get very interested.

M____   I've already proved that I can write, Conrad.

CONRAD SHADOW   Yeah sure, but can you write comedy? That's the big big question to me.

M____   Conrad, have you read anything I've written?

CONRAD SHADOW   No.

M____   But Conrad, I sent you guys my stuff. You got it all, right there at the CBC.

CONRAD SHADOW   I want you to write something just for me, I want you to make me laugh.

M____   Conrad, fuck off.

CONRAD SHADOW   No one has ever said that to me before.

M____   Well, maybe it's about time someone did. (*hangs up*) This time I've really escaped.

ACTOR   But next day…

> *Half-ring, picks up.*

M____   Conrad's assistant.

ASSISTANT   If you get down on your knees and apologize—

ACTOR   Those were her very words.

ASSISTANT   —Conrad will probably option your show.

M____   What does that mean?

ASSISTANT   A cheque for several thousand dollars. (*ching-ching*)

M____   I'll think about it.

ACTOR   I had still not escaped. I wanted the money. I wanted the easy TV money I kept hearing so much about. I wanted to sell my property and get rich. I wanted to get rich writing.

M____   What a stupid idea. How stupid to conceive of my writing as property— saleable property.

ACTOR   Although, of course, it is property, my property, and it is something I can sell, with luck, but that is not the way to conceive of it.

M____   I am my writing.

My writing is me.

And I am not property. I am not for sale.

ACTOR   And yet perhaps I was for sale at The Collaborative Vision. I put myself on the market and I was for sale.

M____   I am property.

ACTOR   But I took myself off the market before making the sale. And I escaped. More or less. For in the end, after months of idiotic and sickening negotiations, I again told Conrad to fuck off and that time it worked.

M____   If you want to escape…

ACTOR   I reflected as I sat in my sturdy Adirondack chair.

M____   …you must give up all thoughts of selling your property. Only then will you escape. You must give up all thoughts of selling yourself. You must learn this and then each day you must learn it again, until finally it is second nature.

ACTOR   But, the real truth is, if you truly want to escape, you must give up the whole idea of property.

M____   You must give up property!

ACTOR   And yet, I cannot do it. Will not.

M____   I cannot give up property. Not completely. Not yet.

ACTOR   I made a run for it, I am still alive, but I had not escaped.

M____   *(sings)* You can run but you can't hide

Run run run run run—

Glances at letter.

Fuck Property!

Drawn in.

ROBERT CROW   "The neighbours are getting upset."

ACTOR   Continued the letter from Robert Crow, the letter that entered my house through the mail slot and then exited through the front door, the letter, crumpled and stained, that now lay drying on the wide arm of the Adirondack chair, the letter about my property.

ROBERT CROW   "The grounds are thick with bushes that need trimming, the weeds are flourishing."

M____   Bobby honey, we're talking here about a lawn on a run-down property on a crooked street in a modest but pretentious middle class neighbourhood in

London Ontario. It does not have grounds, Bob, it has a lawn. It is not Windsor Castle, Bob. It does not have grounds, and you do not have grounds on your property either, Bob. If you would just go out your front door and look around you would discover a front lawn, Bob, you will not find grounds. There are no grounds on Blackpool Drive, Bob.

ACTOR   As I leaned back on the wooden slats of my Adirondack a gust of wind lifted Bob's letter and carried it off the porch.

> *Laughs hysterically.*

M____   I don't know why I'm laughing.

ACTOR   I hauled myself out of my Adirondack chair and peered over the porch railing. The letter had landed below on a juniper bush—it looked like a piece of ordinary trash. As I lumbered down the stairs to retrieve it, the wind came up again and blew it into the street. I waited at the curb as several vehicles drove over it.

M____   *(sings)* Have you any wool?
Yes sir, yes sir,
Three bags full…

ACTOR   I sauntered into the street and repossessed the letter that had ruined my day, stuffing it into the pocket of my greenjeans—*(notices pants)*—an act that gave me pleasure, like all acts associated with my greenjeans.

M____   I loved and dreamed of greenjeans since I was a kid but I could never get myself a pair. I could not even get anyone to listen to me on this small dream. I was not an acquisitive child. I rarely asked for things. But I urgently required greenjeans. They were simply crucial to me.

ACTOR   That's how kids are. And who can blame them? As time passed I of course forgot this dream. But when I saw the greenjeans in the store, I remembered and I bought them. And they give me great pleasure, just as I dreamed they would.

M____   Sometimes things work out.

ACTOR   I reflected as I drifted in the direction of nearby Main Street where I came upon a ruckus attended by two police officers, a Chinese woman in grey business attire, and the object of their attention, and older woman, perhaps seventy, in a white sundress emitting horrid screeching cries like those of an agitated parrot in a cage—pitiful cries that filled the air with torment and foreboding. I wanted to run from this sound. But I was paralyzed. The woman in white was sparring with some invisible enemy, flailing against it with her thin white arms. She stepped off the curb and plunged into the vehicular traffic on Main Street. The police watched impassively. But the Chinese woman followed into the traffic and brought the old woman safely back to the sidewalk. The high-pitched screeching continued unabated.

And, against my will, I remembered where I heard those sounds before.
Storming through the house tearing books throwing lamps smashing furniture.
I watched the woman in white, but I could only see my mother—my frail and
aging mother—who screeched like a parrot, and tried to smash the world.

M_____   The suffering of women.

ACTOR   I felt the words forming on my lips.

M_____   The suffering of women.

The suffering of London Ontario.

ACTOR   The woman in the white sundress was in Vancouver, but she was really
lost in London Ontario.

M_____   There is no escape.

There is no escape.

ACTOR   I turned away and dragged myself back up the lane to my property.

M_____   *(sings)* One for my master,
One for my dame,
But none for the little boy
Who cries in the lane.

ACTOR   I momentarily considered the inviting contours of my Adirondack chair,
but instead lay down on the polished wood floor of my front hall. I lay with my
head in the very place where the letter had fallen. If the letter, that languished
crumpled and stained in the pocket of my greenjeans, had come through the
mail slot at this point, it would have smacked me right in the face.

Shudders, moans, cries.

M_____   I don't know why I am crying. I don't know why.

ACTOR   But in truth I knew. I was crying for the woman in the white sundress,
I was crying for my mother whose whereabouts I did not know, I was crying
for my physician father who died in his forty-sixth year utterly worn out, I was
crying for my poor brother who, after a mysterious screaming altercation with
my mother, threw himself under the wheels of a train, I was crying for my
brilliant cousin who might have been a great man but instead got utterly lost,
I was crying for my grandmother who willed me my property in London
Ontario, I was crying for a family that had arrived in the new world at the
turn of the century with high hopes—a family that took root, grew and at
length decayed, but never flowered—a family that failed.

I was crying for myself—an additional indulgence that filled me with self-
loathing.

Fifteen rings—counts, toddles to phone, answers.

M____   It's Ariadne. Ariadne. From Arizona.

She saw the rodeo *and* the big cats at the Wild Kingdom in the desert.

The rodeo was revolting.

The big cats are magnificent.

She's having a wonderful time with her family.

ACTOR   I told Ariadne about the letter that had dropped through the mail slot and ruined my day. I told her about how the lawn was proliferating in London Ontario, I told her about Robert Crow's use of the word "grounds." Ariadne laughed. *(laughs)* We laughed in unison although we were thousands of miles apart.

M____   The telephone is an indispensable apparatus.

ACTOR   I said to myself as I laughed.

M____   It's a great invention.

ACTOR   I resolved to plug my telephone in more frequently.

M____   This thing with my mother and that house goes on and on, I cannot escape.

ARIADNE   You can escape, you've escaped before, tomorrow you will escape again.

Hesitation.

If only you had sold that property last summer, it would be easier. But your stupid cousin made sure that didn't happen. Your stupid cousin had to make his little point. Sure he helps your family. He likes doing it. As long as it's done his way. It makes him feel noble. But when it isn't done his way, his way exactly—

M____   That's not why he does it, Ariadne, the guy has convictions, ideas of how things should go, ideas of duty.

ARIADNE   Yeah, like when he wanted you to kill that cat. You wouldn't kill that cat. He doesn't like cats, your stupid cousin, they do things their own way. He wanted you to kill that cat because he knew if you would kill that cat for him, you would do anything. And when you wouldn't, he found a way to punish you for granting that cat the boon of life. And last summer when you wouldn't go along with his programme on the property, he found a way to punish you for that too. That poor little cat of your mother's cost you over a thousand dollars in the end.

M____   Meoooooow.

ARIADNE   Do you know that your stupid cousin is constipated? I saw him sneaking into the kitchen and eating his guilty bowl of Red River Cereal. He's got all that money and he can't even shit! And you know why? He's stopped up inside. He's constipated by the life he's led. Your stupid cousin has got all those brains and all that creativity and it can't flow out. He can't let go of it. That's why he's stupid.

M____   Ariadne, just because the guy likes Red River Cereal. That doesn't prove anything. I like Red River Cereal. I like what it does for me. It's real Canadian. I like it a lot.

ARIADNE   He could have done something new for the country of Canada, he's one of the few people I've ever met with that kind of ability, he could have done almost anything with that *brain* of his. But a brain without a heart is a useless thing. You can have the biggest brain in the world, but you're just a dickhead if you haven't got *heart*. It's heart that keeps a family together. A family without heart is despicable.

M____   He's got heart. He dragged my mother out of the mire dozens of times.

ARIADNE   Your mother. When you first told me about your mother, I thought you were exaggerating. But you were not. She is indeed a special case among mothers. She is heartless. She is mean. She is a killer. Your family is a heartless family. That's why they're trying to break you, because you have heart. Your grandmother had heart too, and that's why she left you that property. Your stupid constipated cousin couldn't stand it that you got that property, and he can't stand it that you've gone ahead and had a career as an artist.

M____   But he doesn't give a good shit about my career.

ARIADNE   There is too much *light*. And your mother is harbouring all the darkness. Each night your stupid cousin goes down into his sepulchre, pulls out his jewels, and puts on his eyepiece to magnify the light. The darkness is somewhere far away in the psychiatric hospital. You are light and dark. You make your living from your *darkness*. That's what every artist does. But it frightens him and he runs down into the basement and stares at those glittering points of light. You sleep with the big cats. Your stupid cousin does not sleep with the big cats.

Hesitation.

I saw the big cats today. I left the barbaric rodeo and went to see the big cats at the Wild Kingdom in the desert. That couple who run the Wild Kingdom get along fine with the big cats. When the big cats had cubs, that couple slept inside the compound for two months so that the big cats would let them become part of the pride, part of the family. They became one with the big cats. Those people at the Wild Kingdom live in harmony with the darkness. Those people have heart. Those people are heroes.

Not like the mean little shits at the rodeo. They hate the animals at the rodeo. The way they bang those animals around—every one of those animals needs major chiropractic work after those shows—you should see what they do to them, and I'm sorry, as romantic as the rodeo might seem, it's just some cruel fucking way to wrestle the animal spirit and throw it to the ground, that's all it's about. It is not heroic to mangle dumb animals. There is no heroic journey in that. There is no trip to the heart of the labyrinth to confront the monster. They treat them as if they were monsters, but they are just poor animals. These rodeo guys, they're no fucking heroes, these mean little bastards with their little pointy-prick cowboy boots. It's all in their heads. The labyrinth is in their heads.

They are all like my ex-husband Dexter. He wore those pointy little-prick cowboy boots. And he thought when he married me that he had a beast that he could throw to the ground, he thought that he could tie me up and cripple me. He thought I was his livestock. I hate that bastard, that cowboy bastard. I'll never forgive him, never. You don't tie up the big cats. You sleep with the big cats. The beast is wild and free and she just walks out on that rodeo and she does not have any regrets and she does not belong to anybody! You know my great-grandfather was a giant—probably six foot seven, he was a titan—he had to marry a woman right off the Mongolian plains. She was the only woman who was wild enough for him—so don't ever, ever try to tie me up!—that's all I have to say to you.

> *Pause.*

M____   I'm not sure I follow you Ariadne.

ARIADNE   Phone somebody up and get them to cut the lawn. You weren't thinking of going there to cut the lawn were you?

M____   Oh heck noooooo.

ARIADNE   Good. You can't go there without me. You'll have an accident. When you're in London Ontario I'm the driver. I'm glad you didn't kill that cat. I'll call you tomorrow. Don't ever kill a cat.

> *Dial tone—hangs up, unplugs phone.*

> *Pulls letter from pocket, violently tears it, and throws it into the toilet.*

M____   That fucking cat! My mother and that fucking cat!

ACTOR   My brilliant cousin wanted me to kill a cat, a cat that I had never seen, a poor stray that used to hang around my mother's house.

M____   It was not my cat, but I was supposed to kill it. It was not my property. It was not my mother's property. It was nobody's property. It was not property. It was a cat—an innocent stray that had the misfortune of coming under the influence of my mother.

ACTOR   When my mother began her annual sojourn at Club Demento, one of her friends, one of her helpful chums, phoned the Humane Society and got that cat a suite in the Cat Hilton.

M____   Probably looked good to that cat: free food, nice company, exercise equipment, lots of time to sleep. Didn't look like death row to that cat. The Club probably looked good to my mother too, for similar reasons.

ACTOR   My mother thought that she had killed that cat. But she had not. She thought that she had killed my brother. And perhaps she did. She thought that she had killed my father. And perhaps she didn't. But she definitely did not kill that cat. In the end that cat cost me a thousand dollars to bail out. In the end I lost track of my mother altogether. And so I saved the cat and lost my mother.

In truth I didn't care at all about that cat. If that cat were squashed by some anonymous bus or garbage truck it wouldn't bother me in the least. Thousands of people are mangled every day in torture chambers, thousands of people every day are butchered in wars, slaughtered in highway accidents, annihilated in natural disasters, exterminated by incurable viruses, blown away in their own suburban homes—I can hardly be expected to care deeply about some marginal pussycat.

And yet I fought for that cat's life.

M____   That's how things go.

ACTOR   I reflected as I stared at the bits and pieces of Bob Crow's letter lolling in the water of my toilet.

M____   You wind up fighting for the cat.

ACTOR   The truth is I am glad I saved that cat—the cat my mother thought she had killed.

M____   My brilliant cousin could have killed that cat himself. He didn't even have to consult me. He had power of attorney too. But he didn't want to commit felicide. He wanted me to commit felicide. But I did not commit felicide. He wanted me to commit suicide.

ACTOR   He did not really want me to commit suicide, he just wanted me to roll over and play dead.

After a day of lixiviating my house in London Ontario, the house left to me by my grandmother, the house in which my currently missing mother holds a life interest, Ariadne would drive me to my brilliant cousin's house in the distant suburbs, and he would lean back in his La-Z-Boy and create diversions.

By the way. He would begin, and lo and behold there would be a new diversion that would waste a morning or a day or more. Absent savings bonds, missing pension cheques, a certain piece of jewellery or furniture that had belonged to the family, a trip to the safety deposit boxes.

By the way. He would begin, leaning back in his La-Z-Boy, and then a new diversion. By the way.

But finally my house was saleable. I called a real estate company and in less than five minutes Don, the real estate guy, pulled into the driveway. With offers! *(tap-dance)* There's no business like property business.

I went to the house of my brilliant cousin that night, and told him that there were offers. I was exhausted, I was happy. I had navigated the twists and turns. I was at the end of the journey. I was at the heart of things.

My brilliant cousin congratulated me. He leaned back in his La-Z-Boy and began to talk about diamonds—how you cut diamonds, how you sort diamonds, how you sell diamonds. And then, just as he finished his dissection of diamonds, just before bedtime, my brilliant cousin paused, and leaned back in his La-Z-Boy one last time.

BRILLIANT COUSIN   BY THE WAY. We have to set up a little contract regarding the property. It's a minor detail.

ACTOR   That's how it is when you deal with a guy like my brilliant cousin. You have to keep taking care of certain minor by-the-way details.

BRILLIANT COUSIN   No big deal. When you sell the property you simply replace it with a guaranteed equivalent. It's a normal procedure. You have to guarantee your mother's living arrangement for the rest of her life. That's what a life interest is all about.

M____   No problem. I'm happy to do that.

ACTOR   And I was. After all, my mother brought me into the world and I'm grateful for that. She brought me into the world, fattened me up, and then she tried to kill me.

BRILLIANT COUSIN   You must put up security in order to back the guarantee of your mother's living arrangements. That is the way I read Grandma's will. So, I'm going to draw up a little contract and you will put up the property in Vancouver as security. That's the way it's done. You will make a contract with your mother. Ariadne will sign too of course. It you fail to fulfill your commitment, your mother has the right, as mortgagor, to seize the property in Vancouver.

ACTOR   As he spoke I found myself getting sleepy. I was ready for bed. I struggled to stay awake. I struggled to think. I knew something critical was underway, and yet all I really want to do was sleep.

M____   *(yawning)* I have given my word that I will pay my mother a good income for the rest of her life, and I will sign an agreement to do so, but I will not enter a contract with my mother that puts my property in Vancouver at risk. That's just stupid. My mother is a dangerous woman. One does not enter into that kind of deal with a person like my mother. Do you think I'm crazy?

BRILLIANT COUSIN *(chuckles)* Well, I know how you feel about your mother, and I agree that she is a difficult case, and frankly I wouldn't let her hold a mortgage on my property either, and luckily there is a viable alternative, a preferable alternative: you will place the money of the sale of your house in a trust fund for your mother. And everybody lives happily ever after.

M____ I won't do that either. I plan to use that money to pay off my house in Vancouver.

BRILLIANT COUSIN You have no choice.

M____ But that is not the right dream. You know about my dream. My dream is that I sell my property in London give some of the proceeds to my mother pay off the house in Vancouver give her money every month the money I save on the mortgage.

BRILLIANT COUSIN You don't understand what you are asking of me. I am legally obligated to your mother. I am a trustee. If you should misappropriate your mother's funds, I, as power of attorney, would be legally obligated to replace them. I can hardly be expected to put myself at that kind of risk, can I?

M____ Then why don't you withdraw from the power of attorney, then you won't be at risk.

BRILLIANT COUSIN I am not in a position to do that.

M____ This doesn't seem right to me. It is my property, after all.

BRILLIANT COUSIN Not exactly. In a sense it's really your mother's property. This is what a life interest means.

M____ If it's my mother's property, why is it in my name. Why did Grandma will it you me.

ACTOR My brilliant cousin turned to Ariadne.

BRILLIANT COUSIN Is he always this stubborn?

ACTOR Ariadne looked at him impassively and did not reply. My brilliant cousin turned back to me.

BRILLIANT COUSIN I have power of attorney. You can't make a move without me. You either sign the contract which I will draw up, or you put the money in a trust.

You are about to be fucked—

ACTOR Said my brilliant cousin.

BRILLIANT COUSIN —in the bum.

ACTOR   He didn't really say this—and yet he did.

There was a long silence out there in the distant suburbs. I felt confused, lost, sleepy, and sadly, somewhat titillated. I was, after all, on the verge of being violated.

I looked at Ariadne. She looked back with an eerie knowing smile. It was that smile that saved me. It was a smile that said:

ARIADNE   You can find your way out of this if you want to.

ACTOR   It was a smile that startled me.

M____   *(surprised)* I am not going to sell the house.

> *Silence.*

ACTOR   Ariadne continued to smile.

BRILLIANT COUSIN   You have no choice.

M____   I am not going to sell the house.

BRILLIANT COUSIN   You have no choice.

M____   The way I understand it, if one owns property in this society, one generally has the right not to sell it.

BRILLIANT COUSIN   But you have done all this work to make it saleable. You've put the house on the market, you have offers. You have to sell.

M____   I won't sell. I choose not to sell. The game is over.

BRILLIANT COUSIN   You will sell the house.

M____   No I won't.

ACTOR   My brilliant cousin got up out of his La-Z-Boy.

BRILLIANT COUSIN   Like many artists, you have a tendency to tilt at windmills. But let me assure you, there are no monsters in this household. We, my wife and I, are your friends. We are trying to do what is best for you.

ACTOR   And then my brilliant cousin went to bed.

The next morning Ariadne and I moved out of my brilliant cousin's house in the distant suburbs and went to see a lawyer. The lawyer explained what a power of attorney was, and what a life interest was.

LAWYER   Your brilliant cousin has misled you—more or less.

ACTOR   Said the lawyer.

LAWYER   And yet he has told the truth—more or less.

ACTOR   I asked the lawyer if I could sell the house without the approval of my brilliant cousin.

LAWYER   Yes—and no. You can sell it—but there could be legal complications; that is to say, I think you're pretty safe—on the other hand, there are dangers.

ACTOR   I asked the lawyer to draw up an agreement in which I would agree to pay my mother a decent income after the sale of the house and in turn she would agree to let me sell it without encumbrance. He drew it up and said:

LAWYER   You know, of course, this agreement is worthless.

ACTOR   I thanked the lawyer for clarifying the situation. I took my agreement to the London Psychiatric Hospital and presented it to my mother who refused to sign for fear of offending my brilliant cousin. And who can blame her? After all my brilliant cousin had taken her meagre savings and invested them and she now had over two hundred thousand in the bank. I don't blame her at all. Better to offend the son than risk offending someone like that.

The curious thing is that if my brilliant cousin had been straight with me from the beginning, I would simply have accepted his counsel as I always had before and signed his contract or set up the trust fund and then tried to find my way out of London Ontario. I have always had complete confidence in my brilliant cousin. But when I realized that he was not straight, when I realized that he had misled me, more or less, when I realized that by following his directions I had gotten lost in London Ontario, I knew at last that I had to go my own way. The curious thing is:

M____   I don't give a shit about that property. And neither did my brilliant cousin. What he really gives a shit about is manipulating the deal. The truth is he wanted to make a deal. He had a plan for my property in London Ontario, and I was part of his plan. It was not the plan that I had for my property. It was a similar plan, but it was not the same plan. When it's his deal, he feels real, he feels that he is a god, the god of the deal. And for my brilliant cousin, every human transaction finally boils down to a business deal.

ACTOR   And as I stood in my bathroom one year later looking into my toilet and thinking of my brilliant cousin, I was momentarily overcome with a desire to:

M____   Hustle down to the airport, buy a ticket, fasten my seat belt, hail a cab, motor on over to the house of my brilliant cousin and hit him in the face with some common implement such as a baseball bat or a brick, and afterwards take another cab over to the looping swerves of Blackpool Drive and shove the lawn mover up and down a few times.

> *Violent flush.*

ACTOR   I said goodbye to my mother. She did not say goodbye to me.

Ariadne drove me through the distorted streets of London Ontario straight down the 401 to the Toronto airport. And we escaped west toward the dark mountains.

M____   Canada is a big country. There is room to escape in Canada. People are
always escaping in Canada. The whole country is filled with escape artists. That
is the history of Canada. That is the thing I love about Canada.

ACTOR   But it was not a clean escape.

M____   I am still gridlocked in London Ontario.

I own a house that I do not want.

I have a lawn that I do not cut.

I have a mother that I cannot find.

Absurd.

I am an absurd person.

An absurd person from an absurd family.

The family itself is an absurd institution.

ACTOR   I reflected as I stared into my toilet bowl.

To be born into a family places one in an absurd situation. You are born helpless
and the family feeds you and the family wipes your ass. You think that someday
it will end—that you will grow up, and that you will be an adult, and the family
will treat you like an adult but you never grow up, you are always a child—you
have lived the life of a child, an absurd child, and some day you will die your
death like a child. You were born in a hospital where they wiped your ass, and
someday you will die in a hospital where they will once again wipe your ass, and
in between those wipes of the ass you wiped your own ass, but no one really
gave you credit for it. You are still a dirty ass little brat as far as your so-called
loved ones are concerned. You could show them Polaroids of your asshole—
perfectly wiped—and they would say:

LONDON ONTARIO   Who did that for you?

M____   And if, in spite of all, you do something with your life, you find a way to
live, and survive, and perhaps even make a contribution of some kind, they find
you intolerable, even hateful, they would prefer it if you were dead, they would
prefer to murder you, or better, they would prefer you to commit suicide like
my poor brother who one night, after a mysterious incident with my mother,
recognized the absurdity—the permanent absurdity—of his circumstances and
threw himself under the wheels of a train.

ACTOR   And the family liked it that way. They were delighted. At the funeral they
were positively jolly. They were enthusiastic about the seating arrangements,
about who should sit directly in front of the coffin and who should sit in the
front row and the second row. They actually took my mother by the arm and
manhandled her into what they considered the appropriate chair. One of my
cousins took my arm in a firm grip and tried to manhandle me.

M____   If you don't leave me alone, I'm gonna break your arm!

ACTOR   Even in the face of death they do not give up control.

M____   What a heinous enterprise a family is.

ACTOR   Not all families, of course, some rare families are delightful. Ariadne's family is delightful.

M____   But most are heinous.

And this heinous enterprise, the family, is a fundamental unit of our society.

And property too is a heinous thing.

And property too is fundamental to our society.

> *Gags.*

Family and property.

> *Wipes mouth, backs away from toilet, discovers envelope.*

The forgotten envelope. The Queen of England. My mother.

This is what it has all finally come down to, a letter that I will never finish complaining about, the deterioration of Grandma's property, now mine, the property she left to me and my poor dead brother, property that I do not want but will not sell. Perhaps, if I could sell my deteriorating house—just get rid of it—perhaps then I could get rid of my deteriorating family.

ACTOR   And yet I did not really believe it. There are no simple solutions. Except death. The only thing that will really do the job is death. The collective death of my family would do the job. As would mine. And neither party is in a hurry to do the other a favour on this score. And who can blame us?

M____   I am afraid to go to London Ontario with its squirming avenues and sell the house. I am afraid to *die*.

Instead I will let the house sit there on Blackpool Drive, a monument with its memorial lawn, a crumbling weed-strewn memento for my brilliant cousin, for my mad mother, for my failed family, for all those who have lost their way in London Ontario. My property will sit there like an oozing boil on Blackpool Drive envenoming the whole neighbourhood with its noxious toxin. The nightmares of Robert Crow will become reality. And all because it's my property and I do what I want with my property and what I want to do is *kill* my property!

ACTOR   I want to kill my property.

M____   I am no better than my mother.

My mother is a killer. I am a killer. This is the time of killers.

This is the century of killers. Our heroes are killers. Our politicians are killers. Our young people are killers. Our business people are killers. Our scientists are killers, our physicians are killers, our religious leaders are killers. We are all killers. We kill in countless ways. We kill the plants, we kill the animals, we kill the earth we kill the air and kill the water and we kill each other and we kill ourselves and we kill God. We watch killing on the TV, and in the movies, and we read about it in our newspapers and periodicals. Killing is the major study of our time, the major occupation, the major obsession, the major hobby, the major amusement, the major everything. That is where we have put our energy. That is where we have put our money. We have done more killing in this century than in the rest of recorded history. My mother just wanted to get in on the action. And so do I!

ACTOR   And who can blame us? Everybody's doing it. And most of the time we get away with it. Take the instance of a man in Washington named Robert Martens who killed over one million people in Indonesia in 1965. He did this without leaving his office. He got away with it. He was promoted. His story is not unusual. And almost no one knows it, certainly not the oblivious Robert Crow who wants to kill my lawn. Robert Martens compiled a list the size of a phone book—a list of American enemies—and he gave this list to an Indonesian named Achmed Suharto—another killer—who systematically killed every man woman and child on the list and many many more. Achmed got away with it too.

My mother apparently sentenced herself to life in the psychiatric hospital, with occasional paroles, for what seems, in the larger context of the era, to be almost trivial infractions: a couple of alleged killings, and an alleged attempted killing. But the truth is my mother's incarceration sprang from a far more majestic origin: my mother caused World War II.

She came to this realization in the mid-'40s. She announced that she had caused the war. No one believed her. And I don't blame them. After all, she was in London Ontario, a difficult place for a housewife with two small kids to begin a major European conflict. But she continued to proclaim her guilt to all who would listen. Finally, she turned herself in and received a session of corporal punishment in the form of electroshock therapy—the first of many such punishments.

I was not told of my mother's war crimes until the time of my brother's death. My kind and brilliant cousin found it appropriate to regale me with this tale a few days after the funeral. No account of my mother's diverse psychiatric history ever affected me so deeply. For I realized with finality that my mother was indeed mad, or at least had been mad, and that she had likely been mad through most of my childhood—those years when she was supposedly bringing me up. This well-educated and intelligent woman looked at the world and went mad.

M____   Perhaps this is the correct response.

Perhaps we are madder to live out our primly-hedged daydreams and stare at the lawn while the world turns to shit around us.

ACTOR   My mother was shut out of the action and she wanted in. She made herself part of the larger madness. Perhaps in a different family she would have been an artist, or a healer, or a teacher, but no one recognized that she had ability, or imagination, and they married her off to raise kids and rot. So she refused her domestic destiny and entered the great world through the back door of the psychiatric hospital.

M____   My mother is mad.

The legal tenant of my property is mad.

The property itself is mad.

I am mad.

I am in Vancouver, with its dark mountains, and I am mad.

And only death will cure my madness, and my mother's madness, and the madness of the world. And the three of us are well on our way.

> *Pause.*

ACTOR   What a bitter passage, what a bitter passage.

> *Laughs.*

M____   The truth is that in spite of the family, and my brilliant cousin, and the CBC, and the twisted streets of London Ontario, in spite of betrayals and lies and killings, in spite of my property and the world and my crazy mother, in spite of Robert Crow and his letter-writing activities, in spite of the demons of guilt and regret, in spite of all, I go on. I have Ariadne, and my work. And I go on.

ACTOR   And it can only end in nothing.

M____   And I go on. I have the theatre.

ACTOR   An institution not unlike the psychiatric hospital.

M____   And I go on. I have a home.

ACTOR   Still owned mainly by the bank.

M____   And I go on. I have the dark mountains, the dark mountains. And I go on. I have dreams.

ACTOR   Some, like the hopeful dream of last summer, turn to shit.

M____   But others come true. And I go on. In the theatre, one can see dreams come true.

ACTOR   That is why I am in the theatre.

M____   And I go on. And perhaps, some day, I will go back to London Ontario, and try again. I will go back to my property and cut my lawn and make it saleable, I will set up a decent income for my mother and bail her out of the crazy house and set her up in a nice apartment.

ACTOR   And yes, I know it won't work out, and something will go wrong, because something always goes wrong, every time.

M____   But my dream will be strong by that time, it will be irresistible, and I will go on.

ACTOR   And perhaps I will get permanently lost in the twisting ever-twisting streets of London Ontario.

M____   And still I will go on.

ACTOR   I am indeed mad.

M____   But, perhaps… perhaps…

ACTOR   I reflected holding the envelope.

M____   Just once I will make my dream come true.

>   *End.*

Tinka's New Dress

Ronnie Burkett

Ronnie Burkett has been captivated by puppetry since the age of seven, when he opened the *World Book Encyclopedia* to "Puppets." He began touring his puppet shows at the age of fourteen and has been on the road ever since. Ronnie has received numerous awards in Canadian theatre as a playwright, actor and designer for his work with Theatre of Marionettes, including the Herbert Whittaker Drama Bench Award for Outstanding Contribution to Canadian Theatre, and international recognition including a *Village Voice* OBIE Award in New York for Off-Broadway Theatre. From his peers, Ronnie has received three Citations for Excellence in the Art of Puppetry from the North American Center of the Union Internationale de la Marionnette and the President's Award from the Puppeteers of America. Recognized as one of the world's foremost theatre artists, his work has created an unprecedented adult audience for puppet theatre, and continuously plays to great critical and public acclaim in Canada, the U.K., Australia, Germany, Austria, Sweden and elsewhere. His most recent play, *10 Days on Earth*, is the tenth production from Theatre of Marionettes. When not wiggling dollies in front of strangers, Ronnie lives in Toronto.

Tinka's New Dress, produced by Rink-A-Dink Inc./Ronnie Burkett Theatre of Marionettes, premiered at Manitoba Theatre Centre, Winnipeg in November 1994 with the following company:

MARIONETTES   Ronnie Burkett

Music and Sound Designed by Cathy Nosaty
Lighting Designed by Brian Kerby
Stage Managed by Leo Wieser (1994–1997) and Terri Gillis (1997–2002)
Movement Advisory by Denise Clarke
Voice of The Common Good by Dana Brooks
Marionettes, Costumes and Set Designed by Ronnie Burkett

Carousel built by Martin Herbert
Marionettes built by Ronnie Burkett
Costumes and soft sculptures built by Kim Crossley
Marionette controls by Luman Coad
Puppet Workshop assisted by Angela Talbot and Larry Smith

Subsequent runs include the Canadian Stage Company, Toronto; the National Arts Centre, Ottawa; the Belfry Theatre, Victoria; Theatre Network, Edmonton; One Yellow Rabbit, The Secret Theatre, Calgary; Festival de Théâtre des Amériques, Montreal; Das Meininger Theatre, Germany; Usine C, Montreal; Henson International Festival of Puppetry, New York City; Dublin Theatre Festival, Dublin; Images Festival, Holland; queerupnorth, Manchester; Festival Theaterformen 2000, Hanover; The Barbican Centre, London; and The Melbourne Festival, Australia.

Note

Two sections of the play are improvised at each performance. These are the character Carl's underground "Franz & Schnitzel" puppet shows. Ronnie assumes the human portrayal of Carl for these, working on a small stage within the larger set and manipulating a cast of separate characters designed to look decidedly more puppet-like than the naturalistic marionettes in the dramatic body of the play.

The title characters are Franz, a grotesque psycho-clown and his innocent sidekick Schnitzel, an elf-like child who longs to grow fairy wings. Their debates begin each improv section, and usually centre around social and political happenings of the (present) day. Sometimes these debates are silly, bawdy or just comic, other times they carry significant satirical bite, depending on the news of the day, the audience and certainly the performer's whim.

There is also the "fat lady who sings" in the form of Madame Rodrigue, the resident diva. She usually makes an appearance in the first section to berate and bully the audience, training them in the fine points of how to greet a star. In the second improv she sings a song, written that day and commenting on topical news, to one of five standard bedtracks composed by Cathy Nosaty.

Other characters include the critic (usually brought onstage to comment on any particular reviewer not in the performer's favour that moment), Schnitzel's spiritual guide, Larry the Fairy, and The Judge. Interestingly, in over 200 performances to date, The Judge has never been used.

While there is commentary on Carl's performances throughout the play, these two improvised sections have the performer playing to the audience by his wits, and serve to illustrate that Carl/Ronnie is in constant danger of crossing the line. The first section is introductory, light and funny, while the second sequence later in the play is darker and risks a true emotional connection with the audience.

The improvs bring the struggle of the artist as commentator vividly to life and relate directly to the audience. To merely describe them, or the impact of Schnitzel on the audience is impossible, but it is profoundly strong and real, and gives the struggle of Carl and Tinka within the play a deeper resonance for those watching their journey.

For the purposes of the published version of the play, the general structure and content of the improv sections are written down.

Notes on Staging

The set is a carousel, somewhere between human and puppet scale. There are twenty-one animals in two rows on the centre ring, which is flanked by an "acting ring." The entire set floor is a circle, eighteen feet in diameter. The carousel ring, thirteen feet in diameter, is set into this, but upstage of the outer ring. Therefore, the acting ring is greater at the front of the set. The entire puppet cast, including duplicates, hang from the centre poles of each carousel figure, "riding" on the animal. The carousel is faded, almost ghostly, painted in sepia tones like a faded photograph.

At the stage left side of the set, on the acting ring, is the puppet stage for "The Franz & Schnitzel Show." The cast for this segment hang behind the backdrop of the small stage, except for Franz and Schnitzel who hang on the miniature stage. This stage unit rides around the acting ring on a fixed castored system. By simply pushing the unit, it can be moved to centre stage front and off again to either side.

On the front curve of the stage decking, which is one foot high, are wooden cutouts of letters reading *"JAKO SVEDEK A VAROVÁNÍ."* This is the Czech translation of "As a Witness and a Warning."

Preset on the acting ring, and in front of the set, are seven figures, referred to as The Officer, Mother, Thin Woman, Fat Man, Thin Man, Little Boy and Little Girl. They are self-standing, made of cloth, and completely natural in tone with no shading or colour detail. This is "The Populace." During the course of the action these figures are moved around the acting space as silent extras playing a variety of roles.

Stage directions herein are kept to a minimum. The play is performed solely by Ronnie Burkett, and reference to him is throughout the stage directions.

When a number appears after a character's name in the stage directions, such as "Tinka #3," it indicates a character represented by duplicate marionettes. This is most usually for costume changes, which require a separate figure for each. Tinka, for example, is represented by seven different marionettes.

The play progresses from light to dark emotionally, and each scene is assigned a palette dictating colours and tones for costumes to further enhance this.

Cathy Nosaty's score and Brian Kerby's lighting are integral to the overall design and performance, although lighting and sound notes within this text are referred to only when necessary to the reading.

The play is performed without intermission, with a running time of approximately two hours and twelve minutes.

Characters

STEPHAN, an elderly puppeteer
CARL, Stephan's protégé
MRS. ASTRID VAN CRAIG, a wealthy patron
TINKA, Carl's seamstress sister
MORAG, a transvestite cabaret performer
FIPSI, Stephan's other protégé and Carl's rival
HETTIE, a radical poet and writer
BENJAMIN, a friend of Hettie's
ISAËL, Mrs. Van Craig's nephew

Setting

A vaguely European city and an internment camp on the outskirts.

Time

Ostensibly mid-twentieth century, although possibly the present or future.

TINKA'S NEW DRESS

Once the house is open, and until the beginning of the play, the soundtrack consists solely of sporadic announcements from The Common Good. These are referred to as THE VOICE, and are heard throughout the show as well, seemingly with no direct relation to the action. It is intended simply to be the omnipresence of the government.

THE VOICE "For The Common Good, please have your identification card available for inspection at all times. Thank you. This has been a message from The Common Good."

"Compliance is the core of civilization. Resistance to The Common Good results in chaos. Thank you for your civility. This has been a message from The Common Good."

"Remember to travel only in those sectors as indicated on your identification card. This has been a message from The Common Good."

"Non-family groups of three or more must obtain assembly clearance from their zone commander. This has been a message from The Common Good."

"The Common Good represents the best of us all. Please feel free to report those who do not embrace our collective cause. This has been a message from The Common Good."

Once the house is full and the doors are closed, we hear a final announcement:

"This area is now secured. Movement will be monitored and discouraged. Thank you for your co-operation. This has been a message from The Common Good."

Scene One
The Park—Yellow Palette

Music begins. The houselights and stage are preset fade to half, and then to black. After a brief moment in blackout, lights up revealing the faded carousel. Ronnie is standing stage right looking at the carousel. With a change in music, he notices the soft sculpture figure standing beside him. She is referred to as Mother, the only figure off the acting ring. She is standing downstage centre facing the carousel. With the music now playing the carousel theme, Ronnie places Mother on the set. He moves from figure to figure, moving them to their opening positions. The carousel does not move during the beginning of the play, however during the following scenes when the carousel is moved, the animals which have stopped centre front hold the marionettes for the scene. This is what happens on the now static carousel animals centre front. Ronnie takes the puppet of STEPHAN #1 and presents him with the final flourish of the music. It is spring. The music and leafy texture of the lights reveal this. Ronnie walks STEPHAN through The Populace. They do not speak, although he answers them as if they had. Music out.

STEPHAN   Thank you all so very much for coming. The puppets and I appreciate the generosity of your applause, and your pockets.

STEPHAN bends over to talk to a young girl:

Well look who's here today! Tell me my dear, did you enjoy the show? Oh yes, that is funny, isn't it? When Schnitzel tries to fly, it always brings a great laugh. Yes, I will be sure to tell Schnitzel that you love him. I'm quite certain he loves you too.

To the child's Mother:

It is remarkable, isn't it? How the puppets—mere wooden dolls—become so real to the children.

He turns, as if reacting to the Thin Man figure:

Oh yes, we'll be here again next week. With each spring comes a new season of The Franz and Schnitzel Show.

To a Fat Gentleman:

Oh yes, same place. I've performed in this park for… well, for almost fifty years now!

To the Thin Woman figure:

Really? You're little Zina? That precocious girl who would sit in the front row and yell every time Madame Rodrigue began to sing? And now look at you my dear. My dear! Thank you so much for coming to visit me and my players once again. Oh, I see.

He stoops down to address the Little Boy beside the woman:

So, your mother brought you to see my puppets. What did you think of them? Well, Franz isn't really a bad clown, he's just naughty. You're naughty once in a while yourself I would imagine? Yes, I will be sure to tell him that he ought to be nicer. Thank you very much for your thoughts on the matter.

A figure standing stage right of the others is illuminated by light. There is a strain of music, The Common Good theme. Until now this figure has been somewhat in shadow. Once lit, we see that he, while still neutral cloth like the others, is more erect and official in appearance, with his hands clasped behind his back and feet astride. This is The Officer. STEPHAN reacts to him.

No, no Officer, this is not an unsanctioned assembly. I was simply chatting with some of my audience. The puppet show. The Franz and Schnitzel Show. Yes, that's right, I am Stephan. Oh yes, sir, I do have an amusement vendor license. I keep it over here with my puppet stage, if you'd care to see it. Thank you, Officer; thank you very much. That's very kind of you. Yes, I will be sure to avoid creating any such disturbances in the future.

The special on The Officer figure fades. On STEPHAN's following speech, he is hung centre stage as Ronnie moves The Populace to stage right and stage left.

Well, my friends, I'm afraid that we must now part company. Thank you all so very much for coming to see me and my players today. I do hope that I shall see you all again very soon for another performance of The Franz and Schnitzel Show!

Ronnie takes the marionette of CARL #1 from the carousel and walks him toward STEPHAN.

CARL   Well, it appears that even the genteel and beloved Stephan is not immune from the watchful eyes of The Common Good.

STEPHAN   It was nothing, Carl. A simple misunderstanding.

CARL   It's a good thing you had the appropriate papers, Stephan. Or was that business about the amusement vendor license merely a bluff?

STEPHAN   Carl, I would never bluff The Common Good.

CARL   So you actually went out and registered yourself as an amusement vendor?

STEPHAN   Well, it is the law.

CARL   It's an insult.

STEPHAN   Oh Carl, it changes nothing. I still perform my shows. What insult is there in that?

CARL   You're an artist, Stephan! This is theatre.

STEPHAN   Carl, this is a park. And I am merely an old puppeteer performing for children on a sunny day. There is no shame in being an amusement vendor, and if that is how The Common Good needs to classify me…

CARL   Then that is where The Common Good will keep you, Stephan.

STEPHAN   Carl, I'm old. I've had a happy career. And I've been proud to share it with you and Fipsi. Soon, Franz and Schnitzel and all the other characters will belong to you both. To do as you will, and to keep our traditions alive. But I can only pass it along as I know it, Carl. Please, don't ask me to march alongside you in your cause.

CARL I only want to take what you taught me, Stephan, and make it mine.

STEPHAN The puppets become tangled in your ego, Carl. It's not your soapbox. It's just a puppet stage.

CARL No. It's more than that.

STEPHAN What then?

CARL I... I don't know yet.

> *CARL is hung in position. STEPHAN puts his arm around CARL's shoulder.*

STEPHAN Sweet David, do not engage Goliath in a battle unless you know that God is on your side.

> *Ronnie reaches for MRS. VAN CRAIG #1, seated on the carousel.*

MRS. VAN CRAIG My word, Stephan, how bold you are! How revolutionary!

STEPHAN Mrs. Van Craig, you startled me.

MRS. VAN CRAIG On the contrary, Stephan, 'tis you who startles me. Public discussion of God! My word, you are more daring than I would have imagined.

STEPHAN Thank you, madam, but really, since when is discussion of God a public offence?

CARL Since last month, Stephan. The Common Good has forbidden public utterances of God by those not classified as Disciple Brethren or Holy Army Officers.

MRS. VAN CRAIG It's true, Stephan. Didn't you know?

STEPHAN No. No, I didn't. How could I? The Common Good swept to power as God's government. Why would they now ban Him?

CARL It's us they've banned, Stephan. The Common Good has made God in their image. But they don't want their poster boy to be too common.

MRS. VAN CRAIG Bravo, young man! I see you've an opinion on our ruling party.

STEPHAN Carl has an opinion on everything.

MRS. VAN CRAIG Carl. Yes. Your celebrated protégé. Your performance of Franz in this afternoon's show was very interesting. One might almost say... bloodthirsty.

STEPHAN Others might say out of control. Forgive me, madam. Carl, this is Mrs. Astrid Van Craig.

CARL   I know who she is. Slumming, Mrs. Van Craig?

STEPHAN   Carl!

MRS. VAN CRAIG   Please, Stephan. I am not one who takes offence at the umbrage of youth. No, Carl, I often take the sun on days such as this, and for many years I have found enjoyment in the company of your mentor's beloved characters.

CARL   Oh brother...

MRS. VAN CRAIG   Does it dismay you to learn that an old woman finds kinship in the antics of a few puppet players?

CARL   It puzzles me, Mrs. Van Craig, that a wealthy person would find anything in folk art. The voice of the common people.

MRS. VAN CRAIG   I see. You praise the common man, yet you condemn The Common Good?

CARL   It's a convenient slogan.

MRS. VAN CRAIG   The common man?

CARL   The Common Good.

MRS. VAN CRAIG   They are both slogans, Carl. What makes yours the more noble of the two?

CARL   Well I... I think that it's... what I mean is, the struggle of the common man is mirrored by the... no, the good of the common man is no way reflected by the will of the... what I mean is, the common man and The Common Good... well, are... what I mean is... shit....

STEPHAN   His militancy is still somewhat embryonic.

MRS. VAN CRAIG   Then I await the maturity of your ideals, Carl, and the opportunity for the ensuing debate.

> *CARL and STEPHAN are now hung in position. Ronnie reaches back for TINKA #1.*

TINKA   Carl, shouldn't we be going? Oh, hello.

MRS. VAN CRAIG   You must be Stephan's other pupil. Fipsi, isn't it?

TINKA   No, Fipsi is beautiful. I'm Tinka.

CARL   My sister.

STEPHAN   Our seamstress.

TINKA   The puppets' seamstress.

MRS. VAN CRAIG   My dear, are you the one responsible for Madame Rodrigue's stunning new concert gown?

TINKA   Why yes.

MRS. VAN CRAIG   Well my dear girl, you are significantly more than just a seamstress. Tinka, you are a couturier. Tell me, do you ever design for people?

TINKA   No. Well, not other people. Just myself I mean. This one is my good dress.

MRS. VAN CRAIG admires TINKA's dress.

MRS. VAN CRAIG   Just one? Well, the results are lovely. Now, I really must be going. My driver will be wondering what happened to me.

CARL   Held captive by the deviants, no doubt.

MRS. VAN CRAIG   Held captive? No, Carl. Captivated, perhaps.

STEPHAN   Allow me to walk you to your car, Mrs. Van Craig.

MRS. VAN CRAIG   Oh Stephan, do you really think I should be seen on the arm of a known revolutionary such as yourself?

STEPHAN   Why don't you risk it, madam?

She giggles like a schoolgirl.

MRS. VAN CRAIG   Oh Stephan, how you talk! Well, a pleasure to meet you both. Carl. Tinka.

TINKA   Goodbye, Mrs. Van Craig. Carl.

CARL   Bye.

MRS. VAN CRAIG   He's quite eloquent, isn't he? Let the revolution begin!

STEPHAN   This way, madam.

CARL and TINKA are left hanging stage left and stage right as STEPHAN and MRS. VAN CRAIG exit, seated back on their carousel animals.

TINKA   Carl, did you really have to be so rude?

CARL   Yes, Tinka, I did. She needs to learn.

TINKA   What? That you're rude?

CARL   That her wealth is no longer an asset. It's a vulgar handicap.

TINKA   Carl, stop it. You need her, people like her.

CARL   I don't need anyone like her. I don't want my audience to be fat and pink and polite. I'm not a court jester for the rich.

TINKA Carl, you're a performer. And a performer needs an audience who will pay to see them.

CARL Tinka, didn't I promise to take care of you? Haven't I always taken care of you?

TINKA Yes, always, but…

CARL But what then, Tinka?

TINKA Carl, I worry about you. It's not a good time to be controversial.

CARL It's the times that have made me controversial. Oh, Tinka, I can't explain why I need to do it this way, but I know you understand. Don't you?

> *TINKA nods.*

Then let's leave it at that. Please. I can't talk about it. Not now. Not before I have to go and do it.

TINKA Did you tell Stephan?

CARL I was about to, but that woman interrupted us. Look, if it's a success, I'll tell him about it. And if it's a complete failure, he'll never know.

TINKA I'm quite sure he already knows.

CARL How?

TINKA Fipsi.

CARL How did Fipsi hear about it?

TINKA Carl, you're doing a midnight puppet show in a cabaret. It may be offbeat, but it's certainly not a covert activity.

CARL Yet.

TINKA You wish!

CARL Do I, Tinka?

TINKA Sometimes I wonder.

> *Carousel music begins and lights on the acting ring dim. Both puppets are placed in their original starting positions on the animals. Ronnie kneels at centre and pushes the carousel into the second position. Once this is completed, the music and lights shift becoming more "cabaret" in tone, suggesting the world of the nightclub into which we are now being drawn. It is late night, and the lighting reflects the entrance to a seedy club. The Populace are moved into their cabaret positions, children off to the side, the adults by the carousel pillars.*

Scene Two
Outside the Cabaret—Red and Blue Palette

MORAG is obviously male, but dressed in a turban and an elaborate feminine dressing gown. Underneath the loosely-belted gown we see men's boxer shorts and a singlet; fishnets and flat slippers. Ronnie takes the puppets off the animals on the carousel. CARL #2 is placed face out, slightly downstage. MORAG #1 walks toward him as the music flourishes and ends.

MORAG   Darling, there you are! Carl, what are you doing out here? You're on after my next number.

CARL looks at MORAG.

CARL   In that?

MORAG   Let me be the bitch, Carl. I've had far more practice.

CARL   Shouldn't you be padding something, Morag?

MORAG looks at CARL's crotch.

MORAG   Some of us opt for a more subtle approach.

CARL   Sorry hon, no padding there.

MORAG   *Mon Dieu!* A genius, and he's hung! Which will bring you the greater fame, I wonder? Strange, Carl, well-endowed men usually lack ambition. They don't need it. No, ambition is for their admirers. Alas, darling, it's those of us who are genitally challenged who strive so for success.

CARL   You call this success?

MORAG   I'm my own man. I call the shots around this dump and I do things my way.

CARL   Well Morag, that's all I'm after.

MORAG   Well then darling, big or small, I suppose we meet somewhere in the middle.

CARL   And isn't that what society should be?

MORAG   Carl please, I've got to put on a wig, a dress and enough make-up to sink a battleship. Don't get profound on me now.

CARL   Sorry, I'm a bit nervous.

MORAG   Well darling, it's natural to be nervous on one's big opening! Take a tip from the pros. Some do deep-breathing exercises backstage, others say a prayer, most smoke. Me, I pee. I always make a little tinkle before going onstage. And *voilà* darling! I'm a star!

CARL   "Tinkle, tinkle little star…"

MORAG   You really are a hateful man.

CARL   I love you, Morag.

MORAG   And I adore you, old friend. Welcome to the club, Carl!

> *They embrace. MORAG looks at The Officer figure, stage right.*

Wouldn't they just love this little tableaux? Mister and Mister Common Good.

CARL   You be the common, I'll be the good.

MORAG   You'd better be darling, you'd better be. I'm risking my swan-like neck putting you on the bill tonight. What was I thinking? A puppet show. By an unknown. And worse, an unknown with ideals!

CARL   And I appreciate it, Morag.

MORAG   Well then, just remember. If they run us out of town, Carl, there's nowhere left to go.

> *Cabaret music from within, MORAG yells back.*

Keep your knickers on luvvies, I'm coming! There's my cue, darling. I've got to get into my drag. I'm doing the dance of the six veils tonight.

CARL   Six?

MORAG   Cutbacks darling, always cutbacks. Be brave out there tonight, Carl.

> *He starts off.*

And remember, darling, make the bastards laugh. That way, they won't know you said anything important until it's too late.

> *Turning upstage.*

Coming! Oh, and Carl, please don't flush in the middle of my number. It's one thing to play in a sewer, but it's far too embarrassing when the toilet gets a bigger round of applause!

> *MORAG is placed back on the carousel. Ronnie walks though the carousel and picks up the puppet of FIPSI #1 who enters upstage right on the acting ring.*

FIPSI   Carl.

CARL   Fipsi. Hey, thanks for coming.

FIPSI   I'm not here for your little show, Carl. Please pack it all up and let's get out of here before it's too late.

CARL   Relax, Fipsi, they don't enforce curfew in this sector. They just lock it up. I'll walk you home in the morning.

FIPSI Carl, what you're about to do here tonight is dangerous. It's not going to give you any sort of a career.

CARL I don't want a career. Art isn't a vocation Fipsi, it's a discussion.

FIPSI Of what, Carl?

CARL Of the sacred versus the profane. And for that, all I want, all I need, is an audience.

FIPSI At what cost?

CARL Art should be free, don't you think?

FIPSI Well excuse me, Mr. Artiste. My, my, Carl, I'd failed to notice. You've really chosen a temple of art for your debut, haven't you? With a two-drink minimum.

CARL Look, these people have taken a risk to be here. I can't wait to talk to them.

FIPSI Risk! Everything always has to be a risk with you. Why risk everything?

CARL Why not? I can't be like you. "Yes, Stephan, I'll do it exactly the way you do it. No, Stephan, I won't change the characters a bit. Of course, Stephan, they're just puppets." Face it, Fipsi, you never risk a thing!

FIPSI I'm here now.

CARL To save me? Or to watch me fail?

FIPSI How dare you!

CARL Sorry. Look, Fipsi, I appreciate that you're here, but I think we both know what this is really all about. You're jealous. You've always been jealous of me.

She turns quickly and starts toward him.

FIPSI You arrogant…. Do you think it was easy always being the "other" protégé? Do you think it was easy watching you, the gifted boy-wonder, do everything so effortlessly, so artfully, while I struggled to learn mere craft? To do one thing that might make the old man happy? Yes, Carl, I am envious of your gift. But I'm not so jealous that I would let it overpower my admiration for you. Please, Carl, I beg of you, don't do this. Don't go in there. Not with these people.

CARL Fipsi, these are my people.

FIPSI What? Outcasts and perverts and queers?

CARL Come on, Fipsi, you know that I'm…

FIPSI Yes, I know you're… different. But, Carl, you're a decent one. You fit in. Why, you look almost normal. You don't wear your sickness on your sleeve like so many of them do.

CARL Well, maybe it's time I started.

He turns to walk away.

FIPSI   They'll stop you, Carl. Any way they can, they will stop you now.

CARL   What's to lose, Fipsi? Like you said, I'm different. In their eyes, I'm already dead.

    An announcement is played:

THE VOICE   "This sector will be closed, beginning in ten minutes. This has been a message from The Common Good."

FIPSI   All right, Carl, that's enough.

CARL   There's curfew. Go on, Fipsi, get out of here.

FIPSI   Carl, please…

CARL   Goodnight, Fipsi.

FIPSI   Goodbye, Carl.

    She exits.

CARL   Well… here goes.

    There is a brief musical fanfare and we hear MORAG's voice as the lights fade to black. Ronnie replaces the puppets to their original positions on the carousel. He clears The Populace upstage and crosses over to the Franz and Schnitzel stage.

MORAG   *(off)* Ladies and gentlemen, and all you real women too, we have a new performer here at The Penis Flytrap tonight. So I'd like you to put your hands above the table and give our new cummer a warm welcome on his big opening. Darlings, I give you Carl and The Daisy Theatre!

Scene Three
The Franz and Schnitzel Show—
Puppet Palette (Black and White with Orange and Pink)

The quirky theme music for The Franz and Schnitzel Show plays. The lights flash and chase across the carousel as Ronnie moves the Franz and Schnitzel stage into position centre stage.

This scene is improvised, usually lasting approximately twenty minutes in length. The scripted text following is based upon a general format that has evolved through performance.

Lights up on the Franz and Schnitzel stage. Ronnie is standing behind a gold curtain visible from the chest up. He holds FRANZ stage right, and SCHNITZEL stage left, standing in front of the curtain.

FRANZ   Schnitzel, do you smell what I smell?

> *SCHNITZEL sniffs the air.*

SCHNITZEL   No Franz, I don't smell anything.

FRANZ   Ah Schnitzel, it's the most beautiful smell in the world!

SCHNITZEL   What is it?

FRANZ   You have to get close to the source, and inhale.

> *FRANZ moves centre stage and inhales deeply.*

SCHNITZEL   What is it, Franz, what is it?

FRANZ   It's an audience!

SCHNITZEL   What does it smell like?

FRANZ   It's the most beautiful smell in the world, Schnitzel! Some of them are nervous, some are excited. Some are wearing expensive perfume, others have pomade in their hair. Some of them have bathed, others have the scent of a long day on them, but it all combines into one glorious aroma, and oh, Schnitzel, look what it's doing to me now!

> *FRANZ has begun to rock, his pelvis moving back and forth.*

SCHNITZEL   No, no! Not that!

FRANZ   Yes! My diamond pants are doing their magic dance again! I've got a woody, I've got a woody! Okay, Schnitzel, get to work!

> *FRANZ starts to leave.*

SCHNITZEL   No!

> *FRANZ turns.*

FRANZ   What did you say to me?

SCHNITZEL   I… said… no.

FRANZ   Where the hell did you learn a word like that?

SCHNITZEL   I don't know, Franz. It just popped into my head.

FRANZ   That's ridiculous, Schnitzel, your head is empty!

SCHNITZEL   It's true, Franz, it is. I just thought it.

FRANZ   You're a puppet, you can't have thoughts of your own.

SCHNITZEL   Lately I've been having all kinds of thoughts. And right now I'm thinking no. No, no, no!

FRANZ   Schnitzel, don't do this to me. Not now!

SCHNITZEL   I'm sorry, Franz, but I can't do it. I just can't.

FRANZ   But, Schnitzel, you always do it. Every show, it's the same thing. I go backstage while you stand out here and act so cute that invariably after the show one of these good people wants to hug you, to kiss you. And just when they're bending over to cuddle you, I jump them from behind and do my diamond pants dance all over them!

SCHNITZEL   No! I refuse to be a pawn in your sick puppet games ever again!

FRANZ   What are you saying?

SCHNITZEL   I've been thinking that maybe I should, well...

FRANZ   Yes?

SCHNITZEL   That perhaps I should...

FRANZ   What?

SCHNITZEL   That maybe it's time for me to strike out on my own.

FRANZ   Oh, I should have known it would come to this.

SCHNITZEL   What do you mean?

FRANZ   Well, it's pretty obvious what your problem is!

SCHNITZEL   Problem? I wasn't aware that I was the one with a problem!

FRANZ   Oh please, Schnitzel, it's all because of where you stand in life.

SCHNITZEL   What's wrong with where I stand? This is where I've always stood. Stage left.

FRANZ   Yeah, well no one stands on the left anymore.

SCHNITZEL   No? Where do they stand?

FRANZ   Over here, on the right.

SCHNITZEL   What's so great about the right?

FRANZ   There's more of us, and we're organized! And besides, we have God on our side!

SCHNITZEL   God doesn't take sides. He's right in the middle.

FRANZ   Not anymore. But I'll tell you what I'm going to do, Schnitzel. I am going to be such a good friend to you. I am going to trade places with you for a moment so you can try out the wonders of the right.

> *He crosses to stage left.*

But make it snappy, because I can't stand on the left too long. Suddenly I feel warm and gooshy and I love humanity, and I hate that shit!

SCHNITZEL Gee, I dunno, Franz...

FRANZ Come on, move it! Any minute now I may want to hug a tree or care about someone other than myself!

SCHNITZEL Okay, I'm going.

> *He strikes a pose, and with melodramatic underscoring and moody lighting begins a "dramatic" cross to stage right.*

Thus begins my journey to the right! Slowly I push my way through change and progress, saying "Back change, back! Be gone!" as I travel to a time where nothing changes, where everything stays the same...

FRANZ Cut the dramatics, would you!

> *Underscoring ends abruptly. Light restores.*

Okay, there you are on the right. Tell me, Schnitzel, how do you feel?

SCHNITZEL I feel kind of cold.

FRANZ That's good, that's necessary. What else?

SCHNITZEL Suddenly I don't care about anyone but myself.

FRANZ Yes, good, Schnitzel! Anything else? Share. Oh shit, that's a "left" word!

SCHNITZEL Well, is it my imagination, Franz, or, on the right, am I becoming whiter?

FRANZ Ah, Schnitzel, you're on the right track now!

> *SCHNITZEL races back to stage left.*

SCHNITZEL No, I can't stay there! It doesn't feel like home.

> *FRANZ goes back to his side.*

FRANZ Nowhere would feel like home to you. You're a freak, Schnitzel. You don't fit in anywhere. Now look, I have to go backstage and figure out tonight's show.

SCHNITZEL But, Franz...

FRANZ We'll discuss this later, Schnitzel. You want to leave the show, fine. But for now, we have an audience. So you stay here and entertain them, understood?

SCHNITZEL Yes, Franz.

FRANZ Good.

> *He starts to leave.*

Oh, and Schnitzel, while you're at it, do something cute so maybe one of them will come backstage and do the magic pants dance with me!

He exits, laughing maniacally. SCHNITZEL walks to centre stage and addresses the audience.

SCHNITZEL   Ladies and Gentlemen, allow me to apologize for my colleague's unruly behaviour. In case you haven't figured it out yet, I'm the good one. Hi, everybody. Wow, look at you. What a sophisticated, hip, urbane, tony crowd with a high disposable income you are. But no matter how sophisticated you are, I know that ever since I've been standing onstage, you've all been wondering the same thing: "What the hell is that thing!"

He sits on the little chair upstage centre.

Don't worry, it happens to me all the time. Truth be told, my friends, I don't know what I am. I never have. Which is not to say I don't have dreams and aspirations of what I would like to become. You heard Franz. I don't fit in, I don't belong here. I've never belonged anywhere. So I don't want to be here. I want to be up there.

He looks and points upwards.

I want to get above it all. I want to fly. I want wings. I want to be a fairy! I want to soar through the sky with the birds and the planes and the bumblebees, without a care in the world, up there in the air. And I want to swoop through the clouds, looking down on humanity and yell: "Hey people, look at me! It's Schnitzel!"

He makes the sound of a large bulls-eye spit on the crowd. He looks up sheepishly.

But you'll notice upon closer observation my friends…

He turns around.

I don't got no wings. Oh, I know I have a cute little bum, but that's only part of being a fairy.

He sits.

Lately, I've been having the strangest thoughts. And that I should have a thought in the first place is strange in and of itself. My head is literally an empty shell. I shouldn't be thinking anything. So, I've begun to wonder if perhaps these thoughts aren't my thoughts at all. Maybe they've been put there by some greater power. Maybe I am but a vessel to be filled with another's thoughts. Maybe I'm being controlled from on high. Maybe I'm just a spokesperson for someone who's too afraid to come down here and say these things himself. And if that's the case, then sometimes I feel like looking up and screaming…

He stands, looking up.

Why are you jerking me around like this?!

So I've decided. I'm going to climb this gold brocade curtain and see if anything or anyone is up there. I want to see the face of my creator. And if I don't make it, if I should fall to the ground and shatter into a hundred broken pieces before you and still continue to talk, then we'll all know it's greater than just you and me. Wish me luck.

> *He stands on the little chair, and with some effort, climbs up the back curtain. Struggling to the top, he grasps the top of the leaning rail and looks at Ronnie's face.*

Wow. He's real. And much older that you'd expect. Excuse me, I need to ask a favour. I'm Schnitzel and I think you've made a mistake. I don't belong down there. I belong up here, with you. So if you could, please, give me my wings.

> *Ronnie releases the marionette control slightly, and SCHNITZEL begins to slip.*

No! Please, don't do this. Don't make me go back there. Don't let go of me, I beg you. Please!

> *He slides all the way down the curtain, landing onstage.*

I hate when he lets me down.

> *He struggles to his feet, and sits in the chair.*

I'm sorry. I shouldn't expect you'd care. I know you didn't come here tonight to listen to me whine and moan. I know why you're here. You've come to see The Franz and Schnitzel Show! So my friends, you will have the spectacle you've paid money to see. Any minute now, I will raise this gold brocade curtain and dazzle you with the variety of acts for which we have become internationally famous! Clowns, contortionists, jugglers and showgirls! Singers and dancers in an extravaganza the likes of which you've never seen! So, without further ado, let us raise the gold brocade cur…

> *From offstage, we hear MADAME Rodrigue.*

MADAME *(offstage)* Darlings!

> *SCHNITZEL, horrified, leaps to his feet.*

SCHNITZEL Oh no!

MADAME *(offstage)* Oh my beautiful darlings!

SCHNITZEL No, it can't be. That's Madame Rodrigue, the fat lady who sings!

MADAME *(offstage)* Darlings, I'm coming to see you!

SCHNITZEL Oh no, this is terrible! She can't come out now. It's too soon. When the fat lady sings, you know what happens. It's over!

MADAME enters, stage right. Her presence, physically and vocally, is overpowering.

MADAME   Darlings! I'm so happy to see you!

Her bosom heaves and flutters.

And now, I shall sing!

SCHNITZEL   No! Madame Rodrigue, you mustn't sing!

MADAME   But Schnitzel, why not? Look at them. So beautiful, so eager. I cannot disappoint them. They've come to hear their beloved diva.

SCHNITZEL   Yes, that's true, but…

MADAME   And so, I sing!

SCHNITZEL   No, not now. It's too soon.

MADAME   But why make them wait? Why torture them any longer?

SCHNITZEL   Well, because…

MADAME   Yes?

SCHNITZEL   Um, because… well… because… they didn't greet you properly, Madame.

She looks at the audience, then whispers to SCHNITZEL.

MADAME   Schnitzel, you're right. Who are these people?

SCHNITZEL   Bus tour? Subscribers? Americans?

MADAME   Ah! That explains everything. There's only one thing to be done.

SCHNITZEL   Punish them by walking offstage in a huff?

MADAME   No, better than that. I will teach them how to greet a superstar!

SCHNITZEL   What?

MADAME   Schnitzel, it's not their fault. Look at them. They're normal. And I am great. So great that I will rise to the occasion and teach them what they need to know!

SCHNITZEL   Okay. I'll help you.

MADAME   No, I work alone.

SCHNITZEL   But I really think I should.

MADAME   Schnitzel, it takes two hands to make my boobies go up and down, and they love that. So get off the stage!

SCHNITZEL   Um, sure thing, Madame.

He walks to the edge of the stage, and whispers to the audience.

Ladies and gentlemen, it appears that I must vacate the stage, but I must ask you for a favour. Please, no matter what happens out here, do not let Madame Rodrigue sing this early in the show. Do you promise?

Invariably, someone yells "I promise."

Well don't yell it, she'll hear you! Do you promise?

Audience members whisper "I promise."

Thank you, everyone. I'll see you later. Bye!

He runs off stage left. MADAME watches him leave, then fixes her gaze on the audience.

MADAME   My darlings, there are certain rules and traditions in the theatre which must be upheld at all times. One of the most popular, for both audience and artist alike, is the greeting of the superstar diva! Since this didn't happen naturally and spontaneously when I first graced the stage tonight, I shall now have to browbeat and bully you into doing it properly.

But not to worry, my beautiful darlings; Madame Rodrigue will make it easy for you. I will break it down into three easy steps. We shall learn each step individually, and then we'll put it all together. What fun for you. Let's begin!

Step one. Before I came out tonight, I had the great good courtesy to warn you of my impending arrival. I stood backstage and cried, "Darlings, I'm coming to see you!" Now, this is the part of the show when you get so excited you say to yourself, "No! It can't be! Not tonight. Not at these insanely low ticket prices would a superstar diva actually come out onstage and sing for a nobody like me!" But you hear me, calling from backstage, so it must be true. And in your excitement, you nudge the person sitting beside you three times in the ribs, like so:

Her elbow makes a "nudging" action.

"Nudge, nudge, nudge. Could it be? Could it be?!"

Now, we're going to give this a test run. But first, some tips on technique. I find it very helpful if you verbalize the nudge as you physicalize it. So, when doing step one, you must say, "Nudge, nudge, nudge," followed by your squeal of delight with "Could it be? Could it be?!"

Now, of course, if you have people sitting on both sides of you, you will do the double-armed nudge, like so?

She nudges with both elbows.

"Nudge, nudge, nudge," which, by the looks of it, to many of you would be called dancing.

We are going to give this a try. But first, a word of warning. If for any reason some of you decide not to participate in "Nudge, nudge, nudge. Could it be? Could it be?!" be advised that Madame Rodrigue will have the house lights turned up and I will make you stand up one at a time to do it properly. You think I'm kidding? Try me. Don't fuck with a puppet! You'll only get splinters.

I can hear you. I know what you're thinking. "Oh Madame, surely you're not so drunk with power that you would embarrass your beloved audience?" Well I can, and I will. It's one of the perks of being a diva. For you see, back there at the rear of the theatre, is a lovely man operating the lights. And as always happens to Madame when she performs in any theatre, someone on the crew falls hopelessly in love with me. It's true. Why just last night, that dear man pounded on my dressing room door for three hours! I finally let him out. But he adores me nonetheless, and if I ask him to turn the lights up on all of you, he will! So let's all just do it properly the first time and no one will get hurt.

Here we go, on the count of three. One, two, three: "Nudge, nudge, nudge. Could it be? Could it be?!"

> *Depending on how well (or poorly) the audience participates, MADAME will either commend them on their effort, chastise them accordingly, or single out specific culprits to stand up and do the action solo.*

Very good, my beautiful darlings! So, onward. Step two. Once you have heard my voice backstage and start nudging in anticipation, you work yourself up into an absolute frenzy when I actually come onstage. Well, I don't "come" onstage, I *arrive*, but nevertheless it's very exciting for you. I appear from behind the curtain and stand here…

> *She walks to stage right.*

…striking a humble little superstar diva pose like this!

> *One arm is thrust into the air triumphantly.*

Look, I shaved for you people tonight! Seeing me here, standing before you onstage, sends you right over the edge and you involuntarily and spontaneously cry out: "It is! It is! It's Madame Rodrigue!"

Now, my darlings. A tip on getting your voices into the higher octave required to successfully master this step. I myself am a trained professional, but you, my darlings, are merely the public. So listen carefully. I personally find it very helpful if you clench your sphincter with all your might while screaming. How many nights have I said that? But anyway, by tightening up, it allows you to get it up so your voice will sail high and free. Trust me, darlings, master this technique and you will squeal like a twelve-year-old girl on a pony ride!

Let's give it a try, on the count of three. One, two, three: "It is! It is! It's Madame Rodrigue!"

As before, the success of the audience attempt dictates MADAME's response to it. She will often have the men in the audience try it once by themselves.

Marvellous! We have now reached the most exciting part of how to greet a superstar diva. I will make my way to the centre of the stage, but I do not just clomp over there. No! I do not just walk. No! I float, I fly, I sail on the wings of your love, which translated into theatre parlance means you clap.

Don't do it yet, I'm explaining. Now, as I make my way to the centre of the stage, you begin to applaud. I walk, you applaud, I walk, you applaud, I walk walk walk, you applaud applaud applaud. When I reach my destination, a simple little superstar diva spotlight will come on, at which point I will bow a humble little superstar diva bow. I bow to you here, I bow to you there, and I say: "Stop! Stop it! You're too kind, oh stop!"

Now, this is the part of the show when so many people get confused. When Madame Rodrigue says: "Stop! Stop it! You're too kind, oh stop!" some people actually do. No no no no no. Darlings, when a superstar diva says: "Stop! Stop it! You're too kind, oh stop!" you think to yourself "No! My diva is displeased. My adoration is not enough for her. She will leave the stage in a diva-esque rage unless I make her stay!" So, you begin to applaud even louder, you whistle and cheer, you stamp your feet, you clap until your hands bleed, and only when Madame Rodrigue sits down on the little bench, like so…

She sits.

…do you stop applauding. Could anything be simpler? Now, we're going to put all three of these steps together and have a little rehearsal of the entire sequence of how to greet a superstar diva. I'll go backstage, I'll say "Oh my darlings, I'm coming to see you!," you'll say "Nudge, nudge, nudge. Could it be? Could it be?!" I arrive onstage and strike a humble superstar diva pose, you scream "It is! It is! It's Madame Rodrigue!" music will play, I will walk, the spotlight snaps on and you applaud until you faint! Won't this be fun! Let's give it a try.

She runs offstage.

Darlings, I'm coming to see you!

Hopefully the audience knows by now to say "Nudge, nudge, nudge. Could it be? Could it be?!" MADAME sweeps in, striking her pose with one arm in the air. The audience (or part thereof) screams "It is! It is! It's Madame Rodrigue!" Epic fanfare music plays as she walks to centre stage, the spotlight comes on, she bows and all the while the audience applauds.

Stop it! Stop it! You're too kind, oh stop!

The audience goes mad. This is milked with little regard to taste, until finally she sits. The applause subsides.

Now don't you feel like you've gone out for the night?! And what a lovely way
to meet a stranger sitting in the dark beside you! Thank you, my darlings, my
beautiful darlings! And because you have greeted me so warmly, in the only way
that a superstar diva should be greeted, now, my darlings, now I shall give you
what you want. Now I will sing!

> *She stands and strikes a dramatic pose, her head in profile. Upon*
> *her announcement that she will sing, one or many of the audience,*
> *remembering SCHNITZEL's exhortation to them, will blurt out "No!"*
> *MADAME does a slow burn to the audience.*

What?

My darlings, you shock me. You surprise me. I had no idea that you were
sophisticated. Looking at you, who would know? But you do, don't you? You
know that a superstar diva should never sing this early in the show. You know
that she must close the show in a glorious burst of song. My darlings, you have
saved me from humiliating myself!

And I know what you're thinking. You want to cry out "Madame, no! Do not
sing in that shabby, albeit fabulous, tutu you wear backstage. Go, put on your
new concert gown, and come out later looking every inch the superstar diva you
are and always will be!"

Fine. If that's what you want, my darlings, then that is what you'll get! I am but
a humble servant to art and public acclaim. I will go backstage and prepare
myself for my second coming.

> *She starts to leave.*

And just think! When I return later in the show, you already know how to greet
me! Now, send me off with your love!

> *She sweeps off to applause. SCHNITZEL theme music begins.*

SCHNITZEL   Hi everybody! It's me, Schnitzel, and this is my cute re-entrance
music.

> *He does a little dance. He sits on the chair as the music ends.*

Wow, what a terrific audience! Thank you so much, my friends, for ensuring
that Madame Rodrigue didn't sing this early in the show. And because you
have been so helpful, now I will give you what you want. Now you shall have the
fantastic Franz and Schnitzel Show! So, without further ado, let us raise the gold
brocade cur...

> *We hear FRANZ from offstage, and he races in from stage right.*

FRANZ   No, Schnitzel! Don't raise the curtain!

SCHNITZEL   But, Franz, they're a wonderful audience.

FRANZ   Trust me, Schnitzel, there's nothing for them to see behind the curtain.

SCHNITZEL   Don't be silly, Franz, that's where all the stuff is!

FRANZ   No, Schnitzel, there's nothing back there. I got rid of everything.

SCHNITZEL   What are you talking about?

FRANZ   I sold all the scenery and costumes. I fired the band, the showgirls, the novelty acts. Everything. It's all gone.

SCHNITZEL   Why would you do a thing like that, Franz?

FRANZ   Schnitzel, you know how we thought everyone wanted to see our lavish production numbers, comic turns and elaborate stage effects?

SCHNITZEL   Of course, that's what's made us famous!

FRANZ   Well I've been doing some research for tonight's show, Schnitzel, and it turns out that's not what these people want.

SCHNITZEL   But they want a show, Franz.

FRANZ   Yes, but not that old-style entertainment we've been doing.

SCHNITZEL   No?

FRANZ   No.

SCHNITZEL   Then what?

FRANZ   They want post-modern new millennium electronic Dutch dance wank performance art!

SCHNITZEL   Huh. What's that?

FRANZ   No one really knows. And that's the beauty of it, Schnitzel! You can present anything onstage, call it that and they'll love it.

SCHNITZEL   I don't understand.

FRANZ   Neither will they!

SCHNITZEL   It doesn't sound very entertaining.

FRANZ   Oh, it should never be entertaining, Schnitzel. See, if you give them something that's accessible, they'll call it sentimental crap. But if you give them crap that's inaccessible, they'll call it art!

SCHNITZEL   Art?

FRANZ   Art! And that's what we're going to do tonight.

SCHNITZEL   I don't know much about art.

FRANZ   You don't have to. In fact, lack of training is a prerequisite. Never let vision be muddied by technique.

SCHNITZEL   So what are we going to do, Franz?

FRANZ   It's easy. I'll put on some discordant synthesized cello music, turn the lights down and you'll throw yourself around the stage naked!

SCHNITZEL   But that's not about anything, Franz!

FRANZ   Precisely! Which is why they'll read all sorts of things into it!

SCHNITZEL   Franz, I can't.

FRANZ   You have to. We have an audience expecting a show, and we are going to give them a show they'll never forget.

SCHNITZEL   But...

FRANZ   The only butt on this stage will be yours, Schnitzel! You want to leave the show? Fine. But for now, we're in the middle of this show and you're still one half of this team.

SCHNITZEL   Franz, I don't want to. I can't!

FRANZ becomes frighteningly menacing.

FRANZ   Don't make me angry, Schnitzel. You wouldn't want me to get angry in front of your friends out there, would you?

SCHNITZEL   No, Franz.

FRANZ   Good boy. Now, we have to go backstage and rehearse the new show, so say goodbye, Schnitzel, and tell them you'll be back later.

SCHNITZEL   Ladies and gentlemen, um, it appears that there will be a few changes in this evening's performance, so I invite you to join us again later for the second part of the all new...

FRANZ   All nude!

SCHNITZEL   ...Franz and Schnitzel Show!

FRANZ   See ya later!

The spirited Franz and Schnitzel theme music plays again, the lights flashing along in time. FRANZ and SCHNITZEL are hung onstage, Ronnie jumps down and pushes the puppet stage upstage right.

Scene Four
Backstage at the Cabaret—Rust and Blue Palette

Ronnie takes the marionettes of HETTIE and BENJAMIN off of a carousel animal and walks them around the acting ring from upstage right to downstage right as they talk.

HETTIE Benjamin, I cannot begin to tell you how unhappy I am with you right now.

BENJAMIN Oh, Hettie, please.

HETTIE Don't "Hettie please" me, Ben! You knew they closed this sector when you agreed to come with me tonight.

BENJAMIN I know that, Hettie, but it's not a good time for me to be away from home.

HETTIE Then why did you agree to go out with me?

BENJAMIN Have I ever said no to you, Hettie?

> *HETTIE flings herself dramatically against Ronnie's leg.*

HETTIE Take me, Ben! Make me a woman! I want to have your baby!

BENJAMIN No!

HETTIE See, you're perfectly capable of saying no to me. Now, would you relax? Lilly and the kids are already asleep. Once daylight comes, I'll walk you home.

BENJAMIN But where are we going to sleep?

HETTIE Sleep? Oh Ben, that's rich! You don't sleep in this sector. And besides, the night has just begun!

> *BENJAMIN is hung in place stage right, while HETTIE goes upstage centre to the carousel.*

Morag, you old queen! Get your saggy butt out here and let's start the party!

MORAG *(offstage)* Hettie, please! I'm in the middle of my *toilette*!

HETTIE Dames.

MORAG *(offstage)* Dykes.

> *MORAG enters. They embrace.*

Darling!

HETTIE Quite the show tonight, old girl.

MORAG Oh stop! Did you love it?

HETTIE What's not to love? Why, your re-creation of Lot's wife looking back was breathtaking. Art at its highest!

MORAG You know me… anything for a Sodom and Gomorrah theme onstage. Orgies always sell.

HETTIE Your use of feathers to replicate a pillar of salt was magnificent!

MORAG One makes do with what one has. But darling, *qu'est-ce que c'est?*

HETTIE is hung upstage centre. MORAG walks towards BENJAMIN.

HETTIE   Benjamin, meet Morag.

BENJAMIN   Morag? Not the woman who played Mrs. Lot? But you're a...

MORAG   Star?

BENJAMIN   Man!

MORAG   Darling, I'm thrilled the illusion worked for you, but surely you didn't think I was "biological"?

BENJAMIN   Oh... my... word. Wait till I tell Lilly about this!

MORAG   Lilly?

HETTIE   His wife.

MORAG   You have a wife. How... normal. Ben, excuse me for a moment, won't you? Hang around.

   MORAG grabs HETTIE by the arm and walks her stage left.

Hettie, what are you doing? Bringing someone so normal to the show!

HETTIE   Relax, Morag. He's one of us. ·

MORAG   Straight, white, male... married. He's not one of us at all. Why do those people always have to be in our clubs? Don't they have enough places of their own?

HETTIE   By proxy he is one of us. His wife Lilly has just been classified as "racially impure." You can imagine how thrilled The Common Good was with that marriage. Especially after the third kid.

MORAG   Well, why didn't you say so!

   MORAG turns and rushes to BENJAMIN.

Darling, welcome to The Penis Flytrap!

BENJAMIN   Thank you, Miss... I mean, Mister...

MORAG   "Morag" will be fine.

BENJAMIN   Morag. Thank you. Well, Morag, that show tonight was quite a revelation.

MORAG   Revelations are next week, darling. I'm still trying to get through *The Great Broads of the Old Testament.*

BENJAMIN   That's funny!

   Pause.

Isn't it?

MORAG It depends on your point of view, Ben.

HETTIE I don't think The Common Good would find it too hilarious.

MORAG Nor do I find them very amusing. So we're even.

> *MORAG crosses back to HETTIE stage left.*

HETTIE Still, it's pretty dangerous ground you're walking on, Morag.

MORAG Hettie Louise McKinley! You're a fine one to lecture me about dangerous ground. Exactly how many times has your writing caused you to be thrown in jail?

HETTIE Oh, I don't know. Thirty-three.

MORAG Thirty-three! A significant number, wouldn't you say? Especially when it comes to crucifixion.

HETTIE Morag, I'm not being crucified. I'm just misunderstood.

MORAG How I long for the good old days of just misunderstood.

> *CARL calls from offstage.*

CARL *(offstage)* Morag, are you finished in here?

MORAG No darling, I'm not. I'm *en déshabillé*, a disaster in fuzzy slippers.

HETTIE Is that him?

MORAG Carl? Yes.

HETTIE I can't wait to meet him.

MORAG Now, Hettie, please don't eat the young. He's different.

HETTIE Aren't we all.

MORAG Well, I'd better go get my titties off the table before someone cooks them.

BENJAMIN What?

MORAG Rice, darling. They're little bags of rice.

BENJAMIN Huh?

MORAG You really are crashingly naïve for an outcast, aren't you? Come along, I'll show you.

> *MORAG grabs BENJAMIN and starts leading him off toward the carousel.*

BENJAMIN Uh, no that's fine... really...

MORAG Oh come along, Ben, we'll have a gay old time!

MORAG and BENJAMIN are hung together on a carousel animal.

BENJAMIN   Hettie, help!

HETTIE   Relax, Ben. Believe me, you're not Morag's type.

> *HETTIE is left hanging onstage. CARL is taken from his animal and enters.*

So, I finally meet the great man himself!

CARL   Look, if you've waited to critique me, you're too late.

HETTIE   You really are a one-man show, aren't you? Even write the reviews.

CARL   Well, I assume you saw it. Didn't go very well.

HETTIE   No?

CARL   No. At first, I thought it was the audience. But they were fine. It was me. I was trying to say too much, and, as a result, I don't think I said anything at all.

HETTIE   Trying too hard for the laughs?

CARL   That's what I do when I'm nervous.

HETTIE   Well, I'd say you have a lot to be nervous about. Look, you don't know me, Carl, but for what it's worth maybe you *were* trying too hard. You forgot that to most of the audience those were brand new characters. They needed time to digest them, get to know them. But you believed in yourself up there. A little too much at times…

CARL   What makes you think I want to listen to this?

HETTIE   Because it's all about you. And I think that fascinates you. Am I right?

> *CARL is silent.*

I knew I was right. Just like you did tonight. You had something to say, and you were hell-bent to say it. And that's fine, don't get me wrong. But say it through the puppets, kid. Make us believe in them so much that we forget it's you. Don't forget your technique, Carl. That's what supports your voice. Or is it your calling?

CARL   I'm beginning to think it might be.

HETTIE   Pretty lonely thing, a calling.

CARL   Oh? And who are you to know anything about that?

HETTIE   I'm Hettie Louise McKinley.

CARL   The writer?

HETTIE   Oh, essayist, poet, radical, shit-disturber… writer will do just fine. But tonight I suspect I'm Hettie Louise McKinley, Welcome Wagon. Welcome to the club, Carl.

CARL   I don't follow you.

HETTIE   You will. You're in, honey. Or, you're out, depending on how you look at it. You became a card-carrying member of the outcasts the minute you stood on that stage tonight and opened your mouth.

CARL   But I didn't do anything. All I did was a puppet show.

HETTIE   Well, there's no going home now, Carl.

CARL   That's crazy. I have to go home. All my things…

HETTIE   You've got your puppets and your stage. What more do you need?

CARL   My sister, Tinka. She's here too.

HETTIE   Well then, she's in it too.

CARL   But…

HETTIE   You don't understand, do you? Look kid, there were a few Disciple Brethren in that club tonight and you can bet that by tomorrow morning you'll be on the list. If you go home, you'll be in jail. You and Tinka.

CARL   What have I done.

HETTIE   Like you said. Just a puppet show. But hey, they've set up a whole sector just for us! And believe me honey, all the fun people are outcasts. Some call it the ghetto. That's a bit too artsy fartsy for my taste. The Common Good refer to it as the Central Reprocessing Zone, but I find that a bit sterile. No, I like to call it The Camp.

CARL   That's a horrible name.

HETTIE   Not really. If you can think of it as a camp, it makes the mud and the dirt and the cold seem kinda fun, almost outdoorsy. For tonight though, we're stuck in the luxury of this sector.

> *She starts walking toward the carousel.*

See you inside?

CARL   Where else would I go?

HETTIE   You catch on quickly, kid. But don't sulk too long… the party's for you.

> *HETTIE is hung on the carousel. TINKA #2 is taken off and walks to CARL.*

TINKA   Carl, come inside. Let's celebrate your success.

CARL   Oh, Tinka, there's nothing to celebrate.

TINKA   Yes there is. You did it. Tonight you made Franz and Schnitzel your own.

CARL   Tinka, I've done a terrible thing. I didn't think. I only thought about myself. I didn't take care of you.

> *She walks to him and places a hand on his shoulder.*

TINKA   Maybe it's my turn to take care of you, Carl. Maybe that's why I packed our clothes in the puppet trunks this morning. I hear it gets awfully cold in The Camp.

CARL   How did you know?

> *She walks to centre stage.*

TINKA   Carl, I knew. I've always known that when you finally took your big risk, it would be the beginning of a new life for us again. Do you hear me? For us, Carl. We're family. I'm with you, wherever this may lead.

> *Carousel music begins, softly.*

CARL   Tinka, did you enjoy the show?

TINKA   Um, yes. Very much.

> *CARL walks toward TINKA.*

CARL   But?

TINKA   Be careful what you say, Carl. We're in strange territory now.

> *Lights change, dimming instantly on the acting area. Ronnie hangs up the two puppets. The music becomes solo accordion, with a decidedly gypsy flavour.*

Scene Five
The Camp—Green and Mauve Palette

Ronnie moves The Populace into new positions, beginning with the Boy, then the Thin Woman, the Fat Woman, the Thin Man, the Fat Man, and finally The Officer. From within the carousel ring, he takes a (puppet scale) trunk and places it upstage centre left on the acting ring. Once this is in place, he moves the carousel into the next position and the lights shift. The season is now autumn.

The figures of both TINKA #3 and MORAG #2 are taken from one animal. MORAG is without a turban or makeup this time, revealing a diminishing pate and a very distinct shadow of facial hair. However, his garb is a wildly exotic, half-finished woman's gown. TINKA is dressed plainly, her clothes somewhat drab.

As the lights and music complete their transition, MORAG is standing on top of the trunk with TINKA at ground level, fiddling with his hem.

TINKA   Morag, would you please stop squirming!

MORAG   I have to be sure that I can move, darling.

TINKA   And I have to be sure that you don't trip the minute you walk onstage. Now hold still.

MORAG   Oh, I'm too excited. Finally, a character worthy of a Tinka gown!

TINKA   Your dress for Mrs. Noah was nice.

MORAG turns and looks down at TINKA.

MORAG   My dear, that was not a dress. It was a boat. No, I will not be sad to say goodbye to the women of the Old Testament.

TINKA   Turn please.

MORAG turns around again.

Five months is a long time to do the same show.

MORAG   And that's the edited version! At least I had the sense to skip Esther. I mean really, I ask you Tinka, what kind of queen would call herself Esther in the first place?

TINKA   Well, I think you've made the right choice with Jezebel.

MORAG   Sometimes I feel as though Jezebel has chosen me.

TINKA   Oh? Because she too was a queen known for her hideous end?

MORAG jumps off the trunk and sits on it.

MORAG   Good one! I think a certain young miss has been spending far too much time with me these past few months.

TINKA sits on the other edge of the trunk.

TINKA   Well, Morag, I guess I can't get enough of a good thing.

MORAG   Nor I, petal, nor I.

MORAG puts his head on her lap.

No, Jezebel was an outsider. A foreigner. A scapegoat. Thrown to the street as mere dog food. With each passing day, I begin to understand the old girl a bit more. And with each passing night at the cabaret, their final solution becomes more apparent.

TINKA   What are you going to do?

He sits up and faces front.

MORAG   Exactly what Jezebel did. Paint my face, and greet my enemies as a queen!

TINKA   Oh, Morag.

MORAG   Fear not, beloved. It's just metaphor. I trust there are a few in my audience who still understand that. For Carl, however, I fear it may be his undoing.

TINKA   But he's not at the cabaret anymore. It was your idea that he leave.

MORAG   Yes, and for selfish reasons.

TINKA   You were just protecting him.

MORAG   And myself. Carl was becoming far too dangerous, even for my taste. Night after night, more and more Disciple Brethren coming to see him, more and more Holy Army Officers hovering around. Luckily for us, The Common Good is too wrapped up in its own rhetoric to understand our metaphor.

TINKA   Well, he's safe here.

MORAG   No, Tinka, he's not. You're both in far greater danger here.

TINKA   In The Camp? Morag, who cares about a puppet show for displaced people?

MORAG   The Common Good cares, darling, and they're still watching. Don't you tell me this is mere entertainment. This is not some harmless little puppet show for forgotten people.

TINKA has walked toward stage left, indicating The Populace.

TINKA   But it is, Morag. Every night these people come to see Carl's show. They sit in the dirt and the cold to forget.

MORAG   And to listen. It's dangerous enough that Carl continues to speak, but perilous too for those who will listen.

TINKA   Would you want him to stop?

MORAG   Would you?

TINKA   It's beyond the point of even considering. When we first began, Carl couldn't wait to get onstage, to smell the audience, to talk to them, the sheer thrill of performing. Now, each new day brings another atrocity, another rule enforced, another freedom given away. Taken away. And he has to discuss it through the puppets. He just has to.

She sits on the trunk.

MORAG   But what about you, Tinka? I've already told you that I would protect you, as best I could. Tinka, I love you. I'm in love with you.

> *He turns away. TINKA reaches across the trunk and places her hand on his.*

TINKA Morag. Morag, I love you too. But really, how you go on. I'm not enslaved to Carl. I choose to be here.

MORAG Well then, your honour, she's guilty by association!

> *MORAG throws himself across the trunk, landing in a dramatic, campy position.*

TINKA You're such a drama queen.

MORAG Thank you, darling, it's a living.

TINKA Let's finish the costume tomorrow, okay? I have some repairs to do on the puppets before tonight's show.

MORAG Ooh, and what's on the bill tonight?

TINKA I have no idea, Morag. Carl's out trying to find a newspaper.

MORAG A newspaper? Well, if that's where he gets his inspiration, I'm afraid he's merely reading press releases from The Common Good.

TINKA Not their newspapers, Morag. The underground one that Hettie writes for.

MORAG Ah, Hettie. There's another one whose time is running out.

TINKA Please, Morag, don't.

MORAG I'm sorry, petal. How is the old cow?

TINKA I don't know. We haven't seen her in awhile.

> *An announcement is played, prefaced by The Common Good theme.*

THE VOICE "Free passage in and out of this sector will be forbidden, beginning in fifteen minutes. This has been a message from The Common Good."

MORAG Well, there's my cue. I don't dare saunter through the gates in this ensemble. The guards can barely keep their hands off me as it is. Brutes! So, I'll leave the cossy in your tent. See you tomorrow?

TINKA Uh huh. Have a good show tonight.

MORAG And you, darling, and you. Whatever that brother of yours decides it to be.

> *MORAG walks upstage toward the carousel, where he is hung in his starting position.*

TINKA Bye.

She waves and walks to centre, then looks back to where MORAG has exited. Transition music starts and TINKA crosses to the puppet stage upstage right. She briefly stops in front of The Officer, and looks at him for a moment.

Excuse me.

She passes him and is hung near the Franz and Schnitzel stage. Ronnie walks through the carousel to upstage left, where he takes the marionettes of MRS. VAN CRAIG #2 and ISAËL #1 from a carousel animal. ISAËL is carrying two elaborate gowns. They walk through the figures of The Populace.

ISAËL   Really, Auntie, this is quite mad.

MRS. VAN CRAIG   Then let it be a mad adventure, Isaël.

ISAËL   What adventure could there possibly be in such squalor? Auntie, look at these people!

MRS. VAN CRAIG   Isaël, they are your species. And the people in The Camp are undoubtedly the best and the brightest. You could stand to learn a thing or two from them.

ISAËL   To what end? My own, no doubt.

MRS. VAN CRAIG   They are artists and intellectuals. Thinkers, Isaël. People to whom thought is the very life-breath. Really, why do you people fear them so?

ISAËL   "You people"? Auntie listen to yourself, you're beginning to sound like a... bohemian! Have you forgotten the difference between yourself and these people?

MRS. VAN CRAIG   No dear, I have not. Nor have I forgotten a time when differences were celebrated, not condemned.

ISAËL   Individuality leads to chaos. Only through collective consensus can an ordered society prosper.

MRS. VAN CRAIG   Bravo, Isaël! I had no idea that you had committed The Common Good's mantras to memory.

ISAËL   It's not a mantra, Auntie, it's a will. A unified will.

MRS. VAN CRAIG   Well, will you give me a display of this civility you hold so dear?

ISAËL   But Auntie...

MRS. VAN CRAIG   No buts! Now, I have a very good friend here, and I am not about to let you offend her with your juvenile fervour.

An announcement is played, with the musical sting.

THE VOICE   "Free passage in and out of this sector will be forbidden, beginning in ten minutes. This has been a message from The Common Good."

ISAËL   If your friend was truly of any value, you wouldn't be meeting in a place like this.

> *They have reached centre stage left. MRS. VAN CRAIG indicates the trunk.*

MRS. VAN CRAIG   Oh, Isaël, put the dresses down before you soil them.

> *ISAËL puts the dresses down on top of the trunk.*

ISAËL   This is quite ridiculous. There's your precious cargo. Now please Auntie, let's go.

MRS. VAN CRAIG   You go, dear, and wait for me at the gates.

ISAËL   What? I'm not leaving you here alone.

MRS. VAN CRAIG   I won't be alone. Besides, I've been here many times, dear.

ISAËL   Oh, Auntie, what are you up to?

MRS. VAN CRAIG   Mmm, who knows, Isaël? Perhaps I'm a secret messenger for the outcasts!

ISAËL   That's dangerous talk, Auntie, even in jest. I'm not leaving until I meet this friend of yours.

MRS. VAN CRAIG   You'll meet her, dear. When it's appropriate. I simply needed you to carry the dresses. Now go, I won't be long.

ISAËL   Auntie, for your own good…

MRS. VAN CRAIG   My good! The Common Good! Good God, Isaël! Would you shut up and leave an old woman to her folly!

ISAËL   I'm… sorry.

> *He starts off, toward the carousel.*

Don't miss the curfew, Auntie.

MRS. VAN CRAIG   Isaël. Isaël.

> *He pauses.*

Thank you, dear. I won't be long.

ISAËL   Crazy old woman.

> *ISAËL is hung on a carousel animal.*

MRS. VAN CRAIG   Ah youth.

> *MRS. VAN CRAIG walks toward the puppet stage, stage right.*

Tinka? Tinka, dear? Are you there?

TINKA appears from behind the puppet stage.

TINKA   Mrs. Van Craig.

MRS. VAN CRAIG   Now dear, what have I told you about that?

TINKA   I'm sorry. Hello... Astrid.

MRS. VAN CRAIG   That's better. Now I do hope I'm not interrupting.

TINKA   No, I was just doing repairs on some of the puppets.

MRS. VAN CRAIG   And how are my little friends today?

TINKA   They're fine, Astrid. They survive better in this place than most of us.

MRS. VAN CRAIG   Ah yes, but is survival with a wooden heart a life worth living?

TINKA   It's so good to see you again.

They embrace.

MRS. VAN CRAIG   And you, my dear. Now come, we've not much time and I do want you to see what I've brought for you today.

She leads TINKA toward the dresses on the trunk. TINKA sees them and rushes to them.

TINKA   Oh, Astrid, they're beautiful. They're the most beautiful gowns I've ever seen.

TINKA kneels in front of them as MRS. VAN CRAIG comes up behind her.

MRS. VAN CRAIG   They are very old.

TINKA   But extraordinary.

MRS. VAN CRAIG   At one time they meant a very great deal to me. With your skill, Tinka, I hope you will re-create them into something that will be special to you.

TINKA stands and faces her.

TINKA   No, I couldn't. Thank you, but no. These are too perfect to be changed.

MRS. VAN CRAIG   They are too perfect not to be changed. They should live on, and they are of no use to me now. Once, as a girl your age, I wore this gown to a magnificent party.

She indicates the darker dress.

TINKA   You must have been beautiful that night.

MRS. VAN CRAIG   I think perhaps I was. It was at that party I first met Theo Van Craig. And a year later...

> *She indicates the other dress. It is gold embroidery on aged net, in an old floor-length style.*

...I wore this. My wedding gown. It's faded, but the workmanship endures. And I'm certain there's more than enough fabric to make yourself a stunning new gown.

TINKA   Astrid, I have no need for a dress like this. Look where I am.

MRS. VAN CRAIG   I'm giving a party next week, and I want you there. And don't tell me you have nothing to wear.

TINKA   But I don't have clearance to enter your sector.

MRS. VAN CRAIG   That's all arranged. My driver will pick you up at the gates and bring you safely to my door. And bring Carl, won't you.

TINKA   No. That would be too dangerous for him. And you.

MRS. VAN CRAIG   Yes, I know. I had hoped that Carl might perform at my party, but that's quite impossible. And I know it's old fashioned of me, but I was hoping you'd have an escort.

TINKA   There is someone. A friend. I could bring him, if you wouldn't mind.

MRS. VAN CRAIG   No, not at all. Tell me, Tinka, is he special?

TINKA   Very.

MRS. VAN CRAIG   Then I shall be delighted to meet him.

> *An announcement is played, with musical sting:*

THE VOICE   "Free passage in and out of this sector will be forbidden, beginning in five minutes. This has been a message from The Common Good."

TINKA   Astrid, you should go now.

MRS. VAN CRAIG   Yes, I know. On one of my next visits, perhaps I'll intentionally miss that blasted curfew.

TINKA   Well then, you'd better wear something warmer.

MRS. VAN CRAIG   Yes, autumn is upon us. Next week then?

TINKA   Next week.

> *They embrace. MRS. VAN CRAIG walks upstage, then turns.*

MRS. VAN CRAIG   Tinka, I've sewn some money into the lining of the wedding dress. Keep Carl fed. He'll need his strength.

MRS. VAN CRAIG walks to the carousel, excusing herself to The Populace as she leaves.

Good day, madam. Excuse me, dear, I'm coming through…

MRS. VAN CRAIG is hung in place on an animal. Music in: the Tinka theme. TINKA looks after MRS. VAN CRAIG, then goes to the trunk and picks up the wedding dress. She moves with the music and dances with the dress. Showing it to the rest of The Populace. The action indicates a make-believe party, and TINKA curtsys and flirts with the male figures. Realizing where she is, she places the dress back on the trunk. As the lights fade to a pool over the trunk, TINKA kneels, resting her cheek on the dress. Lights fade slowly on the tableau.

The music changes to the carousel waltz. The acting ring lights have dimmed and the carousel lights have crossfaded up. Ronnie takes TINKA and the trunk and places them upstage centre, behind the carousel pole. He brings out a bench unit from upstage left. He then gathers up The Populace and arranges them on the stage left side. He grabs a bench unit from upstage right and arranges The Populace on that side. These units are two benches with large and ornate picture frames fastened behind them. The frames are empty and The Populace are seen through them. At the top of each frame are hooks from which the marionettes may be hung in a seated position. Upstage of the stage right bench, he places the Thin Man. Downstage left of the other bench he places the Little Girl.

Ronnie grabs the Little Boy figure, regarding him for a moment before placing the boy face down on the carousel ring. The carousel is revolved to the next scene.

Scene Six
The Party—Brown and Gold Palette

Ronnie takes MRS. VAN CRAIG #3 from the animal on which she is seated, lights shift and she sweeps into the centre of the acting ring. She is the consummate hostess, wearing a magnificent, albeit older-style gown. As in Scene One when STEPHAN addressed The Populace, so too does MRS. VAN CRAIG address her "party guests."

MRS. VAN CRAIG   Hello! Thank you all so very much for coming.

She walks to the Fat Man stage left and addresses him.

Doctor, how good to see you. Never better, thank you. And you? Yes, I agree. It is our country which is experiencing the poor health. One wonders whether the cancer can be defeated, or if it has spread too far.

To the Thin Woman beside him:

No madam, I do not blaspheme our government. These are but the autumnal musings of an old woman, longing for her faded springtime. What better remedy for our malaise than a party!

MRS. VAN CRAIG leaves them and crosses the stage, muttering to herself.

I don't recall inviting her.

She reaches the figures stage right, and noticing the Mother figure, does a semi-curtsy to her.

Baroness! My dear, how good of you to come.

She speaks in a more confidential tone:

I've heard your husband's stand against The Common Good. You are both in our hearts. My word, no, I didn't know. Exiled from the land he loves. Yes, we must hold on to that dream. Have you plans to…

Light and music theme up to reveal the figure of The Officer, standing upstage right. MRS. VAN CRAIG takes notice of The Officer, and walks to him.

Good evening, Officer. May I be of some assistance? No need for that, this is a private *soirée*. Really? And since when has The Common Good decided to monitor private affairs? I see. Well, I trust you know how to behave yourself at such an event.

She starts to walk away, but turns to add:

Oh, and Officer, I would appreciate it if you didn't help yourself to the refreshments.

Ronnie takes FIPSI #2 off of an animal. She is wearing a slinky and revealing gold gown.

FIPSI Mrs. Van Craig, what a glittering affair!

MRS. VAN CRAIG Fipsi, what a daring gown! Tell me dear, is this the official garb of our newest State Artist?

FIPSI No, but it is the unofficial gift of a state admirer!

MRS. VAN CRAIG My, you certainly are reaping great rewards.

FIPSI One reaps as one sows Mrs. Van Craig. I've worked very hard to find favour with the right people.

MRS. VAN CRAIG No doubt you have. Well, if you'd like to bring in your equipment for a show, I could have some of the staff assist you.

FIPSI No need for that. My own people are bringing it in now. The Common Good has usurped all sorts of little worker people for such purposes, which gives me ample time to mingle with your elite gathering.

MRS. VAN CRAIG   Well then, we'd best find someone for you to mingle with. Oh look! There's Walter Lichtenfels.

FIPSI   The composer? I've been dying to meet him.

MRS. VAN CRAIG   Yes, well don't lay down yet, dear.

> *MRS. VAN CRAIG leads FIPSI to the stage right bench and addresses the Thin Man figure.*

Walter, this is Fipsi, our newest State Artist. Fipsi, Walter, one of our oldest. Now, get to know each other, have a great chat and excuse me if you will.

> *FIPSI is hung in a static seated position from a hook on top of the picture frame behind the bench. MRS. VAN CRAIG beats a hasty retreat.*

Well, she certainly wears her success… obviously.

> *She crosses left to the other bench and addresses the child figure there.*

My, you're up quite late! How grown-up you must feel.

> *She sits, and is hung on the hook above the bench.*

We'll be having a puppet show later. No, it's not the old man from the park, but they are the same characters. Yes, Franz and Schnitzel. I like Schnitzel best too, because he wants to fly!

> *Ronnie leaves MRS. VAN CRAIG in her seated position and goes upstage to the carousel. He takes the marionettes of TINKA #4 and MORAG #3 off their animals. They walk a few steps into the upstage acting ring.*
>
> *TINKA is wearing a beautiful dress made in the same fabric as MRS. VAN CRAIG's wedding gown. We now see MORAG in complete drag for the first time… bead and feather headdress, full make-up, heels and a slinky gown made from the fabric of the other dress in the previous scene.*

MORAG   Well, *tout le* town is out tonight! Tinka, be honest. Do you think I pass?

TINKA   Morag, you're the most beautiful man here tonight. I'm so proud to be on your arm.

MORAG   I'm so nervous.

TINKA   It's all right, Morag.

MORAG   Let's hope, darling. When I'm nervous, I'm really bitchy. Heaven help these poor people!

TINKA   Shall we?

MORAG   Oh why not. It'll be a nice memory to tell the boys in prison.

TINKA   Morag!

MORAG   I feel as though everyone is looking at me.

TINKA   Morag, you're a drag queen. That's what you want, isn't it? Besides, they're just jealous that I have the most beautiful escort. Now, you wait right here. I'm going to find Astrid so I can introduce you.

MORAG   Tinka, don't leave me alone. You know I can't use the ladies' room without you!

TINKA   Relax, Morag. Nothing bad will happen. Not tonight. You're my knight in shining evening wear!

> *MORAG is hung on the upstage centre hook, facing toward the carousel. TINKA sees MRS. VAN CRAIG seated on the bench and walks toward her.*

Astrid? Astrid, hello.

> *MRS. VAN CRAIG turns, still seated.*

MRS. VAN CRAIG   Tinka! Look at you! Child, you take my breath away.

TINKA   Well then, you'd best remain seated. Thank you for inviting me, Astrid.

> *Ronnie's eyes sweep across the audience, taking them in.*

I've never seen a more beautiful group of people. Are you having fun?

MRS. VAN CRAIG   Yes, it's good to do this again. Although…

TINKA   Yes?

MRS. VAN CRAIG   It's different now. In the old days, we gathered simply to be together. These days, everyone seems to have taken a side.

> *TINKA sits on the bench.*

TINKA   Well, I'm at yours.

MRS. VAN CRAIG   And I can't tell you how happy that makes me. But enough of an old woman's reminiscences. Tinka, don't keep me in suspense any longer. Where is he? Where is this boy of yours?

> *TINKA turns to MORAG.*

TINKA   Morag, I'd like you to meet Mrs. Astrid Van Craig.

> *MORAG turns grandly and bows to MRS. VAN CRAIG.*

MORAG   *Enchanté* darling.

MRS. VAN CRAIG   Morag? But, you're a…

MORAG   Man?

MRS. VAN CRAIG   A star!

MORAG I love this woman!

TINKA I knew you would.

MRS. VAN CRAIG You're the cabaret *artiste*!

MORAG You've heard of me?

MRS. VAN CRAIG Who hasn't? I've seen you, many times…

> *She looks around to be sure no one is listening.*

…at The Penis Flytrap. Tell me, dear, have you gotten through *The Great Broads of the Old Testament* yet?

MORAG Oh, please! I'm skipping entire sections of that dreary tome.

MRS. VAN CRAIG Well, I simply adored your portrayal of the burning bush!

MORAG Thank you, darling. There's not much one can do with the Ten Commandments.

MRS. VAN CRAIG Yes, they are written in stone, aren't they?

MORAG *Touché*, old thing! Tinka, where on earth did you find this heavenly creature?

TINKA She found me.

MRS. VAN CRAIG And I never intend to let her go. Morag, I'm delighted to meet you. Although I'm sad to admit, that dress never looked so good on me.

MORAG Go on, you old silly, we're practically twins!

MRS. VAN CRAIG Come, let me introduce you around.

MORAG But, darling, don't you think I'll create a stir?

MRS. VAN CRAIG Let's hope. This party needs a bit of a lift.

> *MRS. VAN CRAIG stands.*

Tinka?

TINKA I'll entrust him to your safekeeping, Astrid. I'd like to sit and watch for a while.

MRS. VAN CRAIG Very well, if you can trust a she-devil like me with a she-devil like he! Morag, shall we?

MORAG Why not, old girl? Let's create a scandal!

> *MRS. VAN CRAIG extends her elbow. They cross to upstage left.*

MRS. VAN CRAIG Morag, when I saw you perform the parting of the Red Sea, I swear I've never seen so much red chiffon in my life. You really are a genius!

MORAG Oh stop! You're just saying that because it's true!

They are hung on the carousel. TINKA remains seated on the bench. When Ronnie returns to the main acting area, he animates the figure of FIPSI, also still seated. She sees TINKA and turns toward her.

FIPSI   Tinka? Tinka, darling! Is it really you? Well, you're the last person I expected to see tonight.

Ronnie moves to centre stage, kneels, and plays the following by turning his head from one to the other, speaking for both TINKA and FIPSI but animating neither.

TINKA   Hello, Fipsi. My, we certainly are hearing great things about you lately.

FIPSI   Of course you have. I've been made a State Artist. My work is officially sanctioned by The Common Good, I've been given a fabulous home, a new atelier, a staff, my name is positively everywhere and, have you heard? Next week, I begin a tour of the entire country. Fully funded.

TINKA   Yes, but are you well, Fipsi?

FIPSI   Tinka, I'm a success. How could I not be well?

TINKA   And Stephan, do you ever see him?

Ronnie moves toward FIPSI and she stands, beginning to cross to TINKA stage left.

FIPSI   Stephan works for me now. I felt I owed it to the old boy. And as I'm sure you've heard, Tinka, street vendors are illegal. Besides, I'm using Franz and Schnitzel now.

TINKA   For propaganda?

FIPSI   For education, dear. I like to think that I enlighten and enrich my audience.

TINKA   That's what Carl tries to do.

FIPSI   My work is nothing like Carl's.

TINKA   No. How could it be.

She starts to walk away.

FIPSI   Well, lovely seeing you again, Tinka, but I really must get ready. I'm performing this evening you know.

TINKA   Yes, so I'd heard.

FIPSI   I have the most elaborate little puppet stage! Thank goodness I've a staff to assist me. It allows me to concentrate on my acting.

TINKA   Yes, improvisation is so difficult.

FIPSI   I never improvise, Tinka. I follow the script.

TINKA   I didn't know there was one.

FIPSI   There is now, dear.

> *FIPSI starts to walk away, then turns to TINKA.*

Tinka, if you ever feel like following the script yourself, I may be in a position to help you.

TINKA   Thanks, Fipsi, but I could never learn the lines as well as you have.

FIPSI   Maybe you should stop reading between them.

> *As FIPSI walks away, Ronnie steps on the train of her gown with his right foot, which stops her abruptly.*

TINKA   Fipsi, give my love to Stephan.

FIPSI   And my… regards to Carl.

> *FIPSI sweeps off to the carousel and is hung on an animal. ISAËL #2 enters. En route, he talks to the Thin Male figure upstage of the stage right bench.*

ISAËL   Walter you old dog! I can't believe they let you in the door! Good to see you again, old man.

> *He sees The Officer.*

Officer, very reassuring to see you here tonight.

> *ISAËL notices TINKA from across the room and crosses to her.*

Good evening.

> *TINKA turns, a bit startled, interrupted from her thoughts.*

TINKA   Oh, hello.

ISAËL   Lost in thought, or simply watching the parade?

TINKA   A bit of both. I'm just waiting for a friend.

ISAËL   I'm looking for my aunt. Mrs. Van Craig.

TINKA   You must be Isaël!

ISAËL   Guilty, I fear.

TINKA   Astrid has spoken of you many times.

ISAËL   Are you a friend of my aunt?

TINKA   I like to think so.

ISAËL   Odd that we've not met.

TINKA   Not really. My world is significantly different from your aunt's.

ISAËL And yet, you've become close?

TINKA We have mutual friends.

ISAËL Ah, perhaps I know them.

TINKA Perhaps. Franz and Schnitzel.

ISAËL What? On no. You're that girl from The Camp.

>   *He takes a step back. She stands.*

TINKA I'm Tinka.

ISAËL What are you doing here?

TINKA I was invited. I'm a guest.

ISAËL No, I mean, how did you get here? Out of your sector.

TINKA Thanks to your aunt's kindness, arrangements were made.

ISAËL Illegal arrangements, no doubt. This could put you both in a great deal of jeopardy.

TINKA Possibly, if someone were to tell. But what a cruel thing to do, don't you think?

ISAËL I'm only thinking of what's right.

TINKA Well, I won't put you or your righteous thoughts at any further risk. If you'll excuse me…

>   *She starts to walk away.*

ISAËL No, please…. Stop!

>   *He/Ronnie steps on the hem of her dress. She stops.*

I'm sorry. That was uncivil of me.

>   *She is silent, her back still to him.*

Allow me to begin again. I'm pleased to meet you. Well, you're a stubborn one, aren't you? Really, I am pleased to meet you. I'm pleased to meet anyone my own age. This party is so dull. Everyone is so old. So stiff. Why even Fipsi's disappeared.

TINKA She's getting ready to perform.

>   *She turns to him.*

Are you a friend of Fipsi's?

ISAËL I'm a great admirer of Fipsi. She does very important work.

TINKA So she tells me.

ISAËL You don't sound impressed by her achievements.

TINKA It's bad enough to do mere entertainment that says nothing and call it art. But it's worse, I think, to do work that says the wrong things, and call it truth.

ISAËL You sound like your brother.

TINKA Thank you.

ISAËL Oh come now, what makes you two think you're so right?

TINKA What makes you think we're so wrong?

ISAËL Your brother's shows are a direct commentary against the efforts of The Common Good.

TINKA I wasn't aware that The Common Good was so fragile that it couldn't withstand a bit of examination.

ISAËL Such examination, as you call it, can be very harmful. It causes people to doubt. And we know what that leads to.

TINKA What?

ISAËL Debate.

TINKA We're having a debate now. I wasn't aware that we were inflicting any real harm on each other.

ISAËL I have no reason to harm you.

TINKA Precisely my point.

> *He comes close to her, lightly touching her back.*

ISAËL None whatsoever. You're… beautiful. And you're certainly spirited. And with a little work, you could even be an asset.

> *She turns.*

TINKA What?

ISAËL Well, look at you. You clean up rather nicely for a camp person. You're special. Not like the others.

TINKA What others?

ISAËL The freaks who contaminate us.

TINKA Stop.

ISAËL I can't stop, Tinka. You should be happy that you fit in. Not like the racially impure, or intellectuals…

TINKA Stop.

ISAËL …or homosexuals and deviants…

TINKA   Stop!

ISAËL   Do you know what I saw tonight? Do you? Here, at this party, I saw a man dressed as a woman!

TINKA   No...

ISAËL   Yes! A freak flaunting his disease, hoping to poison us all!

> *TINKA becomes very agitated.*

TINKA   Oh...

ISAËL   But I protected our kind from him. I did what any decent person would have done.

TINKA   What?

ISAËL   I turned him over to the authorities.

TINKA   No! Morag!

ISAËL   What? You know that... thing?

TINKA   I'm with him.

ISAËL   I see. Well then, you should be with him, shouldn't you? In the dirt, where you belong!

> *ISAËL/Ronnie spits on TINKA. She falls to the ground as the lighting snaps to a pool of red around her. ISAËL storms off, hung on the carousel. TINKA struggles to her knees.*

TINKA   Morag. Morag? Morag!

> *She is whisked off as Ronnie races to the back of the carousel. A fanfare plays and a pool of light hits centre stage. All other lights dim. From behind the central carousel pole, Ronnie has gotten FIPSI #3 and places her in the pool of light.*
>
> *An announcement is played:*

THE VOICE   "Patrons will now quiet themselves for an official presentation by The Common Good."

> *FIPSI is now dressed in a costume which is a bizarre reminiscence of the Court of Versailles, the skirt a wide hoop affair. She talks directly to the audience:*

FIPSI   Thank you, and welcome to another performance of our beloved statesmen, Franz and Schnitzel.

> *A strange, "anthemized" version of the Franz and Schnitzel theme music plays, and continues throughout FIPSI's puppet show. The centre front*

panel on her skirt separates like a theatrical curtain, revealing miniature Franz and Schnitzel puppets against a backdrop inside her dress.

FRANZ   Schnitzel, you seem unhappy. Whatever is the matter?

SCHNITZEL   Oh Franz, I am sad. I'll never be a real fairy!

FRANZ   Well then, there you have it!

SCHNITZEL   What do you mean?

FRANZ   You want the wrong thing.

SCHNITZEL   I do?

FRANZ   Being a fairy won't make you happy.

SCHNITZEL   It won't?

FRANZ   No, it will only make you worse off.

SCHNITZEL   It will?

FRANZ   Of course!

SCHNITZEL   But my friends say I should be a fairy.

FRANZ   Then your friends are bad, and wrong. And they should be reported to the nearest authority at once!

SCHNITZEL   But Franz, if I'm not a fairy, what am I?

FRANZ   You're a worker, Schnitzel! For The Common Good!

SCHNITZEL   Really? That sounds important!

FRANZ   It's the most important thing there is, Schnitzel. Work makes you free!

SCHNITZEL   So by working together we're all working for The Common Good?

FRANZ   Exactly!

SCHNITZEL   I feel so much better now, Franz!

FRANZ   So do I, Schnitzel. See, we have a lot of good in common!

SCHNITZEL   And that's what makes us happy—our Common Good!

FRANZ   Thank you, and goodnight, from your Common Good.

The fanfare plays again as the curtain comes down in FIPSI's skirt. The pool of light fades to black. FIPSI is placed in the centre pillar of the carousel. The carousel music theme plays again, although it is now more sombre in tone, played on an accordion. Dim transitional lighting comes up slowly as Ronnie puts away the benches. The figures of the Little Girl, the Fat Man, and the Thin Woman are repositioned on the acting ring, save for The Officer who stands watch from upstage right.

Scene Seven
The Camp—Grey Palette

The carousel is revolved and the lights crossfade onto the acting area. Time has passed. It is late fall/early winter, late in the day. Ronnie takes the marionette of CARL #3 from an animal. He is dressed in the familiar striped uniform of Holocaust camp inmates. The music fades. CARL is facing the static Mother figure.

CARL So, our numbers are dwindling.

He turns to The Officer.

Tell me, Officer, is it the selection program of our government which causes the audience to shrink, or merely that the showman's appeal is diminishing?

He responds to the Mother figure as if she has spoken to him.

Yes, there will be a show. There's always a show, no matter how cold it gets.

The centre stage carousel light comes up somewhat. We hear the voice of STEPHAN.

STEPHAN *(offstage)* Carl.

CARL turns.

CARL Stephan?

He walks toward the carousel. Ronnie takes the marionette of STEPHAN #2 off an animal and places him in the upstage acting area. They embrace.

STEPHAN Carl!

CARL Stephan, what are you doing here? They haven't…

STEPHAN No, they haven't put me in here… yet.

CARL But how did you… who let you in?

STEPHAN I have a pass. Briefly. So we've very little time, Carl. A Holy Army Officer is waiting for us at the gates.

CARL Us?

STEPHAN I've come to take you out. Please, we'll talk later. But for now, we must simply go.

CARL Go where, Stephan?

STEPHAN To safety. I have convinced Fipsi that you must be saved. And Fipsi has convinced the authorities that you would be valuable in her work.

CARL So, I'll work for the great state artist Fipsi.

STEPHAN   Yes. And Tinka, too. We'll all be together again! Now come.

CARL   Never.

STEPHAN   What?

CARL   I will not work for her!

STEPHAN   Carl, please…

> *CARL walks away, not facing STEPHAN.*

CARL   I have a show to do, Stephan. Too bad you won't be able to stay for it.

STEPHAN   Stop it, Carl! All right, you've made your point. I've noticed. Everyone has noticed, Carl, that's the problem. There's no one left to make an example of but you.

CARL   I'm sure they'll find someone.

STEPHAN   Stop it! You don't understand do you? You don't understand a thing.

> *CARL does not turn to face STEPHAN. Both are silent for a moment.*

So, this is how I'm rewarded. You show your back to your teacher. Very well, Carl. I stand humbled before you. The great artist. The great voice of the people. Perhaps it is I who should now learn from you, Carl. So please, tell me, teach me. I will be a willing student, for I have only one question, master. If you are so right, if yours is the only way, answer me this: where the hell is your audience? I don't see them lining up for your performance, save one, and who knows how long she'll last. Where are they, Carl? And where are all those friends of yours, hmm? Those great revolutionary minds that got you into this in the first place? I'll tell you where they are. They're gone, Carl! They're all gone. Your friend Hettie…

CARL   Hettie has gone underground…

STEPHAN   Hettie is dead! A month ago. And just last night your other friend. They used him as an example all this time, they tortured him, they broke him, and they killed him too.

CARL   Who?

STEPHAN   The fellow from the cabaret.

CARL   Morag?

> *STEPHAN nods.*

No. He was innocent.

STEPHAN   Out there the innocent and the guilty have traded places. Carl, I beg of you, boy, please don't miss this opportunity.

CARL   I miss my generation, Stephan.

STEPHAN   Then choose life, Carl.

CARL   At any cost?

STEPHAN   Yes.

CARL   But their price is my voice.

STEPHAN   If you don't silence it, they will. Carl, this is not what you were trained for. This is not what I taught you. And it's not worth dying for. Carl, they're puppets! They don't think, they don't feel and no one cares about them. Dammit boy, it's just a puppet show!

CARL   Thank you, Stephan.

>   *STEPHAN moves to embrace him.*

Goodbye.

>   *STEPHAN turns to leave. He is stopped by CARL's voice.*

I'm sorry I disappointed you.

STEPHAN   Carl.

>   *He extends his hand once again, then drops it.*

And I'm sorry I… disappointed you too.

>   *A quiet drone begins as STEPHAN leaves. The lights shift to a tight pool stage right. CARL hangs static, facing out. Ronnie stands behind him, talking to the puppet and thinking CARL's thoughts aloud.*

CARL   Happy? You're alone again. You like alone, you're good at it. Fitting in, there's the risk. Getting along, getting by, there's the compromise. And compromise is… death. Always so much death. But it never leads anywhere. I thought it was supposed to lead somewhere.

>   *Ronnie kneels behind CARL, cradling him in one arm.*

Is this what you had in mind? Remember when we…. Go ahead, I dare you. Have a memory. Risk it! Risk everything to remember.

>   *His arm sweeps toward centre stage while turning CARL with the other hand.*

The whole, real moment. Tears optional.

>   *He kisses CARL and stands, leaving the marionette hanging stage right. An odd light surrounds the carousel, giving us the sense of a blurred reality, where memory and present live as one. The drone changes into Tinka's theme music and Franz and Schnitzel all rolled into one theme. The music is continued throughout the following scene. Ronnie takes two puppets from the carousel. They are Carl and Tinka as children. YOUNG*

TINKA runs into the pool of light, followed by YOUNG CARL. She holds a bunch of daisies in her hand.

YOUNG CARL   Tinka, you mustn't run off like that!

YOUNG TINKA   But, Carl, you left me alone after the puppet show.

YOUNG CARL   I went to talk to the man.

YOUNG TINKA   The puppet man?

YOUNG CARL   Yes.

YOUNG TINKA   Did he show you the puppets?

YOUNG CARL   He let me work them. They're heavy!

YOUNG TINKA   Did you ask him for one?

YOUNG CARL   No, silly! But he told me I could come back next week and watch from behind. And that maybe, someday, I could be his assistant!

YOUNG TINKA   Oh, Carl, you're going to be a famous puppeteer!

YOUNG CARL   Yeah, even more famous than him!

YOUNG CARL's arm sweeps, pointing toward the static, hanging puppet of older CARL. He responds to him, as if spoken to, although the hanging puppet neither moves nor speaks.

Yes, sir, I'm Carl. Yes, they told us to wait here. Why? What?

He is agitated. He turns slightly and indicates TINKA.

There. That's my sister. That's Tinka. No, you can't! Let me tell her. I can do it. I never cry.

He walks toward TINKA.

Tinka, this man, he says…

YOUNG TINKA   Is he a friend of Mummy and Daddy's?

YOUNG CARL   No. Well, sort of. He says that we have to go. With him.

YOUNG TINKA   But Carl, we're supposed to wait here for Mummy and Daddy.

YOUNG CARL   They're not coming, Tinka.

YOUNG TINKA   Did something happen to them?

YOUNG CARL is silent.

YOUNG CARL   They're never coming, Tinka.

YOUNG TINKA is absolutely still. She hangs her head and looks at her flowers.

YOUNG TINKA   I have to give Mummy her flowers.

YOUNG CARL   You can't.

YOUNG TINKA   I have to.

YOUNG CARL   Tinka, she's…

YOUNG TINKA   She likes daisies. Remember? She says they're her favourite flower because they grow in the dark. Let me give them to her, Carl. Please.

YOUNG CARL   All right, Tinka, let's go. Let's give Mummy her daisies.

> *They walk upstage, pausing for a moment to look at older CARL. Ronnie hangs the two children on an animal. He takes the marionette of TINKA #5 and places her upstage of the hanging CARL. She is wearing the party dress again, although it is different. The fabric is the same as before, but in a new style.*

TINKA   Carl?

> *The music stops and the light returns to its previous state in a snap.*

CARL   Tinka, we should give Mummy her daisies.

TINKA   What?

CARL   Tinka, it's Morag. They've… he's dead. I killed him. They killed him, Tinka.

> *TINKA is very still.*

Did you hear me? Morag is dead.

> *TINKA walks toward him.*

TINKA   No, Carl. No.

CARL   Stephan just told me.

TINKA   I'm telling you, he's alive. I loved Morag. I love him. And he loved me. I didn't know how to tell you before, Carl. There's going to be… a child.

> *CARL falls to his knees.*

CARL   Tinka, I'm sorry.

TINKA   Don't be. We knew. That's why we… why we have to continue. See, I've remade the dress again. Just like I always do. A new dress for a new show.

CARL   There won't be another show.

TINKA   There has to be. It's all we can do. We continue. There will be another show, Carl. I'm wearing the dress.

> *CARL places his hand lightly on her skirt, feeling the fabric.*

CARL   "O daughter of my people, gird thee with sackcloth, and wallow thyself in ashes: make thee mourning, as for an only son, most bitter lamentation: for the spoiler shall suddenly come upon us."

TINKA   Jeremiah?

CARL   The proclamation of judgment.

> *He faces out.*

Tinka, it's dark.

TINKA   Yes... but things are growing.

> *They stand together as the light fades. In semi-darkness, the marionettes are returned to their carousel animal. Theme music for The Franz and Schnitzel Show begins, although this time it is not as vibrant, somewhat darker and "smaller." The lights come up just slightly, as Ronnie pushes the puppet stage to centre stage front. He puts on a camp jacket, like the one worn by puppet CARL.*

Scene Eight
The Franz and Schnitzel Show—Puppet Palette

Once the puppet stage has been positioned, the lights come up on the stage and Ronnie takes his place behind the chest-high backdrop. FRANZ and SCHNITZEL are standing in front of the curtain.

As before, this scene is improvised around a loose structure of running order and content as follows, and usually runs twenty minutes in length.

FRANZ   All right, Schnitzel, it's time for us to get the new show ready! Look at you, you're not even in costume yet.

SCHNITZEL   But I don't have a costume, Franz.

FRANZ   Ya gotta love performance art! We're going to save a fortune on production costs!

SCHNITZEL   But Franz, I don't think...

FRANZ   Precisely! You don't think, Schnitzel. Thinking gets in the way of survival, and that's a luxury we don't have time for. Understood?

SCHNITZEL   Yes, Franz.

FRANZ   Good. There's only one thing left to do. We have to get rid of the fat lady.

SCHNITZEL   Madame Rodrigue? Oh no, Franz, we can't! She's one of us. She's been here since the beginning.

FRANZ   Schnitzel, just because she's been here since the beginning doesn't make her one of us. She's dangerous. She's different.

SCHNITZEL   She's not different, Franz, she's just like us.

FRANZ   Schnitzel, look at us. What are we?

SCHNITZEL   A couple of white clowns.

FRANZ   Exactly. And the world is set up for white male clowns like us. But Madame Rodrigue is different. She's a singer! She breathes more air than we do, and someday we might want that air and it will be all gone because she took it!

SCHNITZEL   That doesn't make sense, Franz.

FRANZ   It doesn't have to make sense, it's right. There's no room for her now. It's the Franz and Schnitzel Show, remember? We have to look after ourselves! So you have to fire Madame Rodrigue.

SCHNITZEL   Why me?

FRANZ   As long as you are one half of this team, it's about time you took over some managerial responsibilities.

SCHNITZEL   I can't be in management. I'm the good one!

FRANZ   Enough! You'll do what you're told.

SCHNITZEL   But Franz…

> *FRANZ becomes menacing again.*

FRANZ   Need I remind you, Schnitzel, how terrible it would be if I got angry?

SCHNITZEL   No.

FRANZ   No?

SCHNITZEL   I mean, yes.

FRANZ   "Yes" what?

SCHNITZEL   Yes, I'll do what you tell me.

FRANZ   Good boy, Schnitzel! All right, I'm going backstage to get things ready. Fire the fat lady and meet me back there!

> *FRANZ starts off, then turns to SCHNITZEL.*

And Schnitzel, while you're at it, do something cute. Maybe one of these people will want to come backstage and do the diamond pants dance with me!

SCHNITZEL   Franz, how can you think of your pants at a time like this?

FRANZ   I don't know, Schnitzel, but that's the joy of being a big white clown!

> *FRANZ exits, laughing maniacally.*

SCHNITZEL Oh dear.

He turns to the audience.

Ladies and gentlemen, lovers of Thespis, forgive me. I know that you are a genteel and kind group of people, liberal and forgiving in your views, but somehow I don't think you've come out tonight to watch a naked little fairy throw himself around the stage.

And I know, too, that you love Madame Rodrigue. I listened while she bullied you into loving her. But now, I fear that you will never hear your beloved superstar diva sing, for I must now, somehow, fire the fat lady.

Oh dear. What a sour pickle I'm in. If only I could escape. If only I could stop this. If somehow it would just end.

What a minute. End. That's it! It's happening again. I'm having a thought. A thought of my own! Listen everyone, Madame Rodrigue is the fat lady who sings, right? And we all know what happens when the fat lady sings… it's over! I can tell Madame that she's too great for this show. She's too important an artist to wallow in the vulgarity of performance art! And I will give her the opportunity to sing one last time on this stage, for you, her begrudgingly adoring public. No diva could resist that, for the love of an audience, even when it's false, is like a drug.

It's perfect! I'll go backstage, fire Madame Rodrigue, send her out to sing one last time, the show will end, you can go home and I won't have to dance naked. Everyone wins! Wish me luck!

He starts off.

Oh. Even though once the fat lady sings it's technically over, would you mind sticking around a few minutes longer so I can come back and say goodbye? I'd like that.

He exits. We hear a knock backstage.

MADAME *(off)* Yes, who is it? Ah, Schnitzel! I was just getting ready to go out and sing. What? Fired? Terminated? Pink slipped? Sacked? Let go? Fine! I will leave, but before I do I will go out on that stage one last time and give those people what they want! I will sing for them, as only their beloved superstar diva Madame Rodrigue can! I only hope that they remember how to greet a superstar diva when she says:

Oh my darlings, I'm coming to see you!

At which point the audience hopefully says "Nudge, nudge, nudge. Could it be? Could it be?!" MADAME appears stage right, bedecked in a new gown festooned with roses. The audience cries "It is! It is! It's Madame Rodrigue!" at which point the fanfare plays, she walks to centre stage, a spotlight comes on and the audience applauds wildly.

Stop! Stop it! You're too kind, oh stop!

> *This causes the audience to whistle and cheer, clapping even more enthusiastically.*

Stop it! Stop the music!

> *The fanfare dies and the spotlight snaps out returning us to general onstage light.*

Stop. Please. I can't go on with this. Oh my darlings, my beautiful darlings, thank you so very much for greeting me properly. You love me, you really love me! But I can't go on with this charade. My darlings, a terrible thing has happened. But I can't tell you. I won't! No matter how you may beg and plead, no matter how you may cry out "Tell us Madame," you'll never get it out of me! So don't even try!

> *She has posed dramatically facing into the back curtain. An audience member will usually yell out "Tell us!"*

All right, I'll tell you! I'll spill like a cup of coffee. I'll sing like a canary. I'll tell you! My darlings, Madame Rodrigue, your beloved superstar diva is depressed!

> *She flings herself into the back curtain once again. An audience member will yell "No!" or some such thing.*

I know what you're thinking. You look at me and say, "Oh Madame, you look gorgeous! Your hair, your make-up, so tasteful. That stunning new concert gown, so slimming and fabulous! Whatever could be the matter, Madame?" Well my darlings, I have news. A story so shocking, so big in magnitude and horror, that when I tell you this tale of intrigue you will all want to scream out "Say it isn't so Madame!" But please, try to contain yourselves when I tell you the shocking news that Madame Rodrigue, your beloved superstar diva, has been fired!

> *She throws herself into the back curtain again as the audience screams "Say it isn't so!" She turns and sits on the bench.*

Oh save your cheap pity! You think I don't know? You think I'm not aware that Schnitzel concocted this plan to get rid of me out here in front of all of you? That little fairy has a sick codependency with every audience! I know what goes on out here when I'm not onstage, and it disgusts me!

Fine. I'll go. And happily. I've outgrown this shabby show, I'm bigger than this stifling stage. Do I shock you with my candour? Do my words sting your ears? Oh darlings, all I've ever wanted since I was a baby superstar diva Madame Rodrigue, was a life in the theatre. Look where I ended up. The queen of alternative venues.

Oh, I don't criticize you for being here, my darlings. You're not to blame. This is probably all you can afford. And I know that you are the thrill-seeking boob-and-bum kind of fringe crowd that laughs too loud at everything just to prove to everyone around you how smart you are. You don't know better.

So I will go on. I will leave this tomb that has buried me alive and find a place in the real theatre! A real big theatre. Yes, I am going to be in a franchise musical! I want a microphone pack permanently attached to my ass so I won't have to work so hard every night to be heard. I want to be in a show that's already a hit somewhere else so before the audience sees it they already think it's good because it's not from here. I want to be in a show that's so expensive the mere ticket price alone will make you feel privileged to be allowed in. I want to be in a show that takes no risks and says nothing to everyone. I want to be in a show that's the same thing night after night, running like a machine with no connection between the audience and the performer whatsoever. That's real theatre! And that's what I want.

But as I have dreams for myself, so too have I a dream for you, my darlings. I hope that someday you will lift yourself up out of this alternative theatre gutter you wallow in. That you will pull yourself together, work hard, save a few pennies and be able to scrape together enough to buy yourself a ticket to the real theatre. And who knows? Perhaps someday you'll be sitting up there in the third balcony, your nose bleeding from the altitude, and you'll look down to the stage and see a tiny little speck with orange hair and fabulous gown. And as if in communion with the people around you, you'll quietly whisper, "Nudge, nudge, nudge. Could it be? Could it be?!"

And with that prayer in my bosom, I must leave you. I'm too emotional, I cannot sing. Please don't ask me to!

> *The audience begs her to sing.*

All right, I bow to your will! And you have been so beautiful to me my darlings, you deserve a song. Now, as bleak as things have become around here, I will not sing alone. No! As always, I will be accompanied by the house band. Granted, my ego is too large to share the stage with anyone else, but I assure you they are here, behind this gold curtain. The fabulous Harry Bagg Trio! I'm just nuts about Harry and the boys, although after the show I will have to give them the sack. Oh, Harry is going to be so testy, and the boys will bawl. But they'll bounce back, they always do.

And so, a song. A little song I have written just for you my darlings. Hit it, Harry!

> *MADAME sings. Five bedtracks are available, ranging from operetta style to country and western. Given the news of the day, ranging from politics to entertainment, a new song will be written for MADAME to sing at each performance. As she finishes her song, she bows and the audience goes mad.*

Goodbye, my darlings! Goodbye!

MADAME exits. A music-box lullaby version of Schnitzel's theme plays. He enters, dressed in a pink and white striped nightshirt and cap. In one hand he drags a teddy bear.

SCHNITZEL Hi, everybody, it's sleepy time Schnitzel. I just had a terrible thought backstage. So I thought I would come out and share it with you. Oh I'm sorry, I'm being terribly rude. I haven't introduced my bear to you. See my bear? Grrr. Grrr. Grrr. Don't be afraid, he's not a real bear. He's my friend.

The bear is given a new name for each venue, usually based on a politician. In London for example, he was "Tony Bear" (Blair). Given whatever personality the bear is named for, SCHNITZEL will have him do a little dance while he sings a short (unaccompanied) song.

Anyway, I didn't come out here to talk about my bear. I came out here to tell you my terrible thought. Would you like to hear it?

Underscore begins.

My terrible thought, by Schnitzel. See, I was just backstage and I noticed that everything was gone. I don't know how many of you have been backstage in a theatre, but it's the most magical place on earth. The scenery, the costumes, the props. Singers and dancers and actors warming up or complaining about the show. Dressing rooms full of rotting flowers and overflowing ashtrays. Cards from people you love, or from strangers who love you. But Franz got rid of it all, and now it's empty. And I realized that I've spent my whole time looking up there, wanting to get above it all, when in fact I was already at home. And now that it's all gone, I'm empty too.

So I realized something. I may never ascend. I may never get above any of this. I may never fly at all. And that perhaps my destiny in life is simply to become just like you.

He shudders in horror.

And that was my terrible thought.

And that made me hang my head in abject sorrow. But as my head was hanging down, you'll never guess what I saw. My feet. Now, this may not be big news to you normal people who get to belong and fit in everywhere, but to me it was quite a revelation. I've been told my whole life that there was no room for me, that my kind didn't belong, couldn't fit in anywhere. But I look down and see my feet, and there is room for me. My feet are firmly planted on the ground. I'm not stepping on anyone's toes. And my feet can move around, and the more they move…

He walks to the edge of the stage.

...the closer they bring me to you. And the closer I get, the more I realize that... well, the more I feel... what I mean to say is.... Oh this is too weird. I can't look at you and tell you!

He runs upstage and buries his face in the back curtain.

That's better. What I wanted to say, is that...

I love you.

Pause.

Well, don't feel like you have to say it back or anything.

To date, there has been only one audience wherein no one has yelled back "I love you, too." Usually many, several, or just one brave soul will blurt out their affection for Schnitzel. It is pure magic. He turns slowly and walks downstage.

You do? Oh thank you! Thank you. I always thought the theatre was about scenery, or costumes or stuff. But the only stuff here now is what you and I are made of, and that's what counts. And nothing, or no one, can ever destroy this or take it away!

FRANZ *(offstage)* Schnitzel!

SCHNITZEL Oh no.

FRANZ enters stage right.

FRANZ Schnitzel, what the hell is going on out here?

SCHNITZEL I'm having a bonding moment with my audience. They love me, Franz!

FRANZ Oh, Schnitzel, don't be pathetic. They don't love you.

SCHNITZEL Yes, Franz, they do. And I love them!

FRANZ Don't be ridiculous. You can't love, you're a performer. Nothing about you is real.

SCHNITZEL No, you're wrong! I'm real because they love me.

FRANZ They don't love you.

SCHNITZEL Yes they do!

FRANZ Then how come only one or two said it?

SCHNITZEL Those people are representative spokespeople for this entire audience! They love me!

FRANZ No they don't!

SCHNITZEL They do!

FRANZ   They don't!

SCHNITZEL   They do!

FRANZ   No!

SCHNITZEL   Yes! If I was a T-shirt in the lobby they would buy me!

FRANZ   I leave you alone for five minutes, and look what happens. You not only start thinking, you start feeling, too. Well that's not your job, Schnitzel, and it's not what they want.

SCHNITZEL   But Franz…

FRANZ   Shut up! Schnitzel, you are breaking the rules. And I won't have it. Not as long as I am one half of this show. And if it takes me all night, I will teach you how to behave on this stage. Now get down here.

SCHNITZEL   But Franz…

FRANZ   I said get down here.

SCHNITZEL   But Franz…

FRANZ   I said get down here now!

SCHNITZEL   But Franz, can I bring my bear?

FRANZ   Well he's sewn to your fucking hand, I guess you'd have to! Now get down here!

> SCHNITZEL *walks to the edge of the stage. He holds the bear up to* FRANZ.

SCHNITZEL   Grrr.

FRANZ   Stop being cute! Okay, here we are. Tell me, Schnitzel, what's that?

SCHNITZEL   It's the edge of the stage.

FRANZ   And what's beyond the edge?

SCHNITZEL   The big black void.

FRANZ   And what's in the big black void?

SCHNITZEL   People!

FRANZ   Exactly! People sit in the dark. We stand in the light. Those are the rules, Schnitzel. Do not cross the line.

SCHNITZEL   But Franz, I did cross the line. Tonight I flew into the audience.

FRANZ   Schnitzel, don't start this again. You don't have wings.

SCHNITZEL   Yes, I do! They're in my heart!

FRANZ   I hate that kind of talk, Schnitzel.

SCHNITZEL   I flew into the audience, Franz, because they love me!

FRANZ   No they don't!

SCHNITZEL   Yes they do!

FRANZ   I am the only kind of love you'll ever know!

SCHNITZEL   Well that's not good enough for me, Franz.

FRANZ   What do you think you are to these people, Schnitzel?

SCHNITZEL   A benign comic character who embodies hope?

FRANZ   No. You're fourteen inches of fun in the dark, that's all.

SCHNITZEL   Why do you have to make everything dirty, Franz?

FRANZ   Because that's what they want, Schnitzel. You think they love you? No. I'll show you what love in the theatre is about. Watch this.

> *He begins to rock his pelvis suggestively.*

See, Schnitzel? That's what they pay for. The silly clown with his dancing pants! That's what they come to see. They don't want you. You're a freak, you're dangerous. You ask them to think and feel and care, and that's not why people go to the theatre. They don't love you. Look at them. Look at them, Schnitzel. I said look at them!

> *SCHNITZEL slowly turns his head. He and FRANZ look at the audience.*

Poor bastards sitting in the dark, wondering what happens next. But we know, Schnitzel! We know what happens next.

SCHNITZEL   But, Franz, it's always the same thing, night after night.

FRANZ   And that's why we keep moving from town to town! Schnitzel, you're where they want to be. In the light. With me.

SCHNITZEL   I'd rather take my chances in the dark with them than stand in this light with you.

FRANZ   When the lights go up out there, Schnitzel, they won't take you with them. They'll forget about you.

SCHNITZEL   I can't forget about them, Franz. And I can't do this anymore.

FRANZ   Fine. I give up. You want to go? Go. You make me sick. Look at you! Standing out here in your pyjamas. Just what the hell is that all about?

SCHNITZEL   The fat lady sang, Franz. It's over. It's the end.

FRANZ   You stupid fairy. It's not the end, Schnitzel. It's just the beginning.

> *A loud police whistle is heard as a glaring searchlight hits Ronnie's face, beginning a rapid-fire sequence of sound and light cues. The puppet show*

lights snap out, and all light on the carousel and stage begins flashing. Music becomes chaotic, underscored by barking dogs and the sound of glass being shattered repeatedly. Ronnie whisks off FRANZ and SCHNITZEL and disappears behind the puppet stage. The carousel begins to revolve by itself during the continuing chaos. After Ronnie moves the puppet stage upstage left, he steps onto the now moving carousel. After one revolution, he steps off the carousel into the centre of the set. The carousel stops. Sound calms to an eerie drone, lighting becomes cold and stark. After a brief moment, Ronnie moves forward, and hugging The Populace Mother figure, pushes the carousel into its final position.

Scene Nine
The Camp—Black Palette

It is winter now, late in the day. Ronnie places The Officer upstage centre, and takes TINKA #6 from a carousel animal. Dressed primarily in black except for a striped camp jacket, she is in the early, but obvious, stages of pregnancy. She addresses the Mother figure who stands stage right of The Officer.

TINKA   Go away. Why do you keep coming back, day after day? You know the shows have stopped. This is very dangerous. Please go. There won't be another show.

After hanging TINKA stage left, Ronnie moves the Mother figure out to her starting position downstage centre off the acting ring. MRS. VAN CRAIG #4 enters.

MRS. VAN CRAIG   Tinka? Tinka dear, what are you doing?

TINKA   Waiting.

MRS. VAN CRAIG   For what, dear?

TINKA   Spring.

TINKA turns toward MRS. VAN CRAIG. She too is dressed in black, but her outfit is very beautiful with an elaborate cape over her dress.

Astrid, hello. I'm sorry, but there won't be a show today. Carl's been… gone.

MRS. VAN CRAIG   I know. I took your advice, though. See? I dressed warmly this time.

TINKA   For what? Why are you here?

MRS. VAN CRAIG   It's my home now too, dear.

TINKA   Why would you choose to be here?

MRS. VAN CRAIG   I didn't choose, Tinka. Or did I? I suspect it's too late to even wonder anymore.

She indicates TINKA's stomach, either by a look or with a touch.

So, due in spring. There's reason enough to keep each other warm through this bitter winter.

They hold each other, half embrace, half for warmth.

I've brought you a present.

TINKA   Oh, Astrid, I don't need any more dresses.

MRS. VAN CRAIG   No, but perhaps you have a reason to wear the one you have.

TINKA is hung again, face out. MRS. VAN CRAIG exits upstage to the carousel. She trades places with STEPHAN #3, who bows to her as she takes his place on a carousel animal. STEPHAN walks toward TINKA.

STEPHAN   Hello, Tinka.

TINKA turns.

TINKA   Oh, Stephan. You frightened me! I thought you were...

STEPHAN   Carl?

TINKA   No, dead. Carl's dead.

STEPHAN   Oh, really. Then why is this person waiting for a show?

He indicates the Mother figure facing the stage.

Could it be that Carl is alive? That she's waiting for him? He's not dead, Tinka. Not to her. Not to me.

TINKA   Well he is, Stephan. I was there.

STEPHAN   I see. Then tell me, what's behind the stage over there?

TINKA   What? Nothing. Just puppets.

STEPHAN   Just puppets?! It's a good thing Carl's not around to hear you say that.

TINKA   Without Carl, that's all they are. Just puppets.

STEPHAN   I disagree. And I was wrong. So go on, Tinka, get ready.

TINKA   For what?

STEPHAN   Well, I'm not doing a show until you put on that dress of yours. Tinka, tradition! We have to keep it alive.

TINKA   Oh, Stephan, you can't.

STEPHAN   I most certainly can. And I will. All right, I admit, this foolish old… student was slow to learn from the master. But I think I'm ready to give it a try. Won't you help me, Tinka?

He stands beside her.

With each spring comes a new season of The Franz and Schnitzel Show, remember? We continue. And who knows, perhaps today Schnitzel will fly.

He starts off.

Please. Put on your new dress.

He is hung on the stage right side of the Franz and Schnitzel stage. TINKA walks slowly to centre stage as the light dims to a special on The Officer. Ronnie whispers to her.

RONNIE   Tinka.

On this, sensing CARL's presence somehow, she turns upstage and walks toward The Officer. Face to face, she thrusts her head up defiantly. The silent confrontation is held for a moment, then she is placed back on the carousel. Humming the theme music from the Franz and Schnitzel show, Ronnie walks to the puppet stage and moves it downstage centre. During the previous "chaos" scene, TINKA #7 was placed on the stage left side of the puppet stage. Ronnie takes his place on the stage, and walks STEPHAN out in front of the backdrop. This is the first and only time that we see the "human" marionette characters in the "puppet show" realm. STEPHAN talks to The Populace figure of Mother.

Ladies and gentleman… well… madam. Welcome to The Daisy Theatre and The Franz and Schnitzel Show, back by popular demand! Tinka, we have an audience. Are you ready?

TINKA appears from the other side of the backdrop. She is wearing the party dress again, in a style which appears to be a wedding dress.

TINKA   Yes, Stephan, I'm ready.

STEPHAN   Good.

STEPHAN starts to exit.

TINKA   Stephan?

STEPHAN   Hmm?

TINKA   I think you're right. He is here.

STEPHAN   Then let's begin. Again.

They are both hung face to face on the Franz and Schnitzel stage. The lights start to dim, as a circle of light on the puppet backdrop comes up.

TINKA theme music softly plays. When the only light on the set is the puppet stage spotlight, it fades almost to black. Music and light snap out together on the final bell-like note as Ronnie, lifting his face upwards, whispers:

RONNIE   Fly!

The End.

About the Editors

DD Kugler, a Vancouver-based freelance dramaturg/ director in theatre and dance, was the first Canadian president of Literary Managers and Dramaturgs of the Americas (LMDA, 2000–2002). He served eight seasons as Production Dramaturg with Toronto's Necessary Angel Theatre (1985–1993), five seasons as Artistic Director of Edmonton's Northern Light Theatre (1993–1998), and since then has taught in the Theatre Area at Simon Fraser University's School for the Contemporary Arts. Kugler adapted Marc Diamond's *Property* and (in collaboration with Richard Rose) co-authored *Newhouse*, as well as the adaptations of Michael Ondaatje's *Coming Through Slaughter* and Timothy Findley's *Not Wanted on the Voyage*.

Brian Quirt is Artistic Director of Nightswimming and was President of the Literary Managers and Dramaturgs of the Americas (2006–2008). Brian has commissioned more than twenty new works of dance and drama with Nightswimming, many of which have gone on to acclaimed productions in Toronto and across Canada. He directed the premiere of Anosh Irani's *Bombay Black*, commissioned by Nightswimming, produced by Cahoots Theatre, named the outstanding new play of the 2005–2006 Toronto theatre season and nominated for the 2007 Governor General's Literary Award. Brian has been nominated for three Dora Awards, two for Direction and one for his adaptation of the Iranian play *Aurash* with Soheil Parsa. He received LMDA's 2003 Elliott Hayes Award for Dramaturgy in recognition of his work in creating and directing Nightswimming. His own works include the adaptations of Jane Urquhart's *The Whirlpool* and Michael Redhill's *Lake Nora Arms*, and the original plays *The Death of General Wolfe* and *Blue Note*. He directed the premiere productions of two Jason Sherman plays, as well as Michael Healey's first play, *Kicked*, and is currently developing Judith Thompson's latest play and Ned Dickens's seven-play cycle *City of Wine* through Nightswimming.